CULTURAL POLITICS OF GENDER AND SEXUALITY IN CONTEMPORARY ASIA

CULTURAL POLITICS OF GENDER AND SEXUALITY IN CONTEMPORARY ASIA

Edited by Tiantian Zheng

University of Hawai'i Press
Honolulu

21 20 19 18 17 16   6 5 4 3 2 1

Library of Congress Cataloging-in-Publication Data

Cultural politics of gender and sexuality in contemporary Asia / Edited by Tiantian Zheng.
    pages cm
Includes bibliographical references and index.
ISBN 978-0-8248-5296-2 (cloth : alk. paper)—ISBN 978-0-8248-5297-9 (paperback : alk. paper)
1. Sex role—Asia.   2. Gender identity—Asia.   3. Sex—Social aspects—Asia.   4. Asia—
Social life and customs—21st century.   I. Zheng, Tiantian, editor.
GN479.65.C85 2016
305.3095—dc23

2015024798

Composition by Westchester Publishing Services

I dedicate this book to
Dave Grass

Contents

ACKNOWLEDGMENTS

Over the years of my research and writing, I have accumulated a great deal of debt to my professors, colleagues, and friends. I would like to thank my advisers at Yale—Helen Siu, Deborah Davis, William W. Kelly, and Harold W. Scheffler—for their generous mentorship and supportive encouragement of my professional development, without which I would not be where I am today. I was blessed with four advisers who have always shown me an immense amount of support and faith and offered me helpful professional advice. It is their generous mentorship, continuous inspiration, and precious advice that have shaped who I am today as an anthropologist and scholar. I thank them for having taught me, supported me, and encouraged me more than they could realize, for which I am forever grateful.

My thanks also go to the anonymous reviewers for their generous support of the project and for their encouraging, incisive, and constructive comments, which have helped improve the quality of the volume.

I express my gratitude to Vanessa Fong, Ralph Litzinger, Susan Brownell, Mayfair Yang, Federico Varese, Jun Jing, Marc Blecher, Wanning Sun, Mark Selden, and Xin Liu for their continuous inspiration and unwavering encouragement and support. Thank you to all the contributors for their willingness to be involved and their dedication to the volume. Nana Okura Gagné and Xia Zhang have generously contributed their fieldwork pictures to be considered as the cover for the book. I owe special thanks to my life partner Dave Grass for his generous help with the book cover as well as his precious emotional support, positive encouragement, inspirational discussions, and generous patience during my fieldwork in China.

I am especially grateful to my editor at the University of Hawai'i Press, Pamela Kelley, for her enthusiasm about this project, for her insight and ingenuity that have improved its quality, and for her support in guiding me through the editorial process.

Introduction

Gender and Sexuality in Contemporary Asia

TIANTIAN ZHENG

As a researcher on gender and sexuality in China since 1998 and a professor who has taught gender and sexuality in Asia since 2003, I have always lamented the lack of a comprehensive volume that pulls together cultural politics, political economy, gender, and sexuality across Asia. Students in the Asian Studies program at my college often ask me to recommend a wide-ranging book on gender and sexuality across Asia, and I can only suggest books that are more narrowly focused on either gender or sexuality, or that deal with a single specific society or region. There is also a shortage of books that center on the lived experiences of gendered subjects. Indeed, no edited collections have brought together studies of gender and sexuality from across many different societies in Asia. Also, a survey of the existing literature shows that very few books are, in fact, ethnographic accounts of the intersection between gender and sexuality; and very few books focus on the interfaces between political economy and gender and sexuality.

Recent books on gender and sexuality in China often employ a historical and cultural analysis. *Family Revolution: Marital Strife in Contemporary Chinese Literature and Visual Culture* (Xiao 2014), for example, is a cultural and historical analysis of gender relationships and marital strife; *Regulating Prostitution in China* (Remick 2014) applies the same kind of analysis to sexuality; and *Gender in Chinese Music* (Harris, Pease, and Tan 2013) is a cultural analysis of the intersection of gender and music.[1] The same applies to recent books on gender and sexuality in Japan, South Asia, and Southeast Asia. *Modern Girls on the Go: Gender, Mobility, and Labor in Japan* (Freedman, Miller, and Yano 2013) is a historical and cultural analysis of the intersection of gender and labor, while *Gender and Nation in Meiji Japan: Modernity, Loss, and the Doing of History* (Karlin 2014) conducts the same kind of analysis in relation to gender and nationalism. *Gender in South Asia: Social Imagination and Constructed Realities* (Subhadra 2013) is a historical and cultural analysis of construction of gender, while *Sexual Sites, Seminal Attitudes: Sexualities, Masculinities and Culture in South Asia* (Srivastava 2004) similarly analyzes sex and sexualities. *Gender Pluralism: Southeast Asia since Early Modern Times* (Peletz 2009) is a historical and cultural analysis of gender pluralism, while *Gender and Islam in Southeast Asia* (Schröter 2013) applies the same approach to the intersection of gender and religion.[2]

This volume offers a current, grounded, and critical analysis of the complex intersections of gender, sexuality, and political economy across different societies in Asia. Moreover, rather than focusing on institutional and structural policies concerning gender and sexuality (Chant 2012; Ferree 2010; Marchand and Runyan 2010), this volume centers on the stories of the gendered subjects themselves as an entrée into a systematic investigation of the cultural politics of gender and sexuality in Asia. Sexual mores and gender roles are in a constant state of flux in Asia in consonance with the changing economic, political, and cultural forces in the new globalizing era. How have economic shifts and social changes in Asia altered and reconfigured the cultural meanings of gender and sexuality? How have the changing political economies and social milieus in Asia influenced and shaped the inner workings and micropolitics of family structure, gender relationships, intimate romance, transactional sex, and sexual behaviors?

In exploring the cultural politics of gender and sexuality amid rapid social, political, and economic transformations in contemporary Asia, this volume's goal is to interrogate tradition-bound social and gender roles in Asia and demonstrate how meanings of gender and sexuality are in constant flux, shaped by cultural, political, and economic factors.[3] Contributors to this volume have conducted intense ethnographic fieldwork variously in China, Japan, Cambodia, Vietnam, India, Pakistan, Hong Kong, Thailand, and Taiwan. Their grounded, unique research sheds light on how configurations of gender and sexuality are constituted, negotiated, contested, transformed, and at times perpetuated and reproduced in private, intimate experiences.

This volume fills a significant gap in the literature and makes major contributions by not only exploring the intersections of gender and sexuality, but also integrating them with cultural and political economic analysis. As such, chapters in this volume theorize and conceptualize the ways in which gender and sexuality are not only linked to changing cultural meanings, but also inextricably intertwined with shifting power relations and political economy. Each chapter unravels the ways in which intimate/gendered/sexual experiences are impinged upon by state policies, economic realities, cultural ideologies, and social hierarchies.

Cultural Politics of Gender and Sexuality

Gender and sexuality constitute humans' most intimate and personal experiences. Yet the personal is political, just as the cultural is political. As Clifford Geertz (1973) points out, culture permeates every aspect of human experiences. Cultural politics is often defined as a domain where meanings and practices are constituted and negotiated, and relationships between dominance and subordination are defined and contested (see also Jackson 1991). The intersections between the cultural and the political, the ideological and the material, cannot be revealed until culture and politics are regarded not as separate entities, but as a coherent whole.

The interface between personal experiences and power relations evinces the fact that power relations permeate personal lives in the configurations of gender and sexuality. In other words, our most intimate, personal existence is structured by power relations. This volume theorizes the interplay of gender, sexuality, power, and politics in Asia by analyzing ordinary people's private, everyday life experiences relating to their family planning choices, gender relationships, intimate romances, transactional sex, sexual practices, and sexual behaviors.

Despite a biological basis, gender and sexuality are expressed, constructed, and experienced culturally, with their meanings in constant flux across different historical junctures and different cultural contexts (Klein 2003).[4] Even the most taken-for-granted gender behaviors and sexual practices are not universal or ubiquitous to all humans, but are varied and diversified cultural meanings and social practices specific to cultural contexts. Historians have demonstrated that sexual practices and gender behaviors have changed and shifted throughout history, and that these changes are inextricably linked to political, economic, and cultural changes (e.g., Laqueur 1992).[5] Anthropologists have shown from ethnographic research that human beings express vastly variegated articulations of gender and sexuality that are intricately interconnected with their cultural milieu (e.g., Herdt 2005; Mead 1935). The anthropologist Gilbert Herdt (2005), for instance, in his study of masculinity and same-sex practices, argues that boys of the Sambia tribe in Papua New Guinea go through the initiation ritual of ingesting the semen of older men for years to build their masculinity and mature into men. In this cultural context, the same-sex acts do not warrant the label "homosexual"—a personal and social identity with a particular history within the Western cultural context—but must be understood in the Sambia's cultural context. In this context, the same-sex acts are cultural practices that are informed and constituted by gender ideologies of antagonism and cultural beliefs in the finiteness of men's seminal essence and the role of its ingestion in boys' maturation into men. Herdt contends the cultural malleability of sexual activities such as same-sex practices, which are shaped by cultural contexts with diverse meanings.

Anthropologist Margaret Mead (1935) also highlights the cultural nature of sex roles and examines the ways in which sex roles are acculturated and not programmed by nature. Mead portrays the different roles females and males play in different aboriginal societies and argues that culture is a primary factor determining masculine and feminine social characteristics and behaviors. In her research on whether American adolescents' emotional stress and turmoil is biologically inherent or culturally determined, Mead argues that her research of twenty-five young women in three villages in Samoa shows that adolescents there are neither stressed nor constrained. Mead (1935, 234) concludes that adolescence is not necessarily a time of stress and strain, but that cultural conditions make it so. She explains that the stress-free character of adolescence in Samoa results from different cultural and social arrangements, where adolescent women enjoy a casual sexual code and adult caretaking that bestows upon them knowledge of sexuality, birth, and death and helps them maintain mental health.[6]

Gender and sexuality cannot be analyzed or understood without understanding the social and cultural contexts that surround them. Indeed, gender and sexuality are structured and shaped by the social and cultural environment, which defines the rules, customs, and meanings associated with sexual practices, femininities, and masculinities. Anthropologists have investigated and explored the ways in which sexual and gendered behaviors are taught and learned in societies, the malleability of gender and sexuality cross-culturally, and the embeddedness of gender and sexuality in the social and cultural milieu. This volume explores how the rapid social, political, and cultural transformations occurring in contemporary Asia are affecting gender and sexuality. How are the meanings of gender and sexuality in flux in contemporary Asia? In the following sections, I address these issues of gender and sexuality through their intersections with (1) cultural/institutional contexts, (2) power and agency, and (3) political economy.

Gender, Sexuality, and Cultural Contexts

Examples of the cultural contexts in which gender and sexuality are embedded are the state, the family, the workplace, communities, and institutions. Each has power to define and control the meanings of gender and sexuality. How do the state, family, institutions, and communities interact with political policies and economic realities in shaping sexual practices and gendered experiences? How are private experiences of gender and sexuality structured by larger social contexts? How are cultural meanings of gender and sexuality enacted, challenged, and reconfigured by the lived experiences on the ground? In answering these questions, this volume weaves ethnographies into anthropological theories to shed light on the cultural politics of gender and sexuality.

Among the myriad institutions that define and regulate sexuality, the most dominant is the state (Connell 1990; Foucault 1978). The state represents the process that organizes reproductive relations through institutionalization of marriage and shapes culture and ideology associated with gender and sexuality. As a structure of power, the state is both external and internal to gender and sexuality (Connell 1990). Under the process of state regulations that have evolved in different stages throughout the history, the meanings of gender and sexuality have been constructed, constituted, and reconfigured (Foucault 1978). Through laws and administrative arrangements, the state organizes and regulates gender power relations and sexual practices by setting boundaries, promoting proper masculinities and femininities, normalizing conjugal families, and criminalizing specific sexual and gendered behaviors such as domestic violence, same-sex sex, and transactional sex (see also Amar 2013; Carver and Mottier 1998; Connell 1990; Randall and Waylen 2002). The state hence plays a pivotal role in creating and structuring gender and sexuality.

In categorizing, regulating, and policing gender and sexuality, the state seeks to ensure stability and maintain control (see Connell 1990). In China studies, for instance, research has shown that state discourse of gender and sexuality has suppressed and subordinated women and the same-sex attracted population, whose interests have been subsumed under the state-building process (Harriet 1997; Hershatter 2007; Hershatter and Honig 1988; Hua 2013; Yang 1999a, 1999b; Zheng 2009a, 2009b, 2014). Researchers such as Phyllis Andors (1983) and Margery Wolf (1985) have argued that during the Great Leap Forward and Cultural Revolution from the 1950s to the 1970s, the state's slogan "Women Can Hold Up Half of the Sky" on the surface allowed women to participate in the social construction of communism and garner liberation through socializing housework and child care. In reality, however, women's interests were subsumed under the socialist construction project of the state, and women were subject to the double burden of housework and social labor. Women were not equal in working conditions, in pay, and in educational opportunity. The liberation of women, in effect, was rendered secondary to the goal of socialism. Repressed in many ways by the state's political agenda, women found their issues and concerns ignored and unaddressed.

The essential role of the state in the Maoist era is undeniable. Yet in the post-Mao era, scholars such as Mayfair Yang (1999a) observe that although the country is evolving into the fastest-growing capitalist economy in the world, we must pay special heed to the state as well as to the market economy when we study gender in China because the state still plays the most crucial role in economic development. This is because the state regards economic development not as a goal, but as a means to state power (Yang 1999a). Thus an inquiry into gender issues must examine the multiple relations that women and men have with the state. Along this analytical line of inquiry, chapters in this volume investigate the ways in which existing notions of gender and sexuality are linked to the institutional power of the state, which shapes the private sphere of lived experiences.

In Chapter 1, "Sexuality, Class, and Neoliberal Ideology: Same-Sex Attracted Men and Money Boys in Postsocialist China," Tiantian Zheng explores the impact of the state's neoliberal ideology on same-sex men's sexual practices and intimate relationships. Zheng argues that the state legitimizes and consolidates state power through neoliberal political ideology that deems good subjects as economically entrepreneurial and enterprising, sexually normative (heterosexual), self-managing, and politically docile. Zheng investigates the ways in which the state ideology is embraced by same-sex attracted men through engaging in a variety of sexual practices to fashion themselves as ideal postsocialist subjects. As a result, the state ideology helps produce a myriad of sexual practices and shapes the intimate sphere of lived experiences.

In Chapter 5, "Mobilizing the Masses to Change Something Intimate: The Process of Desexualization in China's Family Planning Campaign," Danning Wang focuses on the ways in which the state family planning campaign desexualizes the propaganda discourse and effectively transforms an individual and private issue into a public issue with political economic significance. Wang contextualizes the family planning campaign within the state's efforts to promote late marriage, modern midwifery, and sterilization, and argues that by eliminating the issue of sexuality, the state campaign discourse effectively defines the individual as part of a collective or a family, which in turn strengthens state power.

In Chapter 7, "Labor, Masculinity, and History: *Bangbang* Men in Chongqing, China," Xia Zhang scrutinizes the ramifications of state discourses of masculinity on rural migrant men who are porters or carriers in China. Zhang examines the ways in which the Chinese state in different historical stages has defined and constructed meanings of masculinity, and how these changing dominant gender ideologies contribute to Chinese porters' dynamic experience of gendered identity in contemporary China.

In Chapter 10, "Media, Sex, and the Self in Cambodia," Heidi Hoefinger explores the state's growing emphasis on autonomy that is at odds with more collectivist modes of living and being. This incongruity, as Hoefinger contends, creates a new arena of anxiety for the women, who are caught between the liberating and constraining forces of globalization. Hoefinger argues that women use subactivism in the context of the bar subculture to resist and defy patriarchy while maintaining the status quo of the existing sexual and gendered order.

At the same time that the state plays a central role in experiences of gender and sexuality, the increasing complexity of societies experiencing rapid social, political, and economic transformations in Asia means that other seemingly distant and intangible social institutions and political forces have also come to impact people's most private existence and intimate experiences through setting parameters and defining boundaries for cultural mores of gender and sexuality. In Chapter 2, "Producing Purity: An Ethnographic Study of a Neotraditionalist Ladies' Academy in Contemporary Urban China," Kevin Carrico examines the ways in which the nationwide Chinese institution of Ladies' Academies employs neotraditionalist "ladies' education" (*shunü jiaoyu*) programs to transform contemporary women into "proper ladies" through immersion in traditional culture. Carrico's ethnographic study of one such institution critically reinterprets the search for the traditional lady as an imaginary deification of masculinity in an era of growing social insecurity.

In Chapter 4, "Feeling like a 'Man': Managing Gender, Sexuality, and Corporate Life in After-Hours Tokyo," Nana Okura Gagné investigates the ways in which the institution of hostess clubs in Japan offers complex exchanges of multiple intimacies—including economic intimacy, social intimacy, dependent intimacy, and sexual intimacy. Gagné argues that the institution of hostess clubs engenders the kinds of intimacies that open up the space for romance and love in marriage, as well as producing new challenges through the "transformation of intimacy" within the course of marriage.

In Chapter 6, "Pleasure, Patronage, and Responsibility: Sexuality and Status among New Rich Men in Contemporary China," John Osburg examines the ways in which the institutionalized elite business networks in contemporary China shape a reconfigured intimacy and romance between male entrepreneurs and female mistresses. Osburg explores the tensions between money and romance and argues that the institutionalized male-centered business networks produce a kind of intimacy wherein female mistresses mirror the social status of elite men.

In Chapter 8, "Boyz II Men: Neighborhood Associations in Western India as the Site of Masculine Identity," Madhura Lohokare explores the ways in which the institutionalized neighborhood associations in Western India impinge upon the formation and performance of masculinity by working-class young men. Lohokare contends that neighborhood associations provide the site where working-class young men construct and enact the kind of political and moral masculinity that intersects with class, caste, and place.

In Chapter 3, " 'Tonight, You Are a Man!': Negotiating Embodied Resistance in Local Thai Nightclubs," Danielle Antoinette Hidalgo and Tracy Royce illuminate the ways in which the institution of nightclubs in Bangkok shapes the construction, performance, and contestation of hegemonic Thai femininity and masculinity. Through examining different enactments of masculinities on the dance floor of nightclubs, they argue that these performances of masculinities destabilize and resist normative Thai gender and sexuality.

In Chapter 9, "Marriage and Reproduction in East Asian Cities: Views from Single Women in Shanghai, Hong Kong, and Tokyo," Lynne Nakano explores the ways in which the institution of marriage shapes single women's view of romance, motherhood, and romance in East Asia. Nakano argues that single women in Hong Kong, Shanghai, and Tokyo did not choose to be single. Nor did they contest the entrenched institution of marriage. Rather, they aspired for marriage and motherhood, and considered themselves unfit and ineligible for the marriage market and incapable of reproduction.

In Chapter 11, "Islam, Marriage, and *Yaari:* Making Meaning of Male Same-Sex Sexual Relationships in Pakistan," Ahmed Afzal illuminates the ways in which the institutions of marriage, family, and religion in Pakistan shape modern male same-sex sexual relationships, romance, and eroticism. Afzal argues that modern same-sex romance in Pakistan is constructed, formed, and enacted through varied negotiations with these traditional institutions to find new meanings and expressions.

In Chapter 12, "Racialization of Foreign Women in the Transnational Marriage Market of Taiwan," Hsunhui Tseng highlights the ways in which the institution of the marriage market in Taiwan impinges upon the hierarchal ranking of Vietnamese and Ukraine brides and the subsequent matching of them to men of different classes in Taiwan. Tseng demonstrates that the institution of the marriage market in Taiwan ranks Vietnamese and Ukraine brides according to race, nationality, and political economy, which influences men's desires for, and romance with, these women.

Power and Agency

While social institutions and political forces such as the state enforce sexual mores and gender ideologies, people on the ground actively negotiate, manipulate, and contest the sexual and gender norms.[7] Individual practices beyond gender and sexual norms often times conflict with state hegemony and institutional powers at the levels of families and communities. It is within these private and personal domains where the penetration of power and contestation of power simultaneously coincide and collide with each other.

Anthropologists have written at length about the rift between ideology and practice in the gender and sexuality system (Ortner 1990). Although many researchers have insisted on a universal male dominance in all human societies, other anthropologists have urged us to pay heed to the discrepancy between the ideology of male supremacy and the reality of female power (Ogasawara 1998; Ortner 1990).[8] As Sherry Ortner (1990, 78) contends, just as female power can be found in male-dominated societies, male power can be located in egalitarian societies. Hence neither the ideology nor the behavior patterns are "total."

The gap between ideology and practice leads us to examine not only the impact of institutional forces such as the state on intimate, private experiences, but also the impact of private experiences on the constraining forces and structural norms. The dynamic relationships between structure and agency render individuals both agents and victims. On the one hand, their behaviors and practices in intimate spheres cannot be understood outside of the structure that circumvents, shapes, and victimizes them. On the other hand, the structure cannot be understood without the actions, behaviors, and choices they make as agents to either contest or reproduce the structure in which they are entrapped.

Anthropologist Kira Hall (1996), for instance, in her portrayal of the marginalized Banaras *hijras* (individuals who are discussed by anthropologists as transvestites, eunuchs, hermaphrodites, or a third sex) in India, explores the ways in which *hijras* subvert gender asymmetry by appropriating it for their own benefit. As Hall states, the *hijras* manipulate the socially constructed cultural meanings embedded in the Hindi linguistic gender forms to maintain their solidarity, and assert their social identity as females while at the same time attaining power as males. In so doing, the *hijras* imbue this cultural matrix of gender linguistic forms with new social meanings for their own political self-interests, thus perpetuating and contributing to that mainstream with their agency by reshaping it and infusing it with new social and political meanings.

Along a similar line of analytical inquiry, chapters in this volume unravel the reconfigured notions of gender and sexuality in lived experiences to understand how power is manifested, resisted, produced, and reproduced. In Chapter 1, Zheng explores the dynamic relationships between the same-sex attracted men and the state. On the surface, same-sex attracted men fit themselves into the state hegemony of heterosexual marriage and the heterosexual norm through engaging in heterosexual marriage. Behind the scene, however, they fulfill their personal desires and engage in same-sex practices through clandestine consumption of sexual services and congregation in cruising places to meet potential sexual partners. This kind of seemingly "everyday act of resistance" through surreptitious same-sex practices outside the socially acceptable realm, however, seeks not to overthrow state policies or state regulations, or to mitigate or minimize domination. Rather, it seeks to satisfy both social norms and individual desires. In so doing, it makes same-sex attracted men both agents and victims, who are complicit in reproducing and reinforcing heterosexual marriage and the heterosexual norm in society.

In Chapter 7, Zhang argues that Chinese rural migrant porters contest the state discourse of the dominant meanings of masculinity that marginalizes Chinese rural migrant men. More specifically, Zhang explores the ways in which the Chinese rural migrant porters refashion their masculine identities through paradoxically resisting and adopting the changing dominant meanings of gendered ideals.

In Chapter 10, Heidi Hoefinger unravels the ways in which young women working in entertainment sectors in Cambodia resist social stigma and challenge gender hierarchy through consuming material goods and supporting their families. Hoefinger demonstrates that these young women employed in hostess bars negotiate the empowering and constraining forces of globalization and neoliberal capitalism and choose to work as "professional girlfriends." In so doing, they contest gender asymmetry and redefine boundaries of gendered respectability.

In Chapter 3, Hidalgo and Royce examine three different enactments of masculinities on the dance floor of nightclubs and argue that these performances destabilize, contest, and resist normative, hegemonic Thai gender and sexuality.

Gender, Sexuality, and Political Economy

The emphasis on political economy and ethnographically grounded research in this volume departs from the cultural paradigm in the existing literature and provides theoretical interventions. Studies on gender and sexuality during the second wave of the women's movement and postmodernism focused on either a cultural analysis of gender asymmetry or a misguided Marxist interpretation that deemed cultural "superstructure" to be determined by economic "base." While cultural analysis leaves out a political and economic perspective, economic analysis leaves out a cultural and political perspective. As research has shown, a woman's social status does not increase just because she has raised her economic status (Pun 2005; Yan 2008; Zhang 2001; Zheng 2009a). Rather, we need to take into account the cultural values associated with the type of work she does, the political environment she is in, and the social and political meanings of the space—rural or urban—in which she is positioned (Pun 2005; Yan 2008; Zhang 2001; Zheng 2009a). In a nutshell, we need to provide a nuanced analysis of culture and political economy to understand and theorize gender and sexuality. This volume follows this line of analytical inquiry and contends that gender and sexuality cannot be understood outside of the changing political economies and cultural milieu in which they are embedded.

The intersection between political economy and gender and sexuality is central to the volume. Changes in political economy are inexorably linked to cultural and ideological changes in gender and sexuality. For example, researchers Karen Sacks (1982) and Eleanor Leacock (1988) have argued that male dominance is inseparably intersected with the emergence of private property, privatization of kinship, colonialism, social stratification, and the contact of egalitarian foraging and early horticultural societies with the West. In China studies, scholars (Lee 1999; Walker 1993; Zheng 2009a) have also argued that gender meanings result from a wide array of cultural, political and economic factors that include women's interests subsumed under the state-building project, state discourse on gender and sexuality, gender division of labor, the male head's control of economic resources in the patriarchal peasant economy, the capitalist production regime, globalization, and rising entrepreneurial masculinities.

In queer studies, anthropologists (D'Emilio 1983; Ross and Rapp 1981) have also argued that gay identities and gay communities were historically created and structured by capitalism. As Ross and Rapp (1981) point out, capitalism has led to a vulnerable material foundation of family life, causing individuals to leave their families and reside elsewhere. This kind of displacement has helped lesbian and gay identities and communities to develop. However, at the same time, capitalism enforces heterosexual marriage to ensure reproduction of workers, which leads to reproduction of heterosexism and homophobia. The contradiction implicit in capitalism evinces the intersection between economic and cultural changes (Ross and Rapp 1981).

Chapters in this volume critically analyze not only the intricate relationships between gender, sexuality, and the state, but also the ways changing concepts of gender and sexuality are shaped by economic and global forces. In these essays, the authors address issues such as how same-sex romance, intimacies, and relationships in postsocialist China are implicated by social inequality, class structure, and consumerism; how tenets of femininity and masculinity are reconfigured and transformed in Asia; how sexuality and intimacy are manipulated by outside factors such as the state in family planning campaigns to meet its goals; how the continuing "democratization of marriage" and the private sphere under late capitalism in Japan has opened up the space for romance and love in marriage; and how romance and intimacy between elite businessmen and mistresses in China are shaped by economic networks, cultural division between the public and private spheres, and the tensions between emotional and financial interests. From these diverse accounts of gender and sexuality in various contemporary Asian contexts, this volume traces the ways in which changing cultural values and political economy contribute to and are influenced by changing gender perceptions.

As shown, unlike previous writing on gender and sexuality that focuses on cultural studies and textual analysis, chapters in this volume foreground cross-cultural ethnographic research by anthropologists to critically examine cultural politics of gender and sexuality in various countries and regions in Asia. This volume should be welcomed by researchers and scholars in a number of disciplines including sociology, anthropology, history, political science, and Asian studies. It is also appropriate for adoption in a number of courses in anthropology, sociology, Asian Studies, gender and sexuality studies, women's studies, urban studies, and LGBTQ studies.

Outline of the Book

In "Sexuality, Class, and Neoliberal Ideology: Same-Sex Attracted Men and Money Boys in Postsocialist China," Tiantian Zheng, after conducting twelve months of fieldwork in Dalian, China, unravels Chinese same-sex attracted men's (*tongzhi*) negotiations and interactions with the dominant discourse of the "normal" postsocialist person, and the impact it has on the class structure, career, and romantic relationships among *tongzhi*. While class structure among Chinese *tongzhi* is largely shaped by wealth, higher-class *tongzhi* can practice what Zheng calls "covert gayness" as they can afford to consume and congregate in more secretive places such as high-cost bars. Lower-class *tongzhi* are compelled to practice more "overt gayness" as they tend to cruise in free, open spaces such as parks and public bathrooms. The dominant discourse of the "normal" person also impinges upon choices and intimacies of romantic relationships and career choices of some rural migrant men who work as money boys (sex workers) and plan to accumulate enough money to catapult themselves to a higher-level career such as businessman. Wealth and class are implicated in the selection of partners and in the intimacy of romantic relationships. This chapter argues that *tongzhi* embrace the dominant discourse to pronounce themselves as "normal" postsocialist persons. In so doing, they paradoxically are co-opted by the state apparatus, thereby legitimizing and perpetuating state power.

In "Producing Purity: An Ethnographic Study of a Neotraditionalist Ladies' Academy in Contemporary Urban China," Kevin Carrico discusses how neotraditionalist "ladies' education" (*shunü jiaoyu*) programs have emerged in urban China in recent years. Female students from all over China come to the Ladies' Academy that is the focus of his study to pass their days reading the classics, painting traditional paintings, learning to cook, playing the *guqin* (a traditional Chinese musical instrument), and sewing Han clothing, embodying an image of "five millennia of tradition." Yet interviews with the all-male teaching staff locate students' activities within a constraining image of the traditional lady as pure, reserved, loyal, and aware of her "proper place" in society. Citing mythology, dynastic history, and the classics, teachers ideologically naturalize a fundamental difference between male and female, while at the same time declaring that this balancing difference was lost in modernity. Numerous contemporary social ills, from money worship to poisoned milk powder, are then attributed to the intrusion of the purportedly culturally imperialist concept of gender equality, producing a narrative of decline that portrays the Chinese male as at once an innocent victim and the sole savior capable of recapturing tradition and revitalizing national glory. The exaltation of the pure yet lost traditional lady is thus ironically an imaginary purification and deification of contemporary maleness; yet female students nevertheless come to be invested in this normative yet highly marketable vision of ladyhood.

In "'Tonight, You Are a Man!' Negotiating Embodied Resistance in Local Thai Nightclubs," Danielle Hidalgo and Tracy Royce build upon Adam Isaiah Green's concept of the sexual field and examine how genders and sexualities are embodied, enacted, and contested on nightclub dance floors in Bangkok. Hidalgo and Royce map out and analyze three separate enactments of embodied resistance to the general rules and regulations for doing gender and sexuality: mocking ideal gay masculinity via impromptu tabletop dancing; resisting hegemonic Thai femininity via the cabaret show; and masculine transformation via negotiating the dance floor. In all of these episodes, clubbers or performers located outside of the sexual field (or lower on its tiers of desirability) used humor and playfulness as a means of disrupting the serious business of the club's gender and sexual hierarchies.

In "Feeling like a 'Man': Managing Gender, Sexuality, and Corporate Life in After-Hours Tokyo," Nana Okura Gagné argues that during Japan's rapid economic rise, corporate consumption was conspicuous and promoted through corporate patronage of the "night business" leisure spaces of hostess clubs. Building on Japan's long history of female attendant services and the intensified "gray zone" of Japan's leisure industries under Japanese capitalism, these spaces offered both men and women new opportunities for intimacy and exchange. Moreover, as a social space situated within private social relationships and broader economic relations, the particular function of this "management of intimacies" at hostess clubs draws our attention to larger structural changes in the management of private and public spheres within Japanese political economy. While it is tempting to think of such intimacy and exchange as characteristic of the "transformation of intimacy" under late modernity, which presupposes that all relationships have become utilitarian and based on a "democratic" model of gender equality and mutual self-disclosure, this chapter aims to understand the dynamics of intimacy in late capitalist Japan. Based on her ethnographic research at three hostess clubs, Gagné argues that rather than representing the birth of new subjectivities and new forms of intimacies as a result of a destabilization of individual identities and social roles under late modernity, the kinds of intimacies at hostess clubs highlight how the continuing "democratization of marriage" and the private sphere under late capitalism has opened up the space for romance and love in marriage, and yet it has also produced new challenges in marriages.

In "Mobilizing the Masses to Change Something Intimate: The Process of Desexualization in China's Family Planning Campaign," Danning Wang states that it is well known worldwide that China specializes in utilizing mass movements and political campaigns to target and change individual behavior patterns. From the New Life Movement in the 1930s to the antidrug crusades in the 1950s and 1990s, such public campaigns were organized, with the involvement of both bureaucrats and citizens, to transform living environments and behavior patterns in the realm of public health and hygiene (Dirlik 1975; Zhou 1999). As China's longest campaign, the family/birth planning program shares some basic procedures, symbols, and attitudes of moral correctness with these efforts at mass mobilization (White 2006). Wang focuses on how the formation and implementation of the family planning campaign deliberately produced desexualized propaganda discourses and effectively transformed an individual and private issue into something public with political economic significance. Based on the historical archival data from Tianjin and Beijing in the 1960s, Wang contextualizes the family planning campaign within the state's efforts to promote late marriage, modern midwifery, and sterilization. By removing the aspect of sexuality, the campaign discourses effectively transformed the individual into a member of a collective. This later paved the way for a nationalistic approach to articulating a national strategy of empowerment.

In "Pleasure, Patronage, and Responsibility: Sexuality and Status among New Rich Men in Contemporary China," John Osburg examines the role of mistresses and sex workers in elite business networks in contemporary China. Based on his fieldwork with a group of wealthy entrepreneurs from 2002–2006, Osburg examines the role these women play in mirroring status and forming alliances between elite men. Most of his male informants maintained a strong division between the "outside" world of business, pleasure, and romance associated with their mistresses and the domestic realm of "responsibility" associated with their wives. Paid forms of sex, although an integral part of business entertaining, ranked the lowest among these men's sexual relationships, yet many men supported their mistresses with lavish gifts of cash, cars, and apartments. Osburg analyzes the tensions generated by the ambiguous status of these relationships that operate in a gray area between commodified and uncommodified realms and are rooted in both sentiment and financial interest.

In "Labor, Masculinity, and History: *Bangbang* Men in Chongqing, China," Xia Zhang investigates the connection between gender and history, drawing on the example of contemporary Chinese rural migrant men who are referred to as *bangbang* (porters or carriers) in Chongqing. In particular, Zhang examines the historical basis of the competing meanings of Chinese masculinity through an investigation of the persistent shifts in the national and popular discourse about masculinity during the presocialist, socialist, and postsocialist eras in China. She further examines how the changing dominant gender ideology contributes to the dynamic experience of gendered identity by *bangbang* in contemporary China. Whereas previous studies of masculinity and labor have focused on the impact of transnational migration and localized globalization on men's sense of self, little has been written about the historical changes in the dominant discourse on masculinity in a specific culture in relation to rural men's experience of migration. In Chongqing, *bangbang* experience both masculine domination and marginalization through migration, laying claim to competing models of masculinity in their newly developing urban subjectivities and expressing masculine pride when they return to their home villages. The gender dynamics that they experience during migration are intimately related to the changing notion of masculinity over time in China. Zhang suggests that new theoretical insights can be gained by exploring the fluid and complex relations between masculinity and labor from a historical perspective. Zhang argues for the importance of historical constructions of gender in understanding the decisions and experiences of rural migrant men in postsocialist China.

"Boyz II Men: Neighborhood Associations in Western India as the Site of Masculine Identity," is based on an ethnography of the lives of young men in a lower-caste, working-class neighborhood in the city of Pune. Madhura Lohokare elaborates on the role of local neighborhood associations in mediating the construction and performance of a class-, caste-, and place-specific masculine identity for their male members. The chapter focuses on the moral discourse of mutual help surrounding neighborhood associations and their active enmeshment with local electoral politics in order to highlight the specific masculinity that these discourses and practices generate. Lohokare contends that in the light of their acute marginalization from urban social space, belonging to a neighborhood association provides space for working-class boys and young men to project a collective self-image geared toward upholding a class-based moral code prescribed by the association and preserving self-respect, while simultaneously consolidating a strong sense of belonging to a place.

In "Marriage and Reproduction in East Asian Cities: Views from Single Women in Shanghai, Hong Kong, and Tokyo," Lynne Nakano observes that in

East Asia, marriage represents a significant life step for women and involves expectations that the woman is willing and capable of giving birth. At the same time, rising levels of education and increased work opportunities for women, particularly in urban areas, have led to rising marriage ages and declining birthrates. Based on interviews with women in Hong Kong, Shanghai, and Tokyo, Nakano explores how single women living in these three cities view marriage and its expectations of reproduction. She argues that single women do not resist marriage and the expectation that the wife will give birth. Rather women who remain single past the age of thirty maintain that they are personally ill-suited to the institution of marriage or that they have yet to find an appropriate person to marry. Nakano interviewed women who wanted to marry because they wanted to become mothers as well as women who believed that they did not possess a complete female physical body and felt that they might be incapable of physical reproduction. In these latter cases, women thought themselves to be ineligible for the marriage market, and sought other ways of finding meaning in their lives.

In "Media, Sex, and the Self in Cambodia," Heidi Hoefinger explores the tensions and intersections between sex and intimacy, media and consumption, and the precarity of female individualization in Cambodia. With a focus on "professional girlfriends" and women employed in the Western-oriented hostess bar scene, Hoefinger illustrates how sex and intimacy are used as a means to consume material goods, and how desires for consumption and individualization are heavily influenced by media and globalization. Due to the collectivist nature of Cambodian culture, however, this growing emphasis on autonomy has created a new arena of anxiety for the women, who are left negotiating both the liberatory and constricting forces of globalization and neoliberal capitalism. Hoefinger concludes that despite experiencing constant contradictions around individualization, and relentless stigma for the decisions they make, the women transgress the boundaries of respectability, challenge gendered double standards, and reconcile individualism and collectivity through subactivism and by becoming proud patrons and providers for their families.

In "Islam, Marriage, and *Yaari*: Making Meaning of Male Same-Sex Sexual Relationships in Pakistan," Ahmed Afzal provides a critical ethnographic analysis of cultural constructions of modern male same-sex sexual relationships and eroticism in Pakistan. Afzal examines three intersecting registers for making meaning of modern male same-sex sexual relationships: (1) cultural scripts and histories of homosociality and intimacy in South Asia; (2) conceptions of marriage and familial obligations in Pakistan; and (3) assertions of religious self-identification as Muslims. Afzal argues that the cultural constructions of male sexuality and same-sex sexual relationships and eroticism in Pakistan discussed do not represent a premodern gay identity. Rather, he contends that analysis shows how a range of sexualities are produced and enacted in the non-West and belies common misunderstandings of Muslim and South Asian cultures and societies as inherently intolerant of homosexuality. Drawing on the life experiences of Pakistani men enables a consideration of new ways of accounting for modern same-sex sexual relationships and eroticism in South Asia, and varied negotiations of sexuality with gender, religion, and globalization.

In "Racialization of Foreign Women in the Transnational Marriage Market of Taiwan," Hsunhui Tseng observes that Taiwan has seen a marriage-related migrant flow from China and Vietnam since the late 1990s. In early 2000s, a few matchmaking companies targeting East European women as a new foreign bride group were formed. The foreign bride phenomenon has drawn the public's and scholars' attention to its social consequences in the past decade. Tseng focuses on the marriage market: How does the market mechanism differentiate foreign brides' value according to their race and nationality and match them with potential clients from different classes in Taiwan? Tseng explores how representations of "foreign women" of different nationalities were produced and reproduced by proprietors, mess media, and other social groups to meet a kind of social imaginary. Tseng argues that the reason why Vietnamese women as ideal wives can be successfully marketed by the marriage brokerage companies is that they provide a nostalgic space for traditional families to perform their patriarchic imaginaries as they were in early Taiwanese society, in which the core value of the family was secured by the unequal gender dynamics.

In a nutshell, this volume offers a grounded, critical analysis of the complex intersections of gender, sexuality, culture, and political economy in contemporary Asia. In so doing, it contributes to the existing literature on a myriad of topics, including gender and sexuality in cultural contexts, the economic, social, and political changes in contemporary Asia, relationships between gender/sexuality and sociopolitical, economic, and familial institutions, questions of power and agency, and political economy.

Notes and References

1. See also Chen (2014), Du and Chen (2013), Evans (2007), Hershatter (2007, 2014), Jeffreys (2004, 2006), Mann (2011), Micollier (2003), Rofel (2007), and Sang (2003).
2. See also Arondekar (2009), Banerjee (2012), Bornstein and Bergman (2010), Burns and Brooks (2013), Derks (2008), Germer, Mackie, and Wöhr (2014), Ikeya (2011), Kimura (2013), Loomba and Lukose (2012), McLelland and Dasgupta (2005), Miller and Bardsley (2003), Saraswati (2013), Sato (2003), Sinnott (2004), and Tickamyer and Kusujiarti (2012).

3. This volume originates from a panel that I organized for the Association of Asian Studies Annual Conference in 2013. I thank the panelists for participating in the exciting panel and contributing their high-quality papers to both the panel and this volume. I thank Kevin Carrico for his constructive comments and careful edits that have improved the quality of this introduction.

4. Laura Klein (2003) notes that the meanings of gender vary at different historical times and in different cultures and societies. Klein examines the ways in which gender is constructed in different institutions such as the family and society, by power, supernatural beliefs, religious ideologies, and the realities of globalization and transnationalism.

5. Thomas Laqueur (1992) provides a model to contrast the body in the industrialized West with the body in the less industrialized Western societies. The less industrialized Western societies, according to Laqueur, have a one-sex model of the body (male sex) and a cosmic hierarchical view of the body, whereas the industrialized Western societies have a two-sex model and a rational scientific view of the body as composed of smaller units.

6. Margaret Mead (1935) discusses the ways in which a casual and positive attitude toward life in the social milieu influences experiences of adolescents in Samoa. She states that adolescents in Samoa enjoy a casual sexual code, despite resistance from missionaries. The Samoan church does press youth hard for participation that would curb their sexual freedom. Sexual jealousy is absent and rape is a foreign idea to them. Mead points out that the less baffling choices of creeds and careers make them less stressful. Also, she argues that Samoan child-rearing practices and attitudes toward sex account for the difference between American and Samoan adolescence, with numerous adult caretakers releasing Samoan children from close attachments to their own parents.

7. Here I offer four examples to illustrate gendered contestations against power. Aihwa Ong (1987) spells out various modes of capitalist control and women's group resistance in Malaysia. As she contends, in addition to the division of labor, new techniques of power operate through controlling a series of spaces, including the body, the shop floor, the state, and the public sphere, to discipline women workers. Women start a "cultural struggle" to contest these disciplinary regimes through family claims on wage labor, moral critique of work relations, spirit possession, and organized group movements. Bianca Petkova (1998, 186), argues that Bulgarian women, though silenced in media discourses, actively reconstruct cultural definitions about them in ways that wage "one of the most quiet and most successful revolts in the history of women." Sheila Rowbotham (1998) examines the ways in which migrant women workers in Europe form community groups and trade unions to mobilize and empower themselves and refuse to be helpless victims. Stacey Burlet and Helen Reid (1998), in their research on Pakistani Muslim women in Bradford in the united Kingdom, show how these women resisted the community decision to only enlist young male representatives and leave out women completely. They mobilized an uprising calling for the representation of diversity, marking a new phase of women's challenge to the patriarchal political hegemony.

8. Yuko Ogasawara (1998) discusses what she calls the "informal power" wielded by office ladies over their male superiors at a major Tokyo bank office. She argues that women's power in the workplace is neither coincidental nor transient but inscribed in the structures of workplace male dominance. This research complicates the simplistic and monolithic approach of oppressed women and powerful men.

Amar, Paul. 2013. *The Security Archipelago: Human-Security States, Sexuality Politics, and the End of Neoliberalism*. Durham, NC: Duke University Press.

Andors, Phyllis. 1983. *The Unfinished Liberation of Chinese Women, 1949–1980*. Bloomington: Indiana University Press.

Arondekar, Anjali. 2009. *For the Record: On Sexuality and the Colonial Archive in India*. Durham, NC: Duke University Press.

Banerjee, Sikata. 2012. *Muscular Nationalism: Gender, Violence, and Empire in India and Ireland, 1914–2004*. New York: New York University Press.

Bornstein, Kate, and S. Bear Bergman. 2010. *Gender Outlaws: The Next Generation*. New York: Seal Press.

Burlet, Stacey, and Helen Reid. 1998. "A Gendered Uprising: Political Representation and Minority Ethnic Communities." *European Journal of Women's Studies* 5 (3–4): 270–287.

Burns, Susan L., and Barbara J. Brooks, eds. 2013. *Gender and Law in the Japanese Imperium*. Honolulu: University of Hawai'i Press.

Carver, Terrell, and Veronique Mottier, eds. 1998. *Politics of Sexuality: Identity, Gender, Citizenship*. New York: Routledge.

Chant, Sylvia H., ed. 2012. *The International Handbook of Gender and Poverty: Concepts, Research, Policy*. New York: Edward Elgar Publisher.

Chen, Ya-Chen, ed. 2014. *Centennial of New Modern Chinese Women and Gender Politics*. London: Routledge.

Connell, Raewyn W. 1990. "The State, Gender, and Sexual Politics: Theory and Appraisal." *Theory and Society* 19 (5): 507–544.

D'Emilio, John. 1983. "Capitalism and Gay Identity." In *Powers of Desire: The Politics of Sexuality*, edited by A. Snitow, C. Stansell, and S. Thompson, pp. 100–113. New York: Monthly Review Press.

Derks, Annuska. 2008. *Khmer Women on the Move: Exploring Work and Life in Urban Cambodia*. Honolulu: University of Hawai'i Press.

Dirlik, Arif. 1975. "The Ideological Foundations of the New Life Movement: A Study in Counterrevolution." *Journal of Asian Studies* 34 (4): 945–980.

Du, Shanshan, and Ya-chen Chen, eds. 2013. *Women and Gender in Contemporary Chinese Societies*. London: Lexington Books.

Evans, Harriet. 1997. *Women and Sexuality in China*. London: Bloomsbury Academic.

———. 2007. *The Subject of Gender: Daughters and Mothers in Urban China*. New York: Rowman and Littlefield.

Ferree, Myra Marx. 2010. "Filling the Glass: Gender Perspectives on Families." *Journal of Marriage and Family* 72 (3): 420–439.

Foucault, Michel. 1978. *History of Sexuality*. Vol. 1. Translated by Robert Hurley. New York: Random House.

Freedman, Alisa, Laura Miller, and Christine Yano, eds. 2013. *Modern Girls on the Go: Gender, Mobility, and Labor in Japan*. Stanford, CA: Stanford University Press.

Geertz, Clifford. 1973. *The Interpretation of Cultures*. New York: Basic Books.

Germer, Andrea, Vera Mackie, and Ulrike Wöhr, eds. 2014. *Gender, Nation and State in Modern Japan*. New York: Routledge.

Hall, Kira, and Veronic O'Donovan. 1996. "Shifting Gender Positions among Hindi-Speaking Hijras." In *Rethinking Language and Gender Research,* edited by V. Bergvall, J. Bing, and A. Freed, pp. 228–266. London: Longman.

Harris, Rachel, Rowan Pease, and Shzr Ee Tan. 2013. *Gender in Chinese Music.* Rochester, NY: University of Rochester Press.

Herdt, Gilbert. 2005. *The Sambia: Ritual, Sexuality, and Change in Papua New Guinea.* Lexington, KY: Cengage Learning.

Hershatter, Gail 2007. *Women in China's Long Twentieth Century.* Berkeley: University of California Press.

———. 2014. *The Gender of Memory: Rural Women and China's Collective Past.* Berkeley: University of California Press.

Hershatter, Gail, and Emily Honig. 1988. *Personal Voices: Chinese Women in the 1980's.* Stanford, CA: Stanford University Press.

Hinsch, Bret. 2010. *Women in Early Imperial China.* New York: Rowman and Littlefield.

Hua, Wen. 2013. *Buying Beauty: Cosmetic Surgery in China.* Hong Kong: Hong Kong University Press.

Ikeya, Chie. 2011. *Refiguring Women, Colonialism, and Modernity in Burma.* Honolulu: University of Hawai'i Press.

Jackson, Peter. 1991. "The Cultural Politics of Masculinity: Towards a Social Geography." *Transactions of the Institute of British Geographers* 16 (2): 199–213.

Jeffreys, Elaine. 2004.*China, Sex and Prostitution.* London: Routledge.

———, ed. 2006. *Sex and Sexuality in China.* London: Routledge.

Karlin, Jason G. 2014. *Gender and Nation in Meiji Japan: Modernity, Loss, and the Doing of History.* Honolulu: University of Hawai'i Press.

Kimura, Aya Hirata. 2013. *Hidden Hunger: Gender and the Politics of Smarter Foods.* Ithaca, NY: Cornell University Press.

Klein, Laura. 2003. *Women and Men in World Cultures.* New York: McGraw-Hill Humanities.

Laqueur, Thomas. 1992. *Making Sex: Body and Gender from the Greeks to Freud.* Cambridge, MA: Harvard University Press.

Leacock, Eleanor. 1988. *Women's Work: Development and the Division of Labor by Gender.* New York: Praeger.

Lee, Ching Kwan. 1999. *Gender and the South China Miracle: Two Worlds of Factory Women.* Berkeley: University of California Press.

Loomba, Ania, and Ritty A. Lukose, eds. 2012. *South Asian Feminisms.* Durham, NC: Duke University Press.

Mann, Susan. 2011. *Gender and Sexuality in Modern Chinese History.* Cambridge: Cambridge University Press.

Marchand, Marianne H., and Anne Sisson Runyan, eds. 2010. *Gender and Global Restructuring: Sightings, Sites and Resistances.* London: Routledge.

McLelland, Mark, and Romit Dasgupta, eds. 2005. *Genders, Trangenders and Sexualities in Japan.* London: Routledge.

Mead, Margaret. 1935. *Sex and Temperament in Three Primitive Societies.* New York: William Morrow.

Micollier, Evelyne, ed. 2003. *Sexual Cultures in East Asia: The Social Construction of Sexuality and Sexual Risk in a Time of AIDS.* New York: Routledge.

Miller, Laura, and Jan Bardsley, eds. 2003. *Bad Girls of Japan.* New York: Palgrave Macmillan.

Ogasawara, Yuko. 1998. *Office Ladies and Salaried Men.* Berkeley: University of California Press.

Ong, Aihwa. 1987. *Spirits of Resistance and Capitalist Discipline: Factory Women in Malaysia.* Albany: State University of New York Press.

Ortner, Sherry. 1990. "Gender Hegemonies." *Cultural Critique* 14 (Winter): 35–80.

Peletz, Michael G. 2009. *Gender Pluralism: Southeast Asia Since Early Modern Times.* New York: Routledge.

Petkova, Bianca. 1998. "Bulgarian Women and Discourses about Work." *European Journal of Women's Studies* 5 (3–4): 437–452.

Pun, Ngai. 2005. *Made in China: Women Factory Workers in a Global Workplace.* Durham, NC: Duke University Press.

Randall, Vicky, and Georgina Waylen, eds. 2002. *Gender, Politics and the State.* New York: Routledge.

Remick, Elizabeth J. 2014. *Regulating Prostitution in China: Gender and Local Statebuilding 1900–1937.* Stanford, CA: Stanford University Press.

Rofel, Lisa. 2007. *Desiring China: Experiments in Neoliberalism, Sexuality, and Public China.* Durham, NC: Duke University Press.

Ross, Ellen, and Rayna Rapp. 1981. "Sex and Society: A Research Note from Social History and Anthropology." *Comparative Studies in Society and History* 23 (1): 51–72.

Rowbotham, Sheila. 1998. "Weapons of the Weak: Homeworkers' Networking in Europe." *European Journal of Women's Studies* 5 (3–4): 453–463.

Sacks, Karen. 1982. *Sisters and Wives: The Past and Future of Sexual Equality.* Urbana: University of Illinois Press.

Sang, Tze-Lan D. 2003. *The Emerging Lesbian: Female Same-Sex Desire in Modern China.* Chicago: University of Chicago Press.

Saraswati, L. Ayu. 2013. *Seeing Beauty, Sensing Race in Transnational Indonesia.* Honolulu: University of Hawai'i Press.

Sato, Barbara. 2003. *The New Japanese Woman: Modernity, Media, and Women in Interwar Japan.* Durham, NC: Duke University Press.

Schröter, Susanne. 2013. *Gender and Islam in Southeast Asia.* London: Brill.

Sinnott, Megan. 2004. *Toms and Dees: Transgender Identity and Female Same-Sex Relationships in Thailand.* Honolulu: University of Hawai'i Press.

Srivastava, Sanjay, ed. 2004. *Sexual Sites, Seminal Attitudes: Sexualities, Masculinities and Culture in South Asia.* New Delhi: Sage.

Subhadra, Mitra. 2013. *Gender in South Asia: Social Imagination and Constructed Realities.* Cambridge: Cambridge University Press.

Tickamyer, Ann R., and Siti Kusujiarti. 2012. *Power, Change, and Gender Relations in Rural Java: A Tale of Two Villages.* Athens: Ohio University Press.

Walker, Kathy. 1993. "Economic Growth, Peasant Marginalization and the Sexual Division of Labor in Early 20th Century China." *Modern China* 19 (3): 354–386.

White, Tyrene. 2006. *China's Longest Campaign: Birth Planning in the People's Republic, 1949–2005.* Ithaca, NY: Cornell University Press.

Wolf, Margery. 1985. *Revolution Postponed: Women in Contemporary China.* Stanford, CA: Stanford University Press.

Xiao, Hui Faye. 2014. *Family Revolution: Marital Strife in Contemporary Chinese Literature and Visual Culture.* Seattle: University of Washington Press.

Yan, Hairong. 2008. *New Masters, New Servants: Migration, Development, and Women Workers in China.* Durham, NC: Duke University Press.

Yang, Mayfair Mei-hui. 1999a. "Introduction." In *Spaces of Their Own: Women's Public Sphere in Transnational China,* edited by M. Yang, pp. 1–34. Minneapolis: University of Minnesota Press.

———. 1999b. "From Gender Erasure to Gender Difference: State Feminism, Consumer Sexuality, and Women's Public Sphere in China." In *Spaces of Their Own: Women's Public Sphere in Transnational China,* edited by M. Yang, pp. 35–67. Minneapolis: University of Minnesota Press.

Zhang, Li. 2001. *Strangers in the City: Reconfigurations of Space, Power, and Social Networks within China's Floating Population.* Stanford, CA: Stanford University Press.

Zheng, Tiantian. 2009a. *Red Lights: The Lives of Sex Workers in Postsocialist China.* Minneapolis: University of Minnesota Press.

———. 2009b. *Ethnographies of Prostitution in Contemporary China: Gender Relations, HIV/AIDS, and Nationalism.* New York: Palgrave Macmillan.

———. 2014. "Contesting Heteronormality: Recasting Same-Sex Desire in China's Past and Present." *Wagadu: A Journal of Transnational Women's and Gender Studies* 12: 15–40.

Zhou, Yongming. 1999. *Anti-Drug Crusades in Twentieth-Century China: Nationalism, History, and State Building.* New York: Rowman and Littlefield.

CHAPTER ONE

Sexuality, Class, and Neoliberal Ideology
Same-Sex Attracted Men and Money Boys in Postsocialist China

TIANTIAN ZHENG

I first met Xiao Dan in the park when he was soliciting clients in 2013. A twenty-year-old good-looking fellow from a rural area outside the Chinese city of Dalian, he self-identified as a heterosexual.[1] Xiao Dan is called "little stammerer" by same-sex attracted men who cruise in the park, as he stammers while talking, presumably as a result of several episodes of epilepsy between the tenth month after his birth and his tenth birthday. His father died from an accident when he was ten. Although he loved reading and enjoyed school, in high school his mother could no longer afford his education. He had to quit school to work in a paper factory at a nearby town.

In the paper factory, although he worked very hard and was exhausted every day, the monthly wage of 800 yuan ($130) was always either withheld or delayed. Sometimes he was given only a one month's wage for half a year's work. Life was hard and he found himself in constant deprivation. When he was seventeen, he quit the job and left for Dalian to pursue a better living and realize his dream of becoming a successful businessman. He stayed at a dirty, crowded hostel that cost only 5 yuan ($0.81) a night and looked for work every day at the city's central labor market, but to no avail. One day, a fifty-year-old guy approached him at the labor market, offering him 2 yuan ($0.33) a night and free meals in his hostel. The guy took him to a nearby restaurant and ordered him some food to feed his empty stomach. Thereafter Xiao Dan became that man's rent boy for half a year. After he turned eighteen, he learned about the career prospects of money boys (sex workers) and left the man.

Xiao Dan lied to his mother and embarked on a career as a sex worker. In the park where I met him, Xiao Dan charged 50 yuan ($9) for hand jobs and oral sex and 300 yuan ($49) for penetrative sex. In the winter when the park is cold, Xiao Dan shifts his work site from the park to a bathhouse to solicit clients. Xiao Dan encountered many clients in the park and at the bathhouse who left without paying for his services, for which he could find no recourse. The work is not easy, as it is psychologically tiring for him to repeat the same acts over and over.

Xiao Dan's dark skin color, rural background, and money boy status invite pejorative and disdaining remarks and comments from same-sex attracted men who cruise in the park. Indeed, he is the recipient of constant ridicule. Same-sex attracted men denigrate Xiao Dan, making fun of his clothes and shoes and calling him "a dirty, lazy, and immoral rural migrant." Xiao Dan, however, responds that it is the urban clients who are immoral and uncivilized when they escape payment for the services they have received from him.

Xiao Dan feels that as long as one can make money, it does not matter through what route the money is made. Money is success and success is money. No one cares about how you earn the money, but the fact that you have money. Despite the low payback and occasional nonpayment for his sex work, Xiao Dan loves the free and mobile lifestyle and quick remuneration that other kinds of work are not able to provide. Xiao Dan is determined to realize his dream to open his own business one day and become a successful entrepreneur in the city. Distant as his dream may seem, he is convinced that he will, down the road, encounter enough wealthy clients to make it a reality.

Sexuality, Class, and Neoliberal Ideology in Postsocialist China

Stories of money boys such as Xiao Dan highlight the relationships between sexuality, class, and political ideology in the increasingly stratified postsocialist China. As I show in this chapter, a rural migrant worker is relegated to second-class citizenship as a result of cultural discrimination, institutional constraints, and economic deprivation. Xiao Dan's engagement in transactional sex is informed by the dominant neoliberal ideology that underscores economic profits, individual responsibilities, and free choice.

Xiao Dan's rationale that the ends justify the means is also informed by the dominant state ideology. In consonance with the country's opening-up and market economy, China's former leader Deng Xiaoping put forth his famous theory that "no matter whether it's a white cat or a black cat, as long as it can catch mice, it's a good cat." This theory prioritizes economic gains and argues that economic development takes precedence over everything else. In other words, it does not matter whether something is capitalist or socialist; what matters is whether it helps with economic development and achieves economic gains. This new neoliberal ideology has steered the country away from class struggle toward making economic profits the state's fundamental principle, and put the blame on individuals for their failure to achieve economic wealth. As we saw in the case of Xiao Dan, the route to economic gains does not matter; what matters is economic success. Xiao Dan follows this ideology in defining success in purely economic terms and justifying the commodification of his body by the end result of his possible ownership of a business.

As a result of China's market reform since the beginning of 1980s, 260 million rural peasants have migrated to cities, forming a massive "floating population" of migrant workers (Solinger 1999). Among these migrants, it has been estimated that over ten million people have chosen to work as sex workers in cities (Fu and Choy 2010).

In general, research on sex work in China has been historically based and public health-focused, centering on female sex workers. There has been a proliferation of scholarship on the history of prostitution and state regulations of prostitution in different historical periods in China, shedding light on the intertwined relationships between prostitution and the state in Chinese history. Examples include *Regulating Prostitution in China* (Remick 2014), *Dangerous Pleasures: Prostitution and Modernity in Twentieth-Century Shanghai* (Hershatter 1997), "State-Sanctioned Aggression and the Control of Prostitution in the People's Republic of China" (Gil and Anderson 1998), *Beautiful Merchandise: Prostitution in China, 1860–1936* (Gronewold 1982), *China, Sex and Prostitution* (Jeffreys 2004), *The Sex Culture of Ancient China* (Liu 1993), *Sex, Law, and Society in Late Imperial China* (Sommer 2000), *A History of Prostitution in China* (Wang 1934), *Sex, Culture and Modernity in China* (Dikotter 1995), *Sex in China: Studies in Sexology in Chinese Culture* (Ruan 1991), and *Chinese Prostitution—Past and Present* (Shan 1995).

In addition to the historical analysis of prostitution in China, a large bulk of literature on sex work stems from the public health realm and focuses on the epidemiological perspective. This set of scholarship identifies sex workers as a high-risk population spreading HIV and STIs to the so-called general population. Public health researchers employ quantitative methodologies such as surveys and questionnaires, investigate the sexual behaviors of the "problem population" of sex workers, and make policy recommendations to monitor and control sex workers' sexual behaviors (Choi et al. 2003; Ding et al. 2005; Hong and Li 2008; Huang et al. 2004; Merli et al. 2006; Rogers et al. 2002; Rou et al. 2007; Ruan et al. 2006; South and Trent 2010; Tucker et al. 2005; van den Hoek et al. 2001; Wang et al. 2009; Xu et al. 2008; Yang and Xia 2006, 2008).

Very little research (e.g., Zheng 2009a, 2009b) has taken an ethnographic perspective and explored the complexity of sex workers' everyday lives, the intersection between gender and sexuality, and the ways in which sex workers' lived existence is situated in, and shaped by, political and economic forces. This chapter fills this gap and makes major contributions to the existing literature by providing an ethnographic account of an understudied population of male sex workers in the context of China's postsocialist culture and political economy. Through focusing on male sex workers' words, stories, backgrounds, and rationales for practicing sex work, I illuminate the intertwined nexus of gender and sexuality, the nuances of male sex workers' lived existence shaped by class hierarchy and postsocialist political and economic factors, and the ways in which economic wealth, social class, and political ideology impinge upon male sex workers' sexual behaviors and choice of sex work.

This chapter is based on eleven months of ethnographic fieldwork in the metropolitan city of Dalian from 2005 to 2013; phone and e-mail contacts with research subjects from 2005 to the present; and archival data of online postings from gay-related websites and LGBT and *tongzhi*[2] (the Chinese term for same-sex attracted men) e-mail lists, and newspaper and magazine articles. My ethnographic fieldwork involved interactions and in-depth interviews with self-identified gay men in cruising places such as parks, gay bars, and bathhouses; participant observations as a volunteer in two local grassroots AIDS organizations whose members were exclusively self-identified gay men; and interviews with health officials and local people. In the grassroots AIDS organizations, I attended a myriad of social events, meetings, and lectures.

I aim to unravel the negotiations and interactions of *tongzhi* with the neoliberal discourse that defines a "normal" postsocialist subject as heterosexual, wealthy, and consumerist, and the impact this has on class structure and career choice as sex workers. Class structure among Chinese *tongzhi* is largely shaped by wealth, with the money boys at the bottom. I argue that their embrace of the neoliberal ideology reproduces the link between success and consumerism and legitimizes state power, which is contingent upon economic growth and consumerism.

I first discuss the neoliberal ideology of a "normal" postsocialist subject in the rapidly transforming China before exploring the internal hierarchies of male sex work and its concomitant diverse practices. I then examine postsocialist social inequalities of rural-urban apartheid and money boys' rationale for sex work and illustrate the ways in which economic wealth, social class, and political ideology impinge upon sexual practices and their career choices as sex workers. I conclude with insights and findings.

A "Normal" Postsocialist Subject: Heterosexual, Wealthy, and Consumerist

In postsocialist China, decollectivization, privatization, and marketization of institutions including education, medical care, and housing have provided opportunities for individuals while simultaneously enforcing responsibilities on them. The economic reform has engendered new spaces for sexual expression and personal desires as long as they are self-circumscribed and self-disciplined within the purview of the state.

The simultaneously authoritarian and neoliberal governance in postsocialist China has created a new "enterprising and desiring" heterosexual subject through imposing new responsibilities on individuals to compete in the market economy and pursue wealth, happiness, and self-expression (Kleinman et al. 2011; Rofel 2007; Zhang and Ong 2008). Neoliberalism, instead of an economic theory or political philosophy, has been conceptualized as a form of governance or "governmentality" in Foucault's term, in order to produce responsible and governable citizens (Brown 2005; Rose 1996; Weiss 2012). In China, economic development and the concomitant making of a "normal" postsocialist subject has been one of the state's strategies to legitimize its political power (see also Hua 2012).

The state resorts to the role of the market to cultivate a consumption-oriented individual whose predominant goal is to maximize economic gains and profits (Kleinman et al. 2011; Kong 2012; Zhang and Ong 2008). Unlike the individuals of the past whose identities hinged upon collectivity and self-sacrifice, the new market individuals seek to maximize their self-interest and fulfill material and sexual desires (Yan 2011). Unlike past individuals whose identities were predicated upon class consciousness, the new market individual is a "desiring subject" who acts on the basis of material and sexual self-interest, and who learns limitations through the proper and improper desires and aspirations expressed by diverse forms of public culture (e.g., soap operas, museums, cosmopolitan fantasies of consumption, magazines, the Internet) (Rofel 2007).

This ideal or "normal" postsocialist subject is economically entrepreneurial and enterprising, sexually normative (heterosexual), self-managing, and politically docile (Kleinman et al. 2011; Kong 2012; Zhang and Ong 2008). This individual is not just "obliged to exercise diligence, cunning, talents, and social skills to navigate ever-shifting networks of goods, relationships, knowledge, and institutions in the competition for wealth and personal advantage" (Zhang and Ong 2008, 8), but is also nationalistic and patriotic in her/his loyalty to the party and the state (Anagnost 2004; Hoffman 2008; Kleinman et al. 2011; Kong 2012; Zhang and Ong 2008).

As I show in this chapter, money boys deploy this dominant discourse and fashion themselves as "normal" postsocialist subjects who are wealthy, consumerist, and economically enterprising.

Xiao Kun: A Money Boy at a High-Class Brothel

While the story told at the beginning of this chapter was about a low-tier money boy who solicits clients in a park, the following story is about a high-tier money boy who works for a high-class brothel (*huisuo*).

I met Xiao Kun in 2013 at a restaurant next to the hotel where he had just completed a session of sexual service. A handsome man in his early twenties, he came to Dalian from a faraway rural area and has been working in the brothel for two years. He enjoys the free and mobile lifestyle provided by sex work, as well as the financial gains.

Self-identified as "half and half" (bisexual), Xiao Kun is very proud of the progress he has made in the city: from a monthly wage of 400 yuan ($65) slowly up to one of 7,000 yuan ($1,130). His first job in the city was as a worker in a bread factory. He then worked in a restaurant with a monthly wage of 700 yuan ($113), and then a sauna bar with a monthly wage of 3,000 yuan ($484). Working as a money boy topped all his previous jobs, with a monthly wage of 6,000–7,000 yuan ($968–$1,130). To Xiao Kun, his dramatically increased monthly salary is a testament to his success, of which he is very proud.

His brothel does not have a physical location. Indeed, appointments are made through phone calls to his boss, who, in turn, calls him. A total of fifteen money boys work in the brothel. Clients vary in age and occupation. One client in his 50s, for instance, had assets of 3 billion yuan ($484 million), and paid Xiao Kun 10,000 yuan ($1,613) for a single service.

It is not easy to be selected for the brothel: "You have to have everything—a handsome face, an appealing appearance, a good body type, and skillful sexual technique." His work is so good that he is guaranteed clients every single day. His boss has heard so much wonderful feedback from clients about his work that he always recommends him to new clients. In fact, his boss is so confident in his work that he promises a return of clients' money if they were not satisfied.

Xiao Kun is very proud of his improved living conditions, which he sees as a token of his success. When he first migrated to the city, he shared a tiny, crowded room with many others with a rent of 400 yuan ($65) a month. He now lives in a two-bedroom apartment with a rent of 1,500 yuan ($242) a month. In two years he has sent home to his family 50,000 yuan ($8,065).

Xiao Kun is en route to realizing his dream of opening his own business as a boss. He was only a couple of months away from saving enough money to launch his own massage parlor (euphemism for a brothel). He has decided to set up business in another city, as he would be able to exchange money boys with his boss to ensure their freshness. His boss has already signed a contract with him on this matter. Xiao Kun is thrilled that he has climbed the social ladder and become a successful businessman with wealth, a high rate of consumption, and a cosmopolitan lifestyle.

Money Boys: Internal Hierarchy

The above two stories illuminate two central themes. First, both rural migrant men have chosen sex work as the path to realizing their dream of success, which is defined by wealth, consumption, and a cosmopolitan lifestyle. Second, the class differences within sex work shapes money boys' experiences, structures their life, and influences their chances to fulfill their dreams. Xiao Dan, who plied his trade in a park, is exposed to the public, open to ridicule, and forced to cope with clients who leave without payment after his services. By contrast, Xiao Kun, who worked in a high-class brothel, led a clandestine and protected life and was always remunerated for his services. Of the two money boys, the money boy at the high-class brothel has a much better chance of fulfilling his dreams.

My research revealed a hierarchy within Dalian's money boys, who were usually rural migrant men around seventeen to twenty-six years old. High-tier money boys usually worked in high-class brothels under the pretext of providing massages and similar services to "cultivate men's body and health." Money boys were advertised as "advanced-level technicians" (*gaoji jishi*), and could earn about 7,000–10,000 yuan ($1,130–$1,613) a night after submitting one-third of the payment to the management. The establishments offered both protection and a stable supply of reputable and wealthy clients. Madams and managers continuously replenished their pool with new money boys to keep their clients intrigued. Applicants to these brothels were required to report their ages, heights, weights, the size of their penis, and bed skills. Attractive money boys were accepted and less appealing ones were denied. Some of these brothels were online and exhibited pictures of numerous half-naked young men, with an employee number assigned to each picture. Customers could contact the establishment's phone number or the 24-hour online customer service. Transactional sex was often completed at five-star hotels.

Medium-tier money boys worked in medium-level brothels, hotels, online chat rooms, bars, and bathhouses. They charged 300–400 yuan ($49–$65) per sexual service or 500 to 2,000 yuan ($81–$323) for overnight, and paid one-third of the earnings to the management, with the exception of online freelance money boys, who could earn more than 3,000–5,000 yuan ($484–$807) a month. Freelance money boys sent out information about their age, height, and weight to all the public chat rooms and waited for private chats. It was in the private chats where they disclosed their identity as money boys and negotiated prices, while engaging in video chats so that clients could confirm their appearance. Clients had to pay for hotels and taxi costs and money boys met them at their designated places. Online solicitation could be perilous and erratic, as clients could leave without paying money boys for their services and could even be plainclothes police officers.

Low-tier money boys solicited customers in the park or on the street next to entertainment places. While the high- and middle-tier money boys were more secretive and clandestine, low-class money boys were more pronounced and out in the open. Charges could range from food and shelter for a night to 50–100 yuan ($9–$17) for oral sex and 100–300 yuan ($17–$49) for penetrative sex. Negotiations were not limited to the price, but the place and the type of service (oral, 1, 0, or versatile).[3] Some money boys I met in the park agreed on sexual services in exchange for a night-stay at a nice hotel. The preference for hotels was not just for comfort, as I was told, but also for their own safety. They expressed a fear of the unpredictable when they were asked to go to a client's place, but felt more in control at hotels. The complaint I heard the most was clients leaving without paying for their services.

Another form of sexual service involved rent boys staying at an apartment with a negotiated monthly payment. These did not self-identify as money boys as the sex-money exchange was not as straightforward as the other forms. This is a testament to the implicit difficulties involved in defining the parameters of sex work (see also Mitchell 2011).

Money Boys: Rural Origin and Historical Baggage

Over 70 percent of the money boys in my research self-identified as heterosexual, and less than 30 percent self-identified as bisexual (in their words, "half and half"). This ratio was similar to those published on online *tongzhi* websites (Xin 2009). This finding reminds us of the 1960s young male sex workers in the United States who served adult gay men sexually but did not self-identify as gay (Reiss 1961).[4] Although young male sex workers in the United States engaged in oral sex with adult gay clients, they construed clients as sexual deviators and did not perceive themselves as such. That demarcated a boundary between "homosexual behaviors/acts" and "homosexual identities" (225).

Money boys in my research came from the countryside. According to them, their lack of marketable skills yielded them only low-wage jobs in factories with hard physical labor. Sex work, however, provided them with a free, enterprising lifestyle that offered the most profits with the least investment. Money boys carry heavy historical baggage because of their rural origins, however. In postsocialist China, 260 million rural people have crossed the rural-urban border due to the intolerable poverty that was engendered by decades of biased government policies against rural people. The house registration system (*hu kou*) divided the population into permanent urban "citizens" with urban residence permits and rural/migrant people without them.[5] Without urban residence permits, rural migrants are denied subsidized housing, health care, employment, education for their children, and other benefits that are associated with urban residence permits (Goodkind and West 2002; Li et al. 2007).

Although the household registration system has gone through reforms since the late 1990s, it continues to lead to rural-urban disparity (Chan and Buckingham 2008; Kong 2012; Li and Piachaud 2006; Wang 2010; Zhu 2007). It is deemed "the most serious form of institutional exclusion against mainly rural residents" in China, producing "rural-urban apartheid" (Chan and Buckingham 2008, 583–587). In Dalian, for instance, the most recent policy dictates that rural migrants who meet the specified requirements can apply for urban residence (Dalian Metropolitan City Government 2009). These requirements include being under forty-five years old, having a legitimate, state-recognized university BA degree, and having a legitimate stable job located in the center of the city or a five-year contract with a company located in the new zone or the satellite zone (the city is divided into the center zone, new zone, and satellite zone). Those rural migrants who are not able to meet these designated requirements need to purchase either an apartment worth at least 800,000 yuan ($129,000) or a business building worth at least 1 million yuan ($161,000) in the center zone to be able to apply for urban residence. In addition, there are restrictions on bank loans to rural migrants, and restrictions on the types of rural/migrants who are allowed to purchase apartments. Only those who have a stable job and are able to provide evidence of having paid at least one year of taxes and social insurance are allowed to purchase an apartment. The policy also restricts the number of apartments—only one apartment per household—that rural migrants are allowed to purchase. A rural migrant who marries someone who holds urban residence still needs to wait eight years and purchase an apartment in the city before she or he is allowed to apply for urban residence (Dalian Metropolitan City Government 2009).

In 1958, the Maoist state institutionalized the household registration system such that every household was required to register all of their members with a local public security station. This constructed a bifurcated hierarchical state structure that classified citizens according to a segregated political, economic, social, and legal resource entitlement (Li 2007; Siu 2007; Solinger 1999). Rural second-class citizens were ruthlessly excluded from urbanites' privileged access to state-subsidized goods (e.g., grains), services (e.g., health care), and opportunities (e.g., jobs, mobility).

For almost three decades, rural people's mobility was severely prohibited, and the countryside was completed isolated as a discrete and static unit. Peasants were condemned as the reservoir of backward feudalism and feudal superstition—a major obstacle to national development and salvation (Brownell 1995; Cohen 1993).

Rural-to-urban migration was only permitted from the beginning of the 1980s in China. Nonetheless, the rural-urban gap is still the dominant contributor to overall inequality (Khan and Riskin 1998). Government policies have intensified rural-urban inequality by promoting a skewed distribution of housing assets and by instituting a regressive rural fiscal policy that has worsened rural poverty, creating greater income polarization and inequality (Khan and Riskin 1998; Khan et al. 1992).[6]

In the cities, despite their great contribution to the national and local economy, migrants still encounter severe institutional constraints (*hukou*) and social denigration (Kipnis 1998; Pun 2005; Pun and Chan 2008; Yan 2008; Zhang 2002). Urbanites deem the city "modern" and consider the countryside "backward" and "barbarian" (Kipnis 1998). Categorized as "outsiders" (*wai di ren, wai lai gong*), migrants are not only secluded and excluded by the state and urbanites, but also mistreated and blamed for all kinds of social problems. For example, in 2003 the college graduate Sun Zhigang was detained by the police due to his failure to show a temporary resident card and was subsequently beaten to death at the repatriation center (Anonymous 2013). In addition to police harassment, wage withholding, reductions of payments, and physical abuse toward rural migrants often drives them to commit suicide (Xu 2003; see also Chan 1993, 1996, 1997, 1998).

Money Boys: Rationale for Sex Work

Social discrimination and a prejudiced policy have forced the vast majority of rural migrant men onto the lowest rung of the labor market. They commonly work as construction workers, garbage collectors, and factory workers. Some have decided to replace low-wage jobs and exhausting physical labor with sex work. Some were introduced into sex work via friends, while others solicited their own clients in different settings or applied to brothels. As they told me, in a city with rampant consumerism, a monthly income of 1,000 yuan ($162) was simply not attractive. Indeed, it was estimated that in the city of Beijing alone, four to ten thousand male rural migrants offered same-sex sexual services (Jeffreys 2007).

Money boys in my research told me that they wished to, in their words, "gain a footing (*lizu*) in the city," with wealth and urban status. With wealth, they could establish their own business and settle in the city as legitimate residents. They could also consume brand-name fashions, build up their bodies, and appear "modern." A modern appearance would help prove their cultural sophistication and heighten their social status. A successful business would help them attain a house, a car, and a high standard of living.

As shown in the two case studies above, money boys harness an entrepreneurial spirit in engaging in sex work as an effective option to reach their goals and achieve success in the city. Ironically, by moving away from "normal" kinds of jobs, money boys achieve status as "normal" citizens (see also Kong 2012; Rofel 2010). In a rural-urban apartheid society, sex work provides them with ample opportunities to accumulate economic capital and proclaim themselves as self-managing, self-reliant, and self-enterprising "normal" postsocialist subjects.

Money boys like the free and laissez-faire lifestyle of sex work, which could not be afforded by lower-paying jobs. As I was told, no one controlled them in their work, so they could quit and resume the work anytime they wished. They are transient and travel from site to site, from city to city, to work as money boys. They are avid consumers of the gym, high-quality cosmetics, and fashionable clothes. The remuneration of sex work allows them to live a cosmopolitan lifestyle.

In my research, quite a few money boys, like Xiao Kun, were able to reap the benefits of sex work and become business owners and house owners in the city. Some rent boys had their urban clients buy them apartments in the city in addition to cash payments. Xiao Sun, another money boy I interviewed, was offered by an urban man 6,000 yuan ($968) a month to rent his services, in addition to an apartment in his own name. At the end of the renting relationship, Xiao Sun had entered sex work. He said, "When I was a factory worker, I was exhausted every night, earning only several hundred yuan ($50–$100) a month. Now I deposit at least 4,000 yuan ($646) every month."

Like Xiao Sun, money boys in my research commented that one client per day could earn them more money than one month of white-collar work. The rationale for sex work was, in their words, "people mock poverty but not prostitution" (xiaopin bu xiaochang). Indeed, the ideology that money mattered, no matter how it was attained, ran through the interviews with money boys in my research. Money boy Xiao Ben, for instance, said, "I want to continue working to strengthen my economic power, to control what I have, and to solve all of my problems. Then I can go to a city I like and live my life as if nothing has happened."

Embracing the neoliberal ideology to become "normal" postsocialist subjects, money boys engage in sex work to enjoy a cosmopolitan lifestyle. Some do achieve upward mobility, despite the risks involved in sex work. As I have discussed elsewhere (Zheng 2009), sex workers are a main target of police raids in China's crackdown campaigns, where sex workers are fined, detained, jailed, or deported to the countryside or to rehabilitation centers. Faced with biased state policies and cultural prejudices against rural migrants and sex work, money boys negotiate the risks and perils associated with sex work through a wide array of strategies. They conceal their work from family and friends, segregate their work from their life, move from one place to another, shift from one type of sex work to another,[7] and endure discriminating insults. Some are able to refashion themselves by transforming themselves from low-status rural migrants to postsocialist successful and wealthy entrepreneurs. As shown above, some earn enough money through sex work to own a business in the city. Sex work has become a niche in the market economy that provides an expedient route to becoming "normal" citizens with wealth and mobility.

Conclusion

Money boys, carrying heavy historical baggage due to their rural migrant status, contest social inequality and cultural stigma by valorizing state ideology and claiming themselves as "normal" postsocialist subjects. Those interviewed in my research reject urbanites' discrimination against them, and castigate urban clients as low-quality, immoral, and uncivilized for escaping payment after using their sexual services. Sex work, for money boys, is an expedient and effective route to becoming "normal" citizens, who are wealthy and successful consumers. Through engaging in nonnormative sex work and sexual practices, money boys are able to participate in urban consumption and a cosmopolitan lifestyle and prove to the urbanites that they, too, can be wealthy consumers. Their success in becoming "normal" postsocialist subjects questions cultural prejudice against migrants.

Money boys' negotiated economic power allows them to climb the social ladder and achieve social mobility. Paradoxically, at the same time money boys' strategic self-fashioning runs the risk of further stigmatizing and excluding rural migrants by validating the correlation between cultural identities and economic purchasing power, consumerism, and market potential. In so doing, money boys divert attention from unequal state policy to individual responsibilities. Obscuring the cultural and political root cause for rural poverty, they contribute to the neoliberal discourse that justifies social inequality by blaming it on migrants' immutable, authentic worthlessness or "low cultural level" (see Zheng 2009, 197–198).

The tension of class differences divides Chinese *tongzhi*. The gulf engendered by class differences creates mutual misunderstanding, stigma, and prejudice. The result is a community that is often fraught with conflict and dissent. As shown in the first case study, urban *tongzhi* relegate rural migrant *tongzhi* and money boys to an illegal and immoral status and disassociate themselves from them. Indeed, they construed money boys as low-class rural migrants who brought disgrace to, and polluted, the *tongzhi* community. The marginalization of money boys within the *tongzhi* community had been attributed to the "quality discourse" (*suzhi*) that marks money boys as uncivilized, uncouth, and immoral (Ho 2009; Jeffreys 2007; Kong 2011a, 2011b; Rofel 2007, 2010). Discriminating comments against money boys were harsh and extreme throughout my fieldwork. In addition to the outright discrimination against money boys, flagrant insults against rural migrant *tongzhi* were ubiquitous.

These entrenched divisions among *tongzhi* prohibit them from uniting together, and their embrace of the neoliberal ideology further reproduces the legitimacy of a heterosexual, self-disciplined, and self-enterprising consumer. The existing hierarchy, prejudices, and discrimination within the Chinese *tongzhi* population may be difficult, if not impossible, to overcome without candid and honest communication that cuts across class barriers.

Notes and References

1. All names in the chapter are pseudonyms.
2. The term *tongzhi,* translated as "comrade," is now most frequently used by same-sex attracted men. *Tongzhi* is a Chinese translation of a Soviet term and originally referred to communist revolutionaries who shared the same aspirations and comradeship in an egalitarian society with no class. Since 1949, *tongzhi* has evolved from a specific term for Communist Party members to a general form of address in everyday discourse. In 1989, *tongzhi* was first publicly deployed by the organizers of the inaugural Hong Kong gay and lesbian film festival to refer to an indigenous Chinese same-sex identity distinct from the global gay identity (Chou 2000; Li 2006; Micollier 2003; Zhou 2000). The term then gained currency in mainland China in the 1990s.
3. 1 means the role of the inserter, and 0 means the role of the inserted (Zheng 2015).
4. Sexual services were, in principle, restricted to oral sex, with the young male sex workers as the penetrators.
5. In Shenzhen, permanent citizens hold a "blue card"; an intermediary category between permanent and temporary residence known as "blue chop" was introduced in 1995 (Wong and Huen 1998 cited in Kipnis 1998).
6. Such inequality has not abated despite the gradually changing household registration system. In the late 1980s, some provinces started selling local urban household registration cards known as blue cards or blue seals to migrant workers. This intermediary category between the permanent and temporary residence started during the national austerity drive (1988–1991) when migrants were desperately seeking protection from expulsion and local governments were just as desperate to raise development funds (Wong and Huen 1998; Woon 1999).

7. Money boys usually change their work settings frequently to protect themselves and gain more clients. Work on money boys in South China also confirms this mobile nature; see Kong (2011b).

Anagnost, Ann. 2004. "The Corporeal Politics of Quality (*suzhi*)." *Public Culture* 16 (2): 189–208.

Anonymous. 2003. "The Death of Repatriated Sun Zhigang." *Nanfang Dushibao* [South Municipal Newspaper], April 25. http://news.sina.com.cn/s/2003–04–25/11111016223 .html.

Brown, Wendy. 2005. *Edgework: Critical Essays on Knowledge and Politics*. Princeton, NJ: Princeton University Press.

Brownell, Susan. *Training the Body for China: Sports in the Moral Order of the People's Republic*. Chicago: University of Chicago Press.

Chan, Anita. 1993. "Revolution or Corporatism? Workers and Trade Unions in Post-Mao China." *Australian Journal of Chinese Affairs* 29: 31–61.

———. 1996. "The Changing Ruling Elite and Political Opposition in China." In *Political Oppositions in Industrializing Asia*, edited by G. Rodan, pp. 161–187. London: Routledge.

———. 1998. "Labor Standards and Human Rights: The Case of Chinese Workers under Market Socialism." *Human Rights Quarterly* 20 (4): 886–904.

Chan, Anita, and Robert A. Senser. 1997. "China's Troubled Workers." *Foreign Affairs* 76: 104–117.

Chan, Kam Wing, and Will Buckingham. 2008. "Is China Abolishing the Hukou System?" *China Quarterly* 195 (September): 582–606.

Choi, Kyung-Hee, Hui Liu, Yaqi Guo, Lei Han, Jeffrey S Mandel, and George Rutherford. 2003. "Emerging HIV-1 Epidemic in China in Men Who Have Sex with Men." *Lancet* 361 (9375): 2125–2126.

Chou, Wah-shan. 2000. *Tongzhi: Politics of Same-Sex Eroticism in Chinese Societies*. New York: Haworth Press.

Cohen, Lawrence. 1995. "The Pleasures of Castration: The Postoperative Status of Hijras, Jankhas, and Academics." In *Sexual Nature/Sexual Culture*, edited by P. Abramson and S. Pinkerton, pp. 276–304. Chicago: University of Chicago Press.

Dikotter, Frank. 1995. *Sex, Culture and Modernity in China*. London: Hurst.

Ding, Yanpeng, Roger Detels, Zaiwei Zhao, Yong Zhu, Guanghui Zhu, Bowei Zhang, Tao Shen, and Xueshan Xue. 2005. "HIV Infection and Sexually Transmitted Diseases in Female Commercial Sex Workers in China." *JAIDS* 38 (3): 314–319.

Fu, Hualing, and D. W. Choy. 2010. "Administrative Detention of Prostitutes: The Legal Aspects." In *Gender Policy and HIV in China: Catalyzing Policy Change*, edited by J. D. Tucker, D. L. Poston, and Q. Ren, pp. 189–200. New York: Springer.

Gil, Vincent E., and Allen F. Anderson. 1998. "State-Sanctioned Aggression and the Control of Prostitution in the People's Republic of China: A Review." *Aggression and Violent Behavior* 3 (2): 129–142.

Goodkind, Daniel, and Loraine A. West. 2002. "China's Floating Population: Definitions, Data and Recent Findings." *Urban Studies* 39 (12): 2237–2250.

Gronewold, Sue. 1982. *Beautiful Merchandise: Prostitution in China, 1860–1936*. New York: Institute for Research in History and Haworth Press.

Hershatter, Gail. 1997. *Dangerous Pleasures: Prostitution and Modernity in Twentieth-Century Shanghai*. Berkeley: University of California Press.

Ho, Loretta Wing Wah. 2009. *Gay and Lesbian Subculture in Urban China*. London: Routledge.

Hoffman, Lisa. 2003. "Enterprising Cities and Citizens: The Re-Figuring of Urban Spaces and the Making of Post-Mao Professionals." *Provincial China* 8 (1): 5–26.

Hong, Yan, and Xiaoming Li. 2008. "Behavioral Studies of Female Sex Workers in China: A Literature Review and Recommendation for Future Research." *AIDS and Behavior* 12 (4): 623–636.

Hua, Wen. 2012. *Buying Beauty: Cosmetic Surgery in China*. Hong Kong: University of Hong Kong Press.

Huang, Yingying, Gail E. Henderson, Suiming Pan, and Myron Cohen. 2004. "HIV/AIDS Risk among Brothel-Based Female Sex Workers in China: Assessing the Terms, Content, and Knowledge of Sex Work." *Sexually Transmitted Diseases* 31 (11): 695–700.

Jeffreys, Elaine. 2004. *China, Sex and Prostitution*. London: RoutledgeCurzon.

———. 2007. "Querying Queer Theory—Debating Male-Male Prostitution in the Chinese Media." *Critical Asian Studies* 39 (1): 151–175.

Khan, Azizur Rahman, and Carl Riskin. 1998. "Income and Inequality in China: Composition, Distribution and Growth of Household Income, 1988–1995." *China Quarterly* 154 (June): 221–253.

Khan, Azizur Rahman, Keith Griffin, Carl Riskin, and Zhao Renwei. 1992. "Household Income and Its Distribution in China." *China Quarterly* 132 (December): 1029–1061.

Kipnis, Andrew. 1998. "The 'Country' as a Foreign Country: Revising Household Registration Policy in the P.R.C." Paper presented at the 97th Annual Meeting of American Association of Anthropology, Philadelphia, Pennsylvania.

Kleinman, Arthur, Yunxiang Yan, Jing Jun, Sing Lee, and Everett Zhang. 2011. *Deep China: The Moral Life of the Person*. Berkeley: University of California Press.

Kong, Travis. 2011a. *Chinese Male Homosexualities: Memba, Tongzhi and Golden Boy*. London: Routledge.

———. 2011b. "Transnational Queer Labor: The 'Circuits of Desire' of Money Boys in China." *English Language Notes* 49 (1): 139–141.

———. 2012. "Reinventing the Self under Socialism: The Case of Migrant Male Sex Workers in China." *Critical Asian Studies* 44 (2): 283–308.

Li, Bingqin, and David Piachaud. 2006. "Urbanization and Social Policy in China." *Asia-Pacific Development Journal* 13 (1): 1–26.

Li, Yinhe. 2006. *Tongxinglian Yawenhua* [Homosexual subculture]. Neimenggu: Neimenggu Daxue Chubanshe [Inner Mongolia University Press].

Li, Xiaoming, L. Zhang. X. Fang, Q. Xiong, X. Chen, D. Lin, A. Mathur, and B. Stanton. 2007. "Stigmatization Experienced by Rural-to-Urban Migrant Workers in China: Findings from a Qualitative Study." *World Health and Population* 9 (4): 29–43.

Liu, Dalin. 1993. *Zhongguo Gudai Xing Wenhua* [The sex culture of ancient China]. Yinchuan: Ningxia People's Publishing House.

Merli, Giovanna, Sara Hertog, Bo Wang, and Jing Li. 2006. "Modelling the Spread of HIV/AIDS in China: The Role of Sexual Transmission." *Population Studies* 60 (1): 1–22.

Micollier, Evelyne. 2003. "HIV/AIDS-Related Stigmatization in Chinese Society: Bridging the Gap between Official Responses and Civil Society, a Cultural Approach to HIV/AIDS Prevention and Care." UNESCO/UNAIDS Research Project No. 20. Paris: UNESCO.

Mitchell, Gregory. 2011. "TurboConsumers™ in Paradise: Tourism, Civil Rights, and Brazil's Gay Sex Industry." *American Ethnologist* 38 (4): 666–682.

Pun, Ngai. 2005. "Global Production and Corporate Business Ethics: Company Codes of Conduct Implementation and Its Implication on Labour Rights in China." *China Journal* (July): 101–113.

Pun, Ngai, and Chris King-chi Chan. 2008. "The Subsumption of Class Discourse in China." *Boundary* 35 (2): 75–91.

Reiss, Albert J. 1961. "The Social Integration of 'Queers' and 'Peers.'" *Social Problems* 9: 102–120.

Remick, Elizabeth J. 2014. *Regulating Prostitution in China: Gender and Local Statebuilding 1900–1937.* Stanford, CA: Stanford University Press.

Rofel, Lisa. 2007. *Desiring China: Experiments in Neoliberalism, Sexuality, and Public Culture.* Durham, NC: Duke University Press.

———. 2010. "The Traffic in Money Boys." *Positions* 18 (2): 425–458.

Rogers, Susan J., Liu Ying, Yan Tao Xin, Kee Fung, and Joan Kaufman. 2002. "Reaching and Identifying the STD/HIV Risk of Sex Workers in Beijing." *AIDS Education and Prevention* 14 (3): 217–227.

Rose, Nikolas. 1996. "Governing 'Advanced' Liberal Democracies." In *Foucault and Political Reason: Liberalism, Neoliberalism and Rationalities of Government,* edited by A. Barry, T. Osborne, and N. Rose, pp. 37–64. London: University College London Press.

Rou, Keming, Zunyou Wu, Sheena Sullivan, Fan Li, Jihui Guan, Chen Xu, Wei Liu, Dahua Liu, and Yueping Yin. 2007. "A Five-City Trial of a Behavioural Intervention to Reduce Sexually Transmitted Disease/HIV Risk among Sex Workers in China." *AIDS* 21: S95–S101.

Ruan, Fang Fu. 1991. *Sex in China: Studies in Sexology in Chinese Culture.* New York: Plenum Press.

Ruan, Yuhua, Xiaoyun Cao, Han-Zhu Qian, Li Zhang, Guangming Li, Zhengqing Jiang, Benli Song, Wei Hu, Shu Liang, Kanglin Shu, Ye Yang, Xinxu Li, Jun Wang, Xi Chen, Chun Hao, Yanhui Song, Hui Xing, Ning Wang, and Yiming Shao. 2006. "Syphilis among Female Sex Workers in Southwestern China: Potential for HIV Transmission." *Sexually Transmitted Diseases* 33 (12): 719–723.

Shan Guangnai. 1995. *Zhongguo Changji: Guoqu He Xianzai* [Chinese prostitution: Past and present]. Beijing: Falü chubanshe [Law Press].

Siu, Helen. 2007. "Grounding Displacement: Uncivil Urban Spaces in South China." *American Ethnologist* 34 (2): 329–350.

Solinger, Dorothy. 1999. *Contesting Citizenship in Urban China: Peasant Migrants, the State, and the Logic of the Market.* Berkeley: University of California Press.

Sommer, Matthew H. 2000. *Sex, Law, and Society in Late Imperial China*, Stanford, CA: Stanford University Press.

South, Scott, and Katherine Trent. 2010. "Imbalanced Sex Ratios, Men's Sexual Behavior, and Risk of Sexually Transmitted Infection in China." *Journal of Health and Social Behavior* 51 (4): 376–390.

Tucker, Joseph D, Gail Henderson, Tian Wang, Ying Huang, William Parish, Sui Pan, S. Xiang, and Myron Cohen. 2005. "Surplus Men, Sex Work, and the Spread of HIV in China." *AIDS* 19 (6): 539–547.

van den Hoek, Anneke, Yuliang Fu, Nicole H. T. M. Dukers, Zhiheng Chen, Jiangting Feng, Lina Zhang, and Xiuxing Zhang. 2001. "High Prevalence of Syphilis and Other Sexually Transmitted Diseases among Sex Workers in China: Potential for Fast Spread of HIV." *AIDS* 15 (6): 753–759.

Wang, Fei-ling. 2010. "Renovating the Great Floodgate: The Reform of China's Hukou System." In *One Country, Two Societies: Rural-Urban Inequality in Contemporary China*, edited by M. K. Whyte, pp. 335–364. Cambridge, MA: Harvard University Press.

Wang, Haibo, Ray Y. Chen, Guowei Ding, Yanling Ma, Jianguo Ma, Jin Hua Jiao, Zhenglai Wu, Gerald B. Sharp, and Ning Wang. 2009. "Prevalence and Predictors of HIV Infection among Female Sex Workers in Kaiyuan City, Yunnan Province, China." *International Journal of Infectious Diseases* 13 (2): 162–169.

Wang, Shunu. 1934. *Zhongguo Changji Shi* [A history of prostitution in China]. Shanghai: Shanghai Life Bookstore.

Weiss, Margot. 2011. *Techniques of Pleasure: BDSM and the Circuits of Sexuality*. Durham, NC: Duke University Press.

Wong, Linda, and Huen Wai-Po. 1998. "Reforming the Household Registration System: A Preliminary Glimpse of the Blue Chop Household Registration System in Shanghai and Shenzhen." *International Migration Review* 32 (4): 974–994.

Woon, Yuen-Fong. 1999. "Labor Migration in the 1990s." *Modern China* 25 (4): 475–512.

Xin, Ling. 2009. "Xingquxiang Yantaohui Jizhe Zao Quzhu" [Reporter driven out of sexual orientation symposium]. *Xinling Kafei Wang* [Psychology Coffee], August 8. http://www.psycofe.com/read/readDetail_6808_1.htm.

Xin, Tong. 2009. "Zhongguo MB Zhong Jin 30% Shi Tongxinglian" [Only 30 percent of MBs in China are homosexuals]. *Xintongwang*, February 14. http://www.1314xt.org/article/66/2395.html.

Xu, Jun Jie, Ning Wang, Lin Lu, Yi Pu, Guo Lei Zhang, Michelle Wong, Zheng Wu, Zheng Lai, and Xi Wen. 2008. "HIV and STIs in Clients and Female Sex Workers in Mining Regions of Gejiu City, China." *Sexually Transmitted Diseases* 35 (6): 558–565.

Xu, Qin. 2003. "Wei Tao Gongqian: Chongqing Mingong Zisha" (Demanding Payment: Migrants Seek Suicide in Chongqing]." *Chongqing Shangbao* [Chongqing Business Newspaper], October 26. http://news.sohu.com/01/53/news214835301.shtml.

Yan, Hairong. 2008. *New Masters, New Servants: Migration, Development, and Women Workers in China*. Durham, NC: Duke University Press.

Yan, Yunxiang. 2011. "The Changing Moral Landscape." In *Deep China: The Moral Life of the Person,* edited by A. Kleinman, Y. Yan, J. Jun, S. Lee, and E. Zhang, pp. 36–77. Berkeley: University of California Press.

Yang, Xiushi, and Guomei Xia. 2006. "Gender, Migration, Risky Sex, and HIV Infection in China." *Studies in Family Planning* 37 (4): 241–250.

———. 2008. "Temporary Migration and STD/HIV Risky Sexual Behavior: A Population-Based Analysis of Gender Differences in China." *Social Problems* 55 (3): 322–346.

Zhang, Li, and Aihwa Ong, eds. 2008. *Privatizing China: Socialism from Afar.* Ithaca, NY: Cornell University Press.

Zheng, Tiantian. 2009a. *Red Lights: The Lives of Sex Workers in Postsocialist China.* Minneapolis: University of Minnesota Press.

———. 2009b. *Ethnographies of Prostitution in Contemporary China: Gender Relations, HIV/AIDS, and Nationalism.* New York: Palgrave Macmillan.

———. 2015. *Tongzhi Living: Men Attracted to Men in Postsocialist China.* Minneapolis: University of Minnesota Press.

Zhou, Huashan. 2000. *Tongzhi: Politics of Same-Sex Eroticism in Chinese Societies.* New York: Haworth.

Zhu, Yu. 2007. "China's Floating Population and Their Settlement in the Cities: Beyond the Hukou Reform." *Habitat International* 31 (1): 65–76.

CHAPTER TWO

Producing Purity

An Ethnographic Study of a Neotraditionalist
Ladies' Academy in Contemporary Urban China

KEVIN CARRICO

Ladies' Academies (*shunü xuetang*), also referred to as Ladies' Training Institutes (*shunü peixun yuan*), have emerged in cities across China in recent years, tasked with the mission of transforming today's women into "ladies" (*shunü*). From the Pearl River metropolises of Guangzhou and Dongguan to the northern cities of Beijing and Shenyang, and from the commercial and tourist capitals of Shanghai, Hangzhou, and Suzhou in the east, to Wuchang, Wuhan, and Changsha in the southern central regions, to Chengdu in the remote west, many of the major metropolitan areas of China have recently witnessed the arrival of such institutions. Some academies, such as the Guangzhou Academy of Women's Elegance (*Guangzhou nüzi youya xuetang*), focus upon producing ladies well-versed in "modern" and "Western" etiquette, who know how to cut their steaks "properly" and how to sit "like a lady" while doing so. Yet by contrast, the majority of these academies are based in an idealization of Chinese tradition, reaching back to images of the lost "traditional Chinese woman" idealized in such volumes as the *Classic on Girls* (*Nü'er jing*) and *Biographies of Exemplary Women* (*Lienü zhuan*) in order to help students, through the study of "tradition," cultivate supposedly lady-like demeanor, etiquette, hobbies, and skills. Accordingly, it was in the midst of my research on the promotion of neotraditionalism and popular cultural-political conservatism in contemporary urban China (Carrico 2013) that I first encountered such traditionalist Ladies' Academies.

The Ladies' Academy that I visited in the spring of 2011 claims to be the first of its kind in post-1949 China.[1] Established in a major metropolitan region in the middle of the previous decade, the academy has over the years recruited female students from the surrounding area for weekend "lady" cultivation courses, and has even brought in students from locations across the country toward its stated mission of re-creating them in the image of the pure and traditional woman: the "lady." A student's day at the academy begins at 6:00 a.m., and continues until 9:30 p.m.: the hours in between are characterized by a rigorous schedule of immersion in the often-cited and celebrated "five millennia of tradition." Students read the classics (especially those focused upon models of femininity), play the *guqin*, a traditional Chinese musical instrument, memorize poetry, learn traditional etiquette, painting, sewing, chess, and the rules of tea ceremony, and, as I noted during my visit, learn to cook for their teachers at lunch and dinner. A typical schedule reads as follows:

6:00	Wake up
7:00	Breakfast
8:00	Study of the classics (*Tao Te Ching* during my stay)
9:00	Etiquette
10:00	*Guqin*
11:00	Lunch
1:00	*Guqin*
2:30	Classics
3:30	Etiquette
5:00	Dinner
6:00–8:00	Study time
9:30	Bedtime

This rigorous schedule has reaped results. The academy was featured in a positive review on China Central Television, multiple articles in the *People's Daily*, and, according to teachers, has also been covered by the Associated Press and Japan's *Yomiuri Shimbun*. Although thorough searches of the Internet provide no evidence to verify these claims of international media exposure, the academy's rapid growth in recent years, moving from a tiny one-room setting in an apartment block to an expansive courtyard-style residence, and expanding its focus from local ladies to a nationwide student body, demonstrates the academy's substantial relevance and influence beyond such unsubstantiated boasting.

In light of this academy's rapid growth and the proliferation of similar institutions in cities across China, I visited this self-declared original Ladies' Academy to find out what exactly constitutes "a lady." And considering that the image of the woman has been a prominent site of national representation and political symbolic contestation in modern Chinese history, I sought to understand what this increasingly determined search for the proper and traditional lady of the past means for the present.

Re-creating the Real China

Approaching the Ladies' Academy on the first day of my visit, I made my way through a winding network of alleys: the air was dense with the pungent odors of street food and motorbike exhaust fumes, and the narrow alleyways were over-flowing with a chaotic mix of pedestrians, bikes, and motorcycles speeding by, ringing bells and honking horns, and ever so narrowly missing one another at the very last moment. Eventually reaching my destination, I found myself standing before a massive traditional-style door closed tightly, as if to shut out the chaotic world beyond. My diligent efforts at knocking on this imposing entryway failed to generate any response, and it was only after I made a phone call to the interior of the academy that a student came to the front to unlatch the heavy door. Bowing and silently gesturing for me to follow her inside as the door closed behind me, I was led through one layer of the courtyard to another to yet another, with each layer seeming to serve as a defense against the city outside, whose clamor eventually faded into the remote distance. Crossing a wooden bridge over a small pond with fish, and then through a set of elaborately carved wooden doors, I arrived at the core of this Ladies' Academy, where I found three men dressed in the neotraditionalist garb known as Han Clothing (*Hanfu*) sitting around a table drinking tea. Lanterns hung from the ceiling and an image of Confucius was placed prominently at the center of the north wall, and a rare and almost eerie silence lingered in this remote room in the heart of this bustling city. "Have a seat," they told me.

Before I had a chance to actually sit down, the three teachers were quick to inquire about my views on contemporary China. What did I think of the cities? What did I think of the food? What did I think of the culture? What did I think of the people? How did I like China? Having answered these questions many times over the years, and eager to avoid controversy before having even introduced myself, I responded to each with a simplistic affirmation: the cities are lively and exciting, the food is delicious, culture is rich, and people are kind. In sum, every-thing is great. But then, to my surprise, they responded, "No, it isn't," proceeding to list a series of dilemmas in each of these fields: the cities are overcrowded, pol-luted, and provide no tranquility or respite for the weary soul; the food is either fake or rotten or poisonous, or all of the above; traditional Chinese culture is long gone; and relations between people nowadays are driven solely by self-interest and the obsessive pursuit of profit. After painting this grim picture, they declared that the China that I was visiting, the China outside of those heavy doors that they had just eagerly denounced, was not in fact "the real China."[2] The real China, a land of rites and etiquette (*liyi zhi bang*), and a global exemplar of morality and harmony, was based in the "Great Way" (*da dao*) that extended from the begin-ning of time to modernity.[3] But this Great Way had been lost decades ago, and had been replaced by an inferior way (*xiao dao*), in which people were solely con-cerned with convenience, ease, speed, money, and their own selfish interests. Now, they told me, the real China of the Great Way could only be found "in here," within the Ladies' Academy. "If you can accept the China out there," they told me, "you will fall in love with the China that we are creating in here."

Deep within this traditional courtyard structure, in a secure and hermetically sealed sphere insulated layer by layer from the chaotic world outside,[4] I sat down around an old wooden table and began weeks of discussion with these three men determined to re-create "the real China." And my initial surprise at their theory of the fundamental unreality of contemporary society was soon surpassed when I learned where they placed the blame for this inauthentic state of affairs: directly on the shoulders of their target students, who were in their opinion the problem and thus had to become the solution.

The Fall from Gendered Paradise

Mourning the loss of the true China, the China of the Great Way, was a refrain that I heard repeatedly throughout my research with neotraditionalist groups. Some blamed this loss upon the disintegration of the imperial system, the sole earthly realization of the transcendent ideals of Chinese civilization; others blamed it upon the New Culture Movement's vernacularization of writing, which in their view severed any link to the glorious sacred past; and others ominously blamed this downfall upon the integration of supposedly uncivilized "barbarian" others into an otherwise pure, homogeneous, and thus harmonious Han nation, embracing a traditionalist anachronism. At this Ladies' Academy, however, the roots of this loss were found elsewhere, much closer to home. The teachers asserted that true Chinese culture had been based upon the delicate balance between *yin* and *yang* that they simplistically yet self-assuredly read as equivalent to a balance between male and female. This perfect balance between *yin* and *yang,* maintained for millennia, had been lost in the past two centuries, thus leading to the loss of the real China. When I asked what they meant by this "loss of balance," the main teacher leaned forward and said quite directly, "nowadays in China, men aren't like men, and women aren't like women." Society, he told me, is backward: this *yinyang* disorder[5] makes people unlike themselves, making the ugly beautiful and the beautiful ugly. And his goal in this Ladies' Academy is to make things right again, so that beauty might again be recognized as beauty, women might again be ladies, and China might then again be the real China.

Drawing upon a mixture of history and mythology to explain this "beauty" and its "reality" to me, one teacher proudly proclaimed that pre-1911 China was the most free and democratic society that had ever existed. It was, he claimed, a society based on balance, or a certain harmony between the heavens, the earth, and the people. Everyone had a clear place within society thanks to the Confucian cardinal relationships, which established clear principles for interactions between ruler and subject, father and son, husband and wife, elder and younger brothers, and friends. As a result of this thorough mapping of relationships and the proper behavior expected of each, premodern society ran smoothly, like a well-oiled machine. This is of course a retroactive idealization benefiting from distance: in the now idealized Ming Dynasty (1368–1644), scholars were already concerned about the degradation of culture and particularly of women (Carlitz 1991). Nevertheless, this idealized and unitary past seemed very real to this teacher. A core factor in this social machine's supposedly seamless operation was the clearly designated role of women in traditional society; or rather, to be more precise, outside of society. Citing one version of the myth of Nüwa and Fuxi (Birrell 1993, 34–35), the creators of the world according to Chinese mythology, he argued that there had been natural gender differences from the very beginning of time: while Fuxi reigned as the first of the renowned three sovereigns, Nüwa was primarily a creator, or a mother, as nature had intended. Eager to provide further "historical evidence" and avoiding even the slightest hint of subtlety, another teacher pointed to a specific detail on the Han Clothing that he was wearing, which was purportedly first woven at the beginning of civilization and existed unchanged into the present. In Han Clothing, the right side of the robe is placed on the inside, while the left side of the robe crosses over on top: in his analysis, based in the saying *nanzuo nüyou,* right represents the feminine, while left represents the masculine. Reading into this supposedly timeless design, he asserted that Han Clothing's layers embody a fundamental and eternal truth, symbolizing the proper relations between the sexes: left as *yang* as male is meant to be on the outside, while right as *yin* as female is meant to be on the inside. Or in other far more direct words, he told me, women are supposed to be at home. This is how society had been arranged according to "heaven," and how it must therefore be arranged again.

The historical downfall of this state of proper gender harmony and perfect societal balance was attributed to the emergence of what one teacher called the "Western idea of gender equality" in the twentieth century.[6] "You Westerners only have a little over two centuries of history," he dismissively declared, "so what makes you think that you have found the only correct model for the entire world?" This rhetorical turn, rationalizing fundamentally anachronistic gender ideologies through the affirmative ideals of tradition and nation,[7] is worthy of closer analysis. The teachers had expressed their thoughts, which can only be accurately characterized as sexist, in the mystical language of *yin* and *yang,* citing as well the supposed division of labor between the mythical figures Nüwa and Fuxi, and thereby presenting their prejudices as part of a "tradition" extending from the beginning of time to the present.[8] This deployment of tradition conveniently abstracts the ideas at hand from the type of actual experiential human relations that might reveal them for what they are, and thereby naturalizes, eternalizes, and legitimizes the fundamentally experientially illegitimate. Beyond this traditionalist abstraction, however, this rationalization of sexism was further buttressed through the affective deployment of the idea of the nation: by using the term "the Western idea of gender equality," the teachers created an all too appealing (and all too common) binary relationship between China and the West that presents the ideal of equality between the sexes (and other rights-based values) as a non-Chinese idea and hence as unnatural in and even corrupting of an otherwise pure cultural sphere. By appealing to the idea of collective identity in order to rationalize subjugation, the teachers render gender equality as national inequality or cultural imperialism that must be resisted. The dignity of nearly half of the nation's population can thereby be suppressed for the declared dignity of "the nation" as a whole, such that in the name of identity people come to argue for and embrace subjugation not only of their fellow citizens but even in many cases of themselves. And while it may be granted that women's rights were indeed not a prominent component of Chinese traditional culture, we must also note that such rights have not been a prominent component of any premodern culture, and remain solely a point of aspiration for most today; cultures nevertheless change, thankfully. Yet by expressing their ideas through the metaphor of an eternal national tradition, such change is renounced, and sexism is illusorily made to appear not as sexism, but as a "natural" and "correct" viewpoint in need of protection from the cruel depredations of a predatory and imperialist outside world.

This rupture of the imagined unadulterated sphere of traditional culture and its comforting boundaries (Sloterdijk 2005) was metaphorically expressed by one teacher through the story of the old city walls located a few blocks away from the academy. One evening he told me that in the early 1950s, during the period typically referred to as "Liberation," the walls of this city were destroyed, leaving only narrow rivers as the barrier between the city and its external surroundings. The academy's founder ascribed a certain historical-immunizing role to these city walls, asserting that since their destruction, all sorts of "poison" (*du*) had been entering into the city day after day, for decades on end.[9] The rivers that surround the edge of the city, while unable to block the entry of such poisons according to this worldview, nevertheless hinder their exit, such that these poisons linger and build up within the urban surroundings. The result, the academy's teachers informed me, is a thoroughly imbalanced and overly feminine-dominated (*yin*) environment in which the natural balance between *yin* and *yang* has been lost and feminine *yin* poison pollutes the air upon which everyone must rely to survive.

This allegory of the protective city walls, symbolically re-created by the walls of the purified courtyard in which we sat, expresses the sociocultural changes of the past century in the language of pathology (Zhong 2000, 51). And indeed, there has been no shortage of social pathologies in modern China since the rupture of the symbolic shell of tradition. What has been lacking, however, is a clear remedy for any of these issues. Conveniently, within an environment of perceived *yin* pollution, even social issues conventionally attributed to men could be attributed to women, deemed to be the source of all social ills. For example, one day during discussion, a teacher asked me: Why do you think that men in China nowadays go out to dinner every night with colleagues, forcing each other to drink, and then go to nightclubs or barbershops or saunas? Answering his own question on the widely discussed practice known euphemistically as *yingchou*, he told me that the only reason such phenomena exist is because women "are not at home anymore." Even when a woman is physically at home (as is indeed likely true of many spouses whose husbands are out on the town at night), he claimed her heart is not really there (*xin bu zai jiali*): she is either thinking of education, or a career, or even, he claimed with an air of disgust, dreaming of some wealthy, hairy foreign beast who might sweep her off her feet.[10] The result, he asserted, is that men nowadays are similarly not at home, and their hearts also cannot stay at home. This was not an issue, he declared, in traditional China, where everyone knew their proper place. He pointed out that in imperial times women abided by the "three obediences" (*san cong*), meaning that they obeyed their father in childhood, obeyed their husband in marriage, and obeyed their son as widows. "Their lives were planned from start to finish, without a single worry," he asserted, happily declaring, "what a beautiful image!" By contrast, an essay distributed as a handout at the academy described the status of women today as follows:

> Taking a look at women nowadays, all that is on their minds is freedom, liberation, independence, and taking charge. They have long ago lost their genuine selves . . . the hegemony of the Western barbarians' (*xi yi*) ideas of "freedom," "democracy," and "human rights" has erased our natural ways and made the harmony of the past lost forever![11]

Within this discourse of the past and the present, the roots of social issues in contemporary China often associated with men, such as binge drinking, infidelity, or the sex industry, are traced back to women, whose deviation from long-standing traditional and thus correct models of being embody the clearly looming threats to the stability and sustainability of society as a whole.

I witnessed a similarly imaginative analysis of the milk powder scandal of 2008, in which milk powder manufacturers added melamine to their watered-down product to create the appearance of higher protein content for inspections.

This seemingly clever trick sickened nearly 300,000 infants across China (Jacobs 2008),[12] causing many to develop kidney stones, and resulting in at least six documented deaths.[13] The same teacher who explained *yingchou* as the result of women's misbehavior traced the source of this milk powder crisis not to unethical business practices wherein poisonous chemicals could be placed in substandard baby formula in order to ensure greater profits, producing kidney stones in the most innocent of consumers. Rather, to my surprise, the source of this crisis was to be found, in his interpretation, in women. "People aren't supposed to drink cow's milk (*niunai*)," he declared, "they're supposed to drink mother's milk (*muru*)." In traditional China, he told me, a woman would stay at home and feed her baby her breast milk: again, their hearts were in the home. But now, he claimed, women go out to work, or their hearts simply are not "at home," and babies are left with nothing but dry and fundamentally unnatural milk powder. Thus, if women had been doing what they were supposed to do according to "tradition," namely overseeing the home that is their responsibility as inhabitants of the domestic sphere, there would have been no milk powder scandal.

Another teacher followed up on these comments, pursuing a very similar line of argument to analyze materialism in society, attributing the perverse power of money within contemporary Chinese society to so-called money-worshipping women (*baijin nü*). Here, this teacher tapped into a broader misogynistic discourse in contemporary popular culture, wherein the phrase "money-worshipping women" is a common denunciatory saying, while the notion of any corresponding "money-worshipping man" (*baijin nan*) remains unspoken and largely unthought. Even an official *China Daily* editorial from 2010 entitled "We are on the wrong path of money worship" only cites examples of women worshipping money, choosing to portray men as victims of "young girls' mercenary attitude toward marriage" and predicting nothing less than the resulting "degradation of our society" (Gao 2010). However, if one takes a deep breath and a step back to look at the state of contemporary society as a whole, rather than focusing upon women's money worship as potentially degrading society, it would be far more accurate to argue that contemporary Chinese society is a money-worshipping society that therefore naturally contains a number of money-worshipping women, as well as the often overlooked money-worshipping men. In recent decades, the political revolutionary capital that played such an essential role in self-presentation and self-promotion in the Maoist era has been seamlessly replaced by monetary capital, which plays an equally important role in self-presentation; correspondingly, the announcement and celebration of each supernatural accomplishment of the spiritual atomic bomb of Mao Zedong Thought has been replaced by the perpetual announcement and celebration of new celestial economic figures: power and money are intertwined, reproducing the inequalities and tragedies of the Maoist era in a new medium. Within this social context, the widely discussed money-worshipping women are simply part of a larger money-worshipping society. Yet by transferring this immensely discomfiting fact "onto women's bodies and female sexuality" (Zhong 2000, 13), the uncomfortable truth of a money-worshipping society is denied and reversed, misrecognizing the product and the producer by projecting blame onto women as the source of all problems, while by extension portraying the man, the only other component in society, as the eternally innocent victim.

In conclusion, following this review of the less than appealing and indeed often disconcerting ideas of the three male teachers leading this Ladies' Academy, it is worth noting for curious readers that all three were single. "I like rural women," the founder and main teacher told me one evening, "but if they've gone off to college (*daxue*) to be trained in the inferior way (*xiao dao*), I can't even stand to talk with them!"[14]

Educational Uterus for a New Society; or, Men Giving Birth to Ladies

While women are targeted as the source of all problems in contemporary society by the academy's teachers, they are also targeted as the academy's only students. Claiming to have found the source of a wide range of contemporary social issues in imbalanced gender relations and in the modern woman in particular, the teachers maintained that the solution to these issues could only be found in these same women. Women, in their analysis, are to be transformed from modern misrepresentations of womanhood into real ladies, so that modern China, which has thus far only ever been a corruption of the ideal of China, might be transformed into the real China: a charmed land of rites, etiquette, tranquility, and their cherished tradition.

What, then, is a lady? One early morning, I asked the main teacher this question after the daily tea ritual. Unsurprisingly, he was certain that he had the answer, and could provide very clear standards to which a lady must conform. He listed five core characteristics of ladyhood:

1. Diligent (*qinlao*)
2. Kind (*shanliang*)
3. Has a sense of right and wrong, knows "her place" (*you guiju/ zhi tiandi*)
4. Has a tradition to continue, or heritage from the past to deliver to the future (*you chuancheng*)
5. Pure (*chunjie*)

Reviewing these five points, note that the vision of a "lady" presented here is clearly limiting, based solely upon obligations rather than any type of rights. Each is a social obligation that is judged by external observers: whether one is diligent or not, whether one is kind or not, whether one is pure or not, whether one knows one's place or not, whether one passes tradition from the past to the future—and thus whether one's sense of culture conforms to the "appropriate" standards as determined by the teachers at this academy. Enacting this judgment, the teachers unabashedly presumed that these characteristics of the lady were lacking at the precise moment that they were articulated, and that they thus needed to be cultivated at their academy.

But how are these missing values to be realized? There are two revealing features of this academy that stand out from my time conducting research there: first, as readers have undoubtedly already noticed, none of the teachers at this "Ladies Academy" are actually ladies. Ironically, they are all men, teaching women how to be ladies. The ideal of the lady is envisioned, inculcated, and judged by men, and the relationship between male and female is thus transformed into an intentionally paternalistic relationship between teacher and student, superior and inferior. Second, a point that the teachers continually emphasized during our discussions was that the school is designed to be like a home: although this "home" has another quite illuminating layer of meaning to the academy's founder and main teacher. Explaining his conception of the school as a home one afternoon during my stay, he drew the following graph in my notebook, microanalyzing the Chinese characters that formed the words "education" and "awakening," as well as the gendered connotations associated with each.

	家		
教		育	(=Education)
學		覺	(=Awakening)
陽		陰	(Male/Female)

	Home		
Teaching		Development	(=Education)
Learning		Sense	(=Awakening)
Yang		Yin	(Male/Female)

Upon completing this graph, he informed me that education in the past took place in homes, or private academies (*sishu*), creating an all-encompassing sphere of learning in which one would not only study but also live and thereby grow. He contrasted this ideal with the large schools and universities of the present, enacting what he called their "Western industrialized model of education" (*xifang gongyehua jiaoyu moshi*), designed for being a businessman (*zuo shengyi*) rather than truly being a person (*zuo ren*). Based in this ideal of the all-encompassing sphere of learning, this Ladies' Academy was located in a traditional courtyard setting, and was supposed to be like a "new home" for a new vision of society, in opposition to the society locked safely outside. In his graph, immediately below the character for "home," the ideal of the school, the teacher wrote *jiaoyu* (education) as two separate characters, aiming to emphasize the distinction between *jiao* and *yu*. *Jiao*, he told me, is the process of teaching. *Yu*, by contrast, refers to the learning process or the environment through which this process is nurtured. The goal of education, he told me, is not only to provide teaching but also to provide a proper environment to *fayu* (develop). He then paused, looked at me intently, and said, "an environment to develop, just like a baby in a uterus." Thus, *jiao* as education relates to *yang*, the concept associated with masculinity, while *yu* as the environment for development relates to *yin*. The two characters of *xue* and *jue*, making up the word "awakening," similarly reflect this binary division. *Xue* is a process of learning, but it also has to rely on *jue*, which refers to one's sense of one's environment, or one's experience of this uterus-like space that sustains one and supports one's development. Encompassing both sides of the graph was this new "home" that the academy's male teachers had founded and oversaw.[15]

This was all quite puzzling. Yet perhaps the most puzzling aspect was the combination of, on the one hand, having all male teachers and, on the other hand, the metaphor of an educational uterus: the intersection of men and their control over a ladies' educational institution as control over an imaginary uterus giving birth to a newly balanced society unable to be produced through conventional means of birth, which inevitably involves passing through the presumed source of pollution. The male teachers had created a cultural space beyond nature in which they incorporated both sides of this graph that they drew, both the masculine and the feminine, under their own male control. This Ladies' Academy was then envisioned as a home without mothers or even a uterus outside of a mother: it was a pure space owned by all male teachers, who biologically cannot give birth and who inevitably come from women, instead giving birth to new women, or ladies, to save society from the women of the present. Hence, despite its stated goal of educating women, this Ladies' Academy is in fact the ultimate misogynistic fantasy in which all problems are attributed to women, who are out of their natural place; and all of the solutions are in the hands of the men, whose job is to put everything back into its proper place, including even the process of birth: to return to the idealized balance between *yin* and *yang* through their encompassment and control of both.

To provide proof of the happy and healthy babies emerging from their educational uterus, the male teachers showed me two pictures before I departed, smiling like proud parents. The first was of a young woman: her hair was dyed blond, she wore a very short jean skirt and a tank top revealing a belly button ring, and she raised her right hand to display the "V" victory sign with a smile. A second picture showed a woman safely covered in Han Clothing, looking sternly at the camera without even a hint of a smile, standing next to an older woman in a button-down white shirt. Although the women in the two pictures indeed looked completely different, I was informed that they were in fact photos of a single graduate of this academy, taken two years apart. The first photo had been taken prior to her education: the teachers told me that she had been living a "wild life," drinking, using foul language, and running away from her family with boyfriends for weeks at a time. Her parents had no idea how to respond and resolve her "troubles"; desperate to find a solution to this dilemma, they sent her to this Ladies' Academy against her will. And although she ran away from the academy at first, she eventually came back, and was able to develop within the academy's environment to rediscover her so-called true self in ladyhood, eventually quitting her partying ways and taking up the thoroughly ladylike hobby of embroidery. The second photograph showed her and her mother, with whom she had had such a difficult relationship in the past, standing together as "ladies." In light of my corrupted tastes, it is perhaps no surprise that I found the first image considerably more attractive than the second. Yet in light of their preferences, it is also no surprise that the three teachers at the academy could not have been prouder of the second image. One teacher pointed to this image, telling me that for the sake of my research I needed to remember it. "This is how a lady should look," he said, glancing longingly at the stern and almost sad face in his hands with a massive smile on his own.

In discussions with the three female students living at this academy during my time there, they displayed not even the slightest hint of dissent from this official vision of the lady. Besides its inherently limiting nature, the other most striking aspect of the academy's representation of ladies was the degree to which it came to be embraced and internalized by students. For example, a young woman who came from rural Sichuan was completing her month of intensive study during my research visit. Over a celebratory dinner during her last night at the academy, one of the teachers asked what she planned to do upon returning to rural Sichuan. She said that she planned to stay at home, pursuing her new ladylike hobbies, while the males of her village lined up outside her home, eager to marry her.

The main teacher then explained to me all too directly that this student had been unable to find a boyfriend for years, on account of her "rough" (*cu*) nature. Eager to blossom into a true lady in order to appeal to men, she had come to the Ladies' Academy, and in her brief tenure there had worn Han Clothing on a daily basis, mastered the intricacies of traditional etiquette, studied the Chinese classics, and in her own words, "learned all about culture and tea and those types of things, and learned how to cook." Despite the very limiting nature of traditional ladyhood as envisioned by the academy's founders, she and other students had embraced their identities as ladies in training. Yet this traditionalist, seemingly self-cultivated identity was directed toward the very contemporary and immediate externally produced pressures of finding an ideal partner and getting married. As was the case with much of the traditionalism that I encountered throughout my fieldwork, the notion of the traditional "lady" was more of a response to contemporary anxieties and uncertainties on the part of both men and women than a continuation of an actual lasting tradition. Giving voice to this often perplexing mixture of the past and the present, this young lady from Sichuan asked over dinner whether upon graduation she might be issued an official "ladies' certification" (*shunü zheng*), which she could show to potential suitors, similar to the modern state's identity card (*shenfen zheng*), to verify her identity as a lady. The academy's teachers mulled over this possibility briefly, before responding that true ladyhood was a beauty that, as noted above, could only "shine from the inside out."

What are we to make of this constructed beauty of "the lady" shining from the inside of this male-constructed educational uterus outward to cities across China in recent years? This traditionalist Ladies' Academy, purportedly based in millennia of tradition, has clearly emerged primarily from the anxieties, uncertainties, and instabilities of the present. Caught between romanticized imaginings of the past and the stark realities of the present, I agreed with the founder and teachers of this academy that there are many problems in contemporary Chinese society, as is true of any society or system. And in their reflections upon the current state of urban China, they have indeed recognized issues that need to be examined more closely: education, gender relations, family life, materialism, instability, and general distrust between people. Yet in their determined eagerness to find a single root cause for these issues, they have fundamentally misrecognized their origins, and drastically simplified complex problems. And in their self-congratulation at finding a solution to all of contemporary society's dilemmas in a misogynistic fantasy of the rebirth and redomestication of the pure and traditional female, I could not help but feel that they might only be creating a new problem for the present, in the name of the past.

Notes and References

I would like to thank Ai Xiaoming, Ke Qianting, and everyone in Sun Yat-sen University's Comparative Literature Section, where this chapter was first written and presented.

1. Despite this institution's aspirations to further raise its profile, I have refrained from revealing any identifiable aspects of this academy, as well as from citing the academy's website, to protect the anonymity of the institution, its teachers, and its students.

2. This was a common assertion regarding the present state of affairs among a number of traditionalist groups with whom I worked. The paradoxical implications of this supposed "unreality" of contemporary reality are analyzed in more detail in Carrico (2013).

3. This image of timelessness is reminiscent of the discourse of "traditional China" within the "Western" academy, which has been justly criticized; see Teng (1996). Nevertheless, it is worth noting that images of a timeless "traditional China" and a classic "traditional Chinese woman" are by no stretch of the imagination solely products of the so-called Western academy: this study shows that such ideas are equally fetishized within China proper.

4. On the history of culture as the history of the creation and breakdown of insulating barriers or spheres at both micro- and macrolevels, see Peter Sloterdijk's *Spheres* trilogy, in particular *Écumes: Sphérologie plurielle* [*Foam: Plural spherology*] (2005). The prior two volumes, *Bubbles* (2011) and *Globes* (2014) have both been translated into English and published by Semiotexte.

5. The notion of *yinyang* disorder is discussed in Zhong (2000).

6. This idea of the fully equal, or rather "liberated" woman, heralded in the Maoist era through a combination of propaganda and an information blockade, has received quite thorough and thoroughly justified critique in English-language scholarship. See, for example, Wolf (1985). Yet despite the fundamental unreality of this idea of liberation, it continues to find a place in regime rhetoric, where it is praised; and in the male imagination, where it is bemoaned as another unnatural result of that thoroughly absurd era.

7. A similarly reactionary viewpoint on gender relations and "tradition" in a different cultural context can be seen in Afary and Anderson (2004).

8. On the rationalization of inequality as tradition, see Bourdieu (2001).

9. A similarly idealized narrative of a fall from paradise can be seen in Hong Fincher (2014), wherein purported improved gender equality in the Maoist era is followed by reform-era retrenchment (i.e., "women's historic gains of the past are now being eroded in China's postsocialist reform era" (7). Although Hong Fincher's work analyzes the underexamined topic of "leftover women," such a schema of the history of gender relations, invoking another unblemished tradition ("the Maoist era") similar to the traditionalist ideas of the Ladies' Academy teachers, fails to consider that the disconcerting developments of today are not always radically different from those of the past. Regarding the common burdens and assumptions of feminine ideals in the Maoist and reform eras, see Evans (2002).

10. The teachers demonstrated particular hostility toward interracial relationships, and even expressed dislike for interactions between people from other countries to me on a regular basis: "It's not good to have too much intercultural exchange," one teacher told me repeatedly throughout my stay. One day, another teacher unleashed a memorable angry tirade claiming that Chinese women nowadays are only attracted by men who wear "Western suits" (*xifu*) and ties (*lingdai*). Laughing out loud at what he called "savage (*yeman*) taste," he told me, "People think that they have a lot of taste, saying that they like those suits and ties! But do you

know where suits originated? Pirates used to wear them! They're pirate clothing! And do you know how ties originated? Ties originated in the slave trade, they were used to pull slaves and criminals along—think about the design! It's completely savage. Yet these people think they have taste when they are together with a man wearing this pirate clothing with a slave tie." By contrast, he described the Han Clothing that he was wearing as having never been designed, but rather naturally emerging as an expression of people's inner hearts and souls. Because Han Clothing is coordinated with the *qi* (life force or energy flow) in people's bodies, it is not only aesthetically pleasing, but also good for one's health.

11. This idea of conspiratorial collusion between "the West" and Chinese women to destroy the real China, placing blame on the other to portray the Chinese male as eternally innocent, is reminiscent of representations of HIV/AIDS in China as analyzed in Zheng (2009), a discourse saturated with nationalism and male dominance wherein the primary modes of transmission are imagined to be the polluting foreigner and the immoral Chinese woman. Women in this brand of contemporary paternalism and traditionalism are not embodiments of national authenticity as described by Duara (1998), but are in fact viewed as those who "cross . . . boundaries" (Ahern 1975, 209) and are thus blamed for the pollution and downfall of the presumed pure Chinese nation in the present. Hence the degree of attention directed toward this figure of "the woman" in nationalist rhetoric.

12. See also the website www.jieshibaobao.org, which is dedicated to sharing victims' stories, raising funds, and providing assistance.

13. This is the official number of infant deaths reported by the government. As is often the case in such situations, official figures are the object of great doubt and suspicion.

14. Osburg (2013) describes modern businessmen's visions of their wives as relics of the past, trapped in a bygone era that they have left behind. In this ethnographic case, in contrast to such negative matrimonial temporal lag, the women of today are all too contemporary in an impure way, and the ideal wife is envisioned as a "lady" dwelling even further in the symbolic past, prior to the perceived pollution of modernity.

15. On encompassment in such binary relationships as *yin* and *yang*, see Sangren (1987).

Afary, Janet, and Kevin B. Anderson. 2004. *Foucault and the Iranian Revolution: Gender and the Seduction of Islamism*. Chicago: University of Chicago Press.

Ahern, Emily Martin. 1975. "The Power and Pollution of Chinese Women." In *Women in Chinese Society*, edited by Margery Wolf and Roxane Witke, pp. 193–214. Stanford, CA: Stanford University Press.

Birrell, Anne. 1993. *Chinese Mythology: An Introduction*. Baltimore: Johns Hopkins University Press.

Bourdieu, Pierre. 2001. *Masculine Domination*. Stanford, CA: Stanford University Press.

Carlitz, Katherine. 1991. "The Social Uses of Female Virtue in Late Ming Editions of Lienü Zhuan." *Late Imperial China* 12 (2): 117–148.

Carrico, Kevin. 2013. "The Imaginary Institution of China: Dialectics of Fantasy and Failure in Nationalist Identification, as Seen through China's Han Clothing Movement." PhD diss., Cornell University.

Deleuze, Gilles, and Felix Guattari. 1987. *A Thousand Plateaus: Capitalism and Schizophrenia, Vol. 2*. Minneapolis: University of Minnesota Press.

Duara, Prasenjit. 1998. "The Regime of Authenticity: Timelessness, Gender, and National History in Modern China." *History and Theory* 37 (October): 287–308.

Evans, Harriett. 2002. "Past, Perfect, or Imperfect: Changing Images of the Ideal Wife." In *Chinese Feminities/Chinese Masculinities,* edited by Susan Brownell and Jeffrey Wasserstrom, pp. 335–360. Berkeley: University of California Press.

Furth, Charlotte. 1988. "Androgynous Males and Deficient Females: Biology and Gender Boundaries in 16th- and 17th-Century China." *Late Imperial China* 9 (2): 1–31.

Gao Qihui. 2010. "We Are on the Wrong Path of Money Worship." *China Daily,* June 24. http://www.chinadaily.com.cn/opinion/2010–06/24/content_10013634.htm.

Hong Fincher, Leta. 2014. *Leftover Women: The Resurgence of Gender Inequality in China.* New York: Zed Books.

Jacobs, Andrew. 2008. "Chinese Release Increased Numbers in Tainted Milk Scandal." *New York Times,* December 2. http://www.nytimes.com/2008/12/03/world/asia/ 03milk .html?ref=melamine&_r=0.

Luhmann, Niklas. 1995. "Why Does Society Describe Itself as Postmodern?" *Cultural Critique* 30 (Spring): 171–186.

Osburg, John. 2013. *Anxious Wealth: Money and Morality among China's New Rich.* Stanford, CA: Stanford University Press.

Sangren, Steven. 1987. *History and Magical Power in a Chinese Community.* Stanford, CA: Stanford University Press.

———. 2000. "Women's Production: Gender and Exploitation in Patrilineal Mode." In *Chinese Sociologics: An Anthropological Account of the Role of Alienation in Social Reproduction,* pp. 153–185. London: Athlone.

Sloterdijk, Peter. 2005. *Écumes: Sphérologie plurielle* [*Foam: Plural spherology*]. Paris: Hachette.

———. 2011. *Bubbles: Microspherology.* Los Angeles: Semiotext(e).

———. 2014. *Globes: Macrosphereology.* Los Angeles: Semiotext(e).

Teng, Emma. 1996. "The Construction of the 'Traditional Chinese Woman' in the Western Academy: A Critical Review." *Signs: Journal of Women in Culture and Society* 22 (1): 115–151.

Wolf, Margery. 1985. *Revolution Postponed: Women in Contemporary China.* Stanford, CA: Stanford University Press.

Zheng, Tiantian. 2009. *Ethnographies of Prostitution in Contemporary China: Gender Relations, HIV/AIDS, and Nationalism.* New York: Palgrave Macmillan.

Zhong Xueping. 2000. *Masculinity Besieged? Issues of Modernity and Male Subjectivity in Chinese Literature of the Late Twentieth Century.* Durham, NC: Duke University Press, 2000.

CHAPTER THREE

"Tonight, You Are a Man!"

Negotiating Embodied Resistance in Local Thai Nightclubs

DANIELLE ANTOINETTE HIDALGO AND TRACY ROYCE

In the popular imagination, Thailand has become synonymous with prostitution and predation. Images of locales such as Nana Plaza, a Bangkok complex that hosts a large number of heterosexual go-go bars, are sometimes deployed as stand-ins for the capital city itself. Journalists, often aiming to expose the very real harm associated with forced sexual labor, typically populate their stories with downtrodden Thai sex workers devoid of any agency, while depicting the men who supervise and patronize sex workers as coercive and exploitative (Olien 2010). Even a casual reading of mainstream media suggests that for many, Thai sexuality has become conflated with nonvoluntary sexual labor. Considerably more rare are discussions of Thai sexuality that incorporate local practices of sexual agency and reach beyond the scope of sex work.[1]

We would like to tell a different story: one that doesn't perpetuate stereotypes, but instead offers a more nuanced discussion of sexuality and gender. In doing so, we draw upon theoretical and ethnographic work on Thai genders and sexualities (Cardoso 2009; Jackson 1989, 1995, 1997, 2000, 2001; Käng 2014; Knodel et al. 1996; Lindberg Falk 2007; Loos 2006; Morris 1994; Ocha 2012; Sanders 2010; Sinnott 2004; Sullivan and Jackson 1999; Wilson 2004), thus critically analyzing how masculinity and femininity play out in a gay masculine club space and contributing to a broader discussion of Thai femininities and masculinities.[2] Building upon key studies such as Peter Jackson's research on Thai genders and sexualities (1995, 1997) and subsequent research, as well as Adam Isaiah Green's concept of the "sexual field" (2008a), we address how genders and sexualities are realized in and through the sexualized spaces of nightclubs. Whereas Costa and Matzner (2007, 2) challenge "popular Thai and Western imaginations" with regard to "second kind of girls" (*sao praphet song*)[3] via the personal narratives of Thai transgender youth, here we focus on nightclubbers' embodied performances and productions of sexualities and genders in and through a sexualized nightclub space. Further, scholars of Thai genders and sexualities frequently refer to the importance of "context," the definition of the situation, or *kalatesa* (Van Esterik 2000, 40) in making sense of how gender and sexuality is understood and plays out (see, in particular, Costa and Matzner 2007; Van Esterik 2000).[4] For example, Costa and Matzner (2007, 142) offer a challenge to scholars, writing that those "interested in identity might consider the relevance of the local notion of *kalatesa* to the Thai sex/gender system and, in particular, to the core versus surface identities expressed by people." In order to begin to capture *kalatesa,* we focus on embodied interactions in and through space rather than fixed identities. Our approach, spatiotemporal embodied relations, allows us to capture how genders and sexualities can and do shift in and through time and space, are impacted by time and space, and are wholly embodied. Finally, this approach allows us to contribute to discussions and research that offer "a more nuanced understanding of Thai sex and gender relations in general" (Costa and Matzner 2007, 2).

While stories about sexual exploitation in Bangkok make for sensational reports, those stories often perpetuate stereotypes and tell us far less about how "people on the ground actively negotiate, manipulate, and contest . . . sexual and gender norms" (Zheng, introduction to this volume). In order to get a sense of "on the ground" enactments of sexual and gender norms in spaces in Bangkok, Danielle (the first author) conducted ethnographic fieldwork in various nightclub spaces, some catering to men who desire men, others catering to women who desire women, and another set of spaces catering to opposite gender or heterosexual desire. For the purposes of this chapter, we focus on how Thai femininities and masculinities played out in a space where men desiring men reigned supreme. We chose this space in particular because it literally borders the infamous commercial sex spaces of Nana Plaza and offers local, "on the ground" challenges to heteronormativity and gender normativity. Further, while similar Thai nightclub spaces have previously been studied, the particular social practices we highlight here have not.

Stroll only a few blocks away from the largely heterosexual Nana Plaza and you will find yourself in the heart of Silom Soi Sii and Silom Soi Song,[5] two small lanes (*soi*) densely populated with clubs that cater to gay-identified men, both Thai and non-Thai. While sex tourism and other forms of commercial sex between men aren't completely absent from this corner of Bangkok, the Silom area offers a rich array of nighttime spaces in which men who desire other men can choose to explore their same-gender desires and identities apart from the normative expectation of opposite sex and/or opposite gender desire in the context of mainstream Bangkok.

The most popular and most heavily attended of these clubs is BoySpace,[6] a nightclub in which men dance with and for other men. Women, and other feminine people such as "second kind of women" (*phuying praphet song*),[7] are occasionally in attendance. But, as the club's pseudonym suggests, BoySpace is masculine territory.

While weekend nights are typically quite crowded, BoySpace also draws fairly large crowds that can fill every floor of the three-story club on weeknights as well. Clubbers, most of whom arrive anywhere from 11:15–11:35 p.m., line up in the street outside BoySpace, submitting to a cursory ID check and paying the door-man a modest door fee of 200 baht on the weekend (the equivalent of approximately $6 USD in 2008, when Danielle concluded her field research), or 100 baht ($3 USD) on weeknights. In exchange, clubbers receive entrance to the nightclub and one or two tickets, redeemable for mixed drinks or beers like Singha.

Once inside, clubbers who arrive early enough typically watch the twenty-to-thirty-minute cabaret show, which features performers dancing and lip-synching to popular songs recorded in English, Thai, and Mandarin. After the show, patrons can dance and mingle with other clubbers on a large dance floor area situated in front of a stage on the club's ground floor. Other clubbers choose to ascend to the second or third floor, each of which has its own bar, areas to dance or sit, and a view of the lower floors. The second floor features a little alcove with a window overlooking the street below. On more than one occasion, Danielle observed young men eagerly perched there, watching the club's entrance and avidly admiring the new patrons as they filtered in.

The Sexual Field of BoySpace

It may be tempting to assume that nightclubs in Bangkok (or elsewhere) represent little more than a venue for leisure, a place to unwind for an evening and temporarily lose oneself, surrendering to the driving pulse of the music. But clubs such as BoySpace actually serve as an important arena in which men (and women) actively *find* themselves. Clubbers don't simply dance, drink, flirt, and carouse at BoySpace. The *way* they do these (and other) things reveals something about the way they understand themselves, particularly with regard to gender and sexuality (West and Zimmerman 1987). Danielle spent over a year studying how clubbers pursue erotic possibilities that reinforce or undermine existing gender and sexual hierarchies. Clubbers accomplish this through dance and interpersonal interactions on the nightclub floor, stage, and even tabletops.

Green (2008a, 2008b) provides a way to understand how sexual stratification, or the unequal distribution of sexual power and resources, occurs through clubbers' embodied interactions. Consider BoySpace as part of a larger sexual community, what Green calls a "sexual field," with distinct, though often unspoken, sets of norms. Clubbers' behavior, appearance, and sexual desire are all governed by rules set forth by this sexual field. For example, in BoySpace, desire is defined as occurring between two or more men. People embodying masculinity are celebrated; women and others embodying femininity are on the margins of BoySpace and are not considered legitimate objects of desire. In fact, if the "game" of BoySpace is desire between men, then men (and perhaps others possessing masculinity) are the "erotic players" of BoySpace, while women and other feminine people are literally sidelined, essentially outside of the sexual field.

But all men are not considered equally desirable, even in a place like BoySpace where the sexual constraints that prevail outside Bangkok's Silom area are suspended. Clubbers who most closely adhere to an idealized image of gay Thai masculinity have more "erotic capital" or are considered more desirable than men who diverge from those ideals. For example, those clubbers who possess a trim, cut body adorned with fashionable attire have more erotic capital than men whose clothes or hairstyles are out of date, or those whose bodies are less trim. Clubbers who most closely reflect the ideal clubber image (and who therefore have more erotic capital) occupy what Green refers to as higher "tiers of desirability." Imagine a pyramid representing a hierarchy of desirability within the sexual field of the club. Those few men with the most erotic capital occupy the highest tiers, and the many others who have less erotic capital occupy the lowest tiers. In practice, clubbers on the highest tiers of desirability may have access to resources that other clubbers do not: better places to sit, stand, or dance, and opportunities to dance and flirt with a wider array of men. Clubbers with less erotic capital—those who are lower down in the hierarchy of desire—still have a place as erotic players within BoySpace, but aren't as privileged as those with more erotic capital.

Even though BoySpace, like other gay clubs in the Silom area, constitutes a space that defies the sexual norms present in much of the rest of Bangkok and Thailand (i.e., men should desire women and vice versa), the club has constraints and norms of its own. Yet rules are made to be resisted and broken; people always find ways of subverting norms. Here we explore how clubbers and cabaret performers use their bodies to resist dominant patterns of gender and sexual behavior in BoySpace. In particular, we examine men with low erotic capital who dance atop stools and tables, feminine cabaret performers, and Danielle as a woman who transformed into a "man" one night on the dance floor. Using a playful and interactional approach, each succeeded in challenging and subverting bodily norms governing gender and sexuality.

Claiming Space: Impromptu Tabletop Parodies

Each night when the cabaret show drew to a close, the professional entertainers vacated the stage, relinquishing the territory of BoySpace to its eager patrons. House music flooded out of speaker stacks flanking the stage and bar, as men (*chai*)

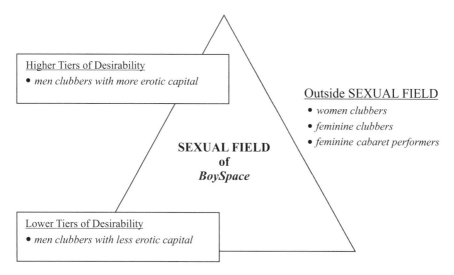

Sexual field diagram for the BoySpace nightclub.

crowded onto the dance floor. As the evening wore on, form-fitting shirts clung ever more closely to trim torsos, moist from the exertion of gyrating to the beat.

Although the majority of the men on any given night were content to groove alongside (and sometimes up against) other clients of the club, on most nights a select few dancers would climb atop barstools or tables, high above the rest of the crowd. From this elevated vantage point, these impromptu, nonprofessional go-go dancers acquired an enhanced view of the club and the other clubbers, but also achieved heightened visibility as other clubbers could clearly see them from most places on the dance floor. Such dancers further pursued the gaze and attention of other clubbers both by performing for and interacting directly with them. Table-top dancers would often lip-synch to the songs playing in the club, strip off their shirts, and flirt with the cheering, appreciative clubbers dancing below them.

For example, one evening Danielle observed a shirtless Thai clubber dancing on a raised platform near the first-floor bar and another *chai* clubber—shirt still on—dancing with him. Their performance consisted of a lot of shifting of the upper torso above relatively static feet and legs, as they were on a raised platform and couldn't move very much within the space. At one point the shirtless *chai* faced away from the dance floor, leaning against the wall using one muscular arm, essentially displaying his butt for the enthusiastic clubbers below. He shifted his hips and butt up and down, side to side, and up and down again, putting on a "sexy performance."

By converting stools, chairs, and other elevated surfaces into their very own improvised stages, clubbers literally and figuratively claimed space. As individuals, they elevated themselves, drawing others' attention to the rhythmic movement of their bodies. They literally "put themselves on a pedestal" as exemplars of the ideal gay Thai male physique and as worthy objects of male attention and desire, asserting a superior position atop the club's hierarchical tiers of desirability. In positioning themselves above others, they were both proclaiming and wielding their erotic capital.

The vast majority of clubbers who engaged in tabletop dancing conformed to the Thai gay masculine ideal: a trim, moderately sculpted body, a funnel-shaped torso enrobed in a tight polo shirt or tank top, and a short fauxhawk hairstyle. Men who in one or more ways diverged from these standards were still erotic players at BoySpace, but they possessed much less erotic and bodily capital than other clubbers. And while these "less desirable" men didn't engage in tabletop dancing with the regularity with which trimmer, more stylish clubbers did, they did sometimes put themselves on display, subverting the standards of desirable Thai gay masculinity in the process.

For example, as Danielle watched the crowd one night, a Thai man in a dark cotton shirt and jeans got up on the stools in front of the ledge and started dancing above everyone on the first-level dance floor. He had unfashionably spiky hair and did not have a trim body, thereby falling outside of the Thai masculine ideal typical of other tabletop dancers. He nonetheless engaged in his own performance, pumping his upper torso with his arms up and his hands framing his round face. He then alternated thrusting his arms forward and then back again, simultaneously switching and shifting his hips in opposite directions as he swung his butt way out in an exaggerated arc. As his performance drew to a close, he giggled loudly, signaling to his friend to jump up and dance with him. Soon his friend, who had been sitting on the nearby ledge, joined in. This friend, also Thai, appeared to be losing his bleached blond hair. He nonetheless sported a long Mohawk—an unruly mane of starchy yellow hair that ended where his neck met his shoulders. The blond Mohawk-adorned man got up and started dancing in unison with his friend; the two pumped their arms back and forth with their hips swaying in opposite directions, giggling together as they simultaneously "performed" to the music. They repeated this synchronized routine before moving on to their own individual performances side by side.

Danielle witnessed similar episodes involving different clubbers on subsequent nights. The playfulness and levity exhibited by these men was absent from the typical tabletop dancers, whose more stylishly clad, thinner bodies more closely approached the Thai gay man's ideal. For men who danced atop not only the tables, but also the club's tiers of desirability, tabletop dancing was a celebration of sorts, but ultimately a serious endeavor. Displayed atop stools and tables, their gay masculinity could hold sway despite the predominance of opposite gender expressions of desire in the world outside the club. But clubbers who did not have an ideal-looking body or whose hair and clothing styles set them apart from this attractive ideal achieved a different goal when they scrambled up stools and speakers. Their gleeful performances, composed of energetic movement and exaggerated poses, asserted their right to claim space in the club despite their reduced erotic capital, while simultaneously poking fun at the dominant standards of gay Thai masculinity. Their antics, always accompanied by grins and laughter, can be understood as a humorous parody of the serious sensual performances offered by most of the club's other patrons. Through their playful interaction with each other, these two men, along with others, flouted the tiers of desirability, subverting the dominant bodily norms of BoySpace, at least for a while.

The BoySpace Cabaret Show: Resisting Hegemonic Thai Femininity

Every night, two to three DJs helped transform BoySpace into a place where men could perform this sweaty celebration (and subversion) of gay Thai masculinities on the dance floor. But clubbers who arrived prior to 11:20 p.m. had the opportunity to begin their evening at BoySpace by watching the cabaret show. This nightly show consisted of second kind of women (*phuying praphet song*) and young *chai* dancers and singers performing about six choreographed pieces as well as bawdy skits. After taking their bows, the performers relinquished the stage to the DJs, and once again masculinity reigned in the club. But for the first twenty to thirty minutes of every evening, femininity took center stage at BoySpace.

The show often began with a *phuying praphet song* performing in the middle of the dance floor, lip-synching while her entourage of other *phuying praphet song* and young boy dancers performed choreography behind her. Just as there was an idealized *chai* clubber look, there were also ideals governing the bodies and movement of *phuying praphet song* performers. Those performers who most embodied the feminine ideal were sleek and slender, with smooth-skinned and hairless bodies, beautiful faces and flawless makeup. Consequently, they routinely delivered dramatic songs in a serious manner that highlighted their femininity (such as Cher's "Believe"). By contrast, performers whose appearance strayed from this idealized image routinely performed "silly" songs and skits that were loud and brash, comedic rather than serious, and were much more overtly sexualized than the numbers performed by more ideally feminine performers.

Typically in these comic numbers, the central performer's body size was significantly larger than the other idealized, thin performers who appeared in most of the other segments of the show. Also, "skits" that were included in these humorous performances were often highly sexualized, featuring the central performer humping another *phuying praphet song* or *chai* performer from behind or sitting on another performer's face while telling dirty jokes. The comic segment came near the conclusion of the nightly cabaret show.

One particular performance featured a Mandarin-language song and starred the less idealized or larger *phuying praphet song* (this particular performer, whom we refer to here as "Aom," appeared to weigh about 200 pounds and always performed the "silly" segments of the show). In this number, Aom acted very demurely, batting her eyelashes and coyly tilting her head to the side as she lip-synched to the song. The popular thin and feminine *phuying praphet song* who usually starred in many of the "serious" numbers (whom we call "Noi") also performed in a supporting role. For example, at one point Aom turned her back to the audience as Noi removed Aom's sheer robe. Underneath, Aom wore red lingerie that revealed a great deal of her body. Aom then faced the audience, standing proudly in the center of the stage. Her exposed belly extended wide and low over her crotch, starkly highlighting her difference from Noi and the other traditionally "feminine" performers.

Aom often undressed throughout her performances, revealing her body in an unapologetic way but nonetheless revealing it in a way that was constructed as humorous, not to be taken seriously, and not desirable. Noi frequently functioned as a sidekick in these comic performances, teasing Aom and providing a point of feminine contrast.

The hypersexualized practices in which performers engaged during these humorous numbers (dry-humping, sucking another performer's extended middle finger) were always reserved for comic rather than "serious" numbers (such as Noi's dramatic performances to songs by Celine Dion and Shakira). In fact, this hypersexualization was central to the comic performances. For example, when Aom performed Madonna's "Like A Virgin," she lolled about on the stage. Aom's rendition of "Like a Virgin" emphasized the most sexualized aspects of the song, rather than other dimensions such as Madonna's glamour or idealized beauty.

The sexualized nature of the comic performances often served to highlight the ways in which Aom's body and behavior diverged from Thai feminine ideals. Costa and Matzner (2007) lay out Thai standards for femininity and womanhood:

> Thai notions of womanhood are informed by a division between "good" and "bad" women. Ideally, the "proper" woman is a chaste daughter, a

faithful wife, or a caring mother. She is expected to follow appropriate modes of speech, dress, and comportment in both her social and sexual lives. Described as *riabroi*, this "virtuous woman" is skilled at household work, has an agreeable demeanour, and is modest in appearance and manner. She is also more mature, dependable, and considerate than her male counterpart. Taught to be hardworking from a young age, this archetypal woman shoulders the responsibilities for taking care of family (including siblings and, eventually, parents) and household. (15)

Taken together, the characteristics described above cohere to form an idealized image of the "good" and "pure" Thai woman. This ideal permeates mainstream Thai culture and constitutes what sociologists refer to as "hegemonic femininity" for this local context (Schippers 2007). Like hegemonic masculinity (Connell 1995), hegemonic femininity sets forth a dominant or hegemonic ideal that individual women may strive to achieve, yet never fully embody. Performers such as Noi, with delicate features, smooth skin, and a slender body, emphasized their proximity to the feminine ideal through their graceful choreography and their selection of dramatic songs, producing serious performances that reinforced dominant notions of Thai femininity.

But Aom, along with other silly performers, embodied a counterpoint to dominant ideals of feminine beauty and demure behavior. Aom overtly mocked feminine ideals by parodying femininity through broad bodily exaggerations, such as furiously batting her eyelashes. But she also offered a different way of doing femininity, one that embraced many of the characteristics that are antithetical to the image of the ideal Thai woman: loudness, bawdiness, immodesty, lewdness. In fact, her bodily appearance and behavior were designed to swerve as far from the traditional feminine ideal as possible. Whereas Noi's body was smooth and hairless, Aom delighted in revealing her forest-like pubic region: unruly black pubic hair that corkscrewed out of the crotch of her bikini underwear. Noi's makeup was flawless, while Aom's garish orangey lipstick was sloppily applied in the general vicinity of her mouth, but with little regard for the boundaries of her lips. Aom's raunchy, sexual style mocked the seriousness of the other cabaret performances. Her very presence subverted traditional expectations of the Thai feminine body.

Why did these humorous performances consistently draw such loud cheers from an audience composed mainly of gay Thai and non-Thai men? It may be that in undermining ideal Thai femininity, Aom and other comic performers simultaneously undermined the ideal that Thai men are expected to desire: the demure and chaste wife and mother. Aom's humorous antics simultaneously skewered femininity *and* (hetero)sexual norms, preparing the way for a night in which gay men's desire took center stage. Without conflating the cabaret shows at BoySpace with Euro-American drag performances and histories (see, in particular, Garber 1992; Newton 1972; Rupp and Taylor 2003), like so many drag and camp performances, this Thai cabaret show produced and played with everyday sexual and gender norms, norms that performers and clubbers were able to make fun of, reenact, and directly challenge. In other words, camp and playfulness in the cabaret show allowed performers and clubbers to critically interrogate gender and sexual normativity in general (Newton 1972). By opposing the sexual norms of mainstream Thai culture (men desiring women and vice versa), Aom validated the sexual field of BoySpace wherein men desiring men was encouraged and supported. However, the centrality of men's desire in BoySpace resulted in some constraints of its own. In the next section, we briefly address how women and feminine clubbers were highly restricted by BoySpace's sexual field and how those constraints were resisted.

"Tonight, You Are a Man!" Masculine Transformation on the Dance Floor

Because the sexual field that predominates in BoySpace is one in which men desire and are desired by other men, women and other people who embody femininity are generally marginalized within the nightclub. Although the cabaret show provided a prescribed time and place in which idealized Thai femininity was both celebrated and parodied, once the cabaret performers ceded the stage to the DJs' driving pulse, masculinity reigned. Men occupied center stage as the club's erotic players, while women and other feminine folks sat or stood on the sidelines.

For example, it wasn't unusual for Danielle, as a woman who is less stereotypically feminine than many, but someone who is nonetheless discernibly "female" (West and Zimmerman 1987) to enter the club and have difficulty finding any place to stand or dance. Night after night, both Thai and non-Thai men breezed past her and were warmly welcomed into social groups of apparent strangers. Men who chose to stand or dance alone were accommodated—as they crossed the crowded club floor, other clubbers adjusted their own bodily positions and moved aside to let them pass. Yet when Danielle (or the few other women or *phuying praphet song* she observed from time to time) attempted to move deeper into the club or find adequate space to dance, other clubbers usually remained unyielding, static obstacles around which she had to navigate. Women who managed to find a small niche in which to dance did so by themselves, watching as men who began the evening by dancing alone were soon joined by eager new companions. Similarly, on nights when Danielle arrived early enough to watch the cabaret show, she often had to crane her neck, stand on tip toes, or otherwise contort herself to see around the men who unapologetically moved into her direct line of sight, blocking her view of the performers.

One extraordinary night, Danielle discovered a way to not only claim a place in BoySpace, but to do so in a way that promoted her inclusion with the men. Earlier that night a visiting Taiwanese *chai* clubber had raised his glass to her, toasting her bravery as a woman adrift in a sea of men. He subsequently invited her to join his group of non-Thai and Thai local friends. Upon returning home that night, an excited Danielle recorded the following episode in her fieldnotes:

> It's a typical night at BoySpace; the dance floor is crowded with men, mostly Thai. Women are few and far between. Large speakers fill the club with a rhythmic, yet ironic refrain: "All the boys and all the girls . . . get on the dance floor." The chorus repeats again and again as I exchange a knowing glance with my new local Thai friend, Thong. I say, "*Dtee mai mii phuying thii nii!* (But there aren't any women here!)." I grin as he scrunches up his face in laughter, nodding in agreement. Our mutual friend, Joe, motions toward me and proclaims, "Tonight, you are a man!" to which I respond, "Okay, tonight I'm a man because I have genitals!" (I mean to say that I have *male* genitals but they understand anyway).[8] I continue laughing and dancing; swaying my legs back and forth a little, I quickly push my crotch forward and cup my hands over it to indicate that I am talking about my "pussy." Joe guffaws and all of the men in our group—Thong, Joe, Jim, and Lou—turn their attention to me as I reiterate, "I am a man tonight." Joe echoes my pronouncement: I *can* be a boy tonight, and I playfully dance back a step, facing the men and exclaiming in Thai, "*Toon nii, mai bpen phuying . . . bpen phuchai!* (Right now, I'm not a woman but a man!). *Bpen phuchai!* (A man!)." We continue laughing while I point at my body and smile wide, as we shift our torsos to the beat.

The episode described above was extraordinary in several ways. Usually, Danielle was literally and figuratively on the margins of BoySpace; however, on this particular night, her new connections with *chai* clubbers, as well as a shared sense of playfulness, facilitated a transformation on the dance floor.[9] Although she wasn't truly desired or actually considered as a potential sexual partner by the men with whom she danced, by playing at "being a man" she temporarily achieved status as an erotic player in BoySpace. Danielle managed this by literally playing with her gender presentation, pretending that she was a man (*bpen phuchai*) for the night, that she magically possessed "male genitals" for the duration of the evening. This focus on Danielle's (imagined) genitalia was mirrored on numerous other occasions, when Thai men proclaimed how much they "didn't like pussy" and "liked dick." "Dick" was not only desirable; possessing one was understood as essential to gay Thai masculinity.

Which suggests the following: clubbers who were read or understood as lacking male genitalia were automatically positioned on the margins of this sexual field. Danielle was usually read in this way, as *not* possessing male genitalia. But through interactional play, she not only transcended but also transformed this limitation. Suppressing any hint of femininity in her gender presentation or movement, she danced with her legs spread apart and her crotch thrust forward, framed by her hands. She used all of the space available to her and let her crotch lead her body toward the group. This highly masculinized form of dance and self-presentation was acknowledged and rewarded by the "other men," who egged her on and laughed with her (rather than *at* her). And importantly, her performance succeeded not only because of her playful approach, but because her movement and dancing were nonintimate—she never initiated any intimate bodily contact with the other dancers. By contrast, had she stepped into the men's close personal space, rubbing up against them (as many of the men on the dance floor did), her newfound (though temporary) position as an erotic player would have immediately lost legitimacy. Danielle's masculinity and "maleness" remained viable only as long as they were nonserious, and actual desire, defined in BoySpace as possible only between two (or more) men, was not imitated or asserted in any serious way.

But the evening retained its air of levity, and Danielle remained a man, if just for the night. She both embodied and parodied masculinity, and as a result was rewarded with its privileges, at least within the context of the club that evening.

Conclusion

In contrast to mainstream Thai society, BoySpace provided its primarily gay patrons with a place in which men desiring men was normative, yet BoySpace contained constraints of its own. Clubbers who embodied femininity were devalued in the space, as were erotic players who failed to live up to a gay masculine ideal. Nonetheless, subversion of bodily and interactional norms routinely occurred.

Although erotic players who closely fit the ideal for Thai gay masculinity monopolized dance-floor bar stools and tabletops, a few clubbers with less than ideal bodies or unfashionable hair and clothes still scrambled atop stools and tables, claiming space to perform with their friends. These men, who did not quite fit the ideal, demanded that other clubbers take notice of them despite their minimal erotic capital, while simultaneously mocking the club's high standards for gay masculinity.

Similarly, cabaret performers who did not fit the ideal for Thai hegemonic femininity used bodily performance to resist norms. For example, Aom frequently and unapologetically flouted expectations of demure, modest Thai femininity in her skits: she told dirty jokes, screamed at the top of her lungs, flipped off the audience, and pretended to have oral and anal sex with other performers on stage. Flying in the face of feminine standards, Aom represented a different way of doing femininity that called into question the relationship between normative femininity and masculinity (Schippers 2007). In turn, Aom's raunchy femininity directly challenged Thai mainstream expectations that situated opposite-gender desire as normative. Aom's embodied performances offered a respite from larger expectations for men (i.e., desiring women) that was welcomed and celebrated by gay erotic players in the club.

Finally, Danielle managed to contest the larger sexual field of BoySpace when she played at "being a man" for the night. Although the success of her performance hinged on its nonintimate nature, she nonetheless challenged the constraints placed on "female" and less desirable bodies by using and playing with space as a man might when socializing and joking with nonintimate friends. She temporarily transformed the space and thus opened up the possibility that bodies presumed to be "female" could in fact be erotic players in certain gay contexts. In all of these episodes, clubbers or performers located outside of the sexual field (or lower on its tiers of desirability) used humor and playfulness as a means of disrupting the serious business of the club's gender and sexual hierarchies.

In order to present a nuanced discussion of Thai genders and sexualities, we have provided an analysis of spatiotemporal embodied relations. Rather than focusing on static identity categories that often conceal more than they reveal, we have highlighted how genders and sexualities are realized, contested, and reimagined in and through a particular space (the BoySpace nightclub), at particular times (the cabaret show versus dancing to house music), and via particular embodied relations. Overall, this research contributes to understandings of Thai genders and sexualities that capture resistance, play, and new possibilities for embodied relations both within the context of sexualized spaces, and as a counterpoint to heteronormativity and gender normativity in mainstream contexts.

Thai Glossary

baht—Thai monetary denomination. At the time of Danielle's fieldwork, $1 USD was the equivalent of about 40 baht.

chai—informal form of *phuchai*

gay—usually used in reference to men who love other men and can embody masculinity (gay king) or femininity (gay queen)

phuchai—man/men

phuying—woman/women

phuying praphet song—feminine-embodied "males" who are considered "a second kind of woman"; also known as *sao praphet song* (a second kind of girl)

Silom/the Silom area—central business district that simultaneously serves as the main gay area of Bangkok with gay nightclubs, bars, and coffee shops

Singha—a Thai beer

soi—small lane; bigger than an alley, but smaller than a street

ying—informal form of *phuying*

Notes and References

1. Further, media depictions rarely tell a nuanced story about sex work in Thailand, often failing to address the many global factors that account for work in the sex industry (for an excellent discussion of these issues, see Kempadoo 2011).

2. See Kitiarsa (2005) for work on Thai masculinities in the context of *Muai Thai;* and Malam (2008) for an exploration of heterosexual masculinity in the context of Thai men working in tourism in southern Thailand.

3. For Thai pronunciation and spelling, we use the work of key scholars of Thai genders and sexualities as a reference point, especially Jackson (2001) and Costa and Matzner (2007). For *phuying,* the "h" is silent and the term is pronounced "poo-ying"; for *phuchai,* the "h" is silent and the term is pronounced "poo-chai." To hear the proper pronunciation of Thai terms, visit http://www.thai-language.com/dict/. Jackson (2001), Sinnott (2004), and Costa and Matzner (2007) occasionally use different spellings of Thai words (e.g., *phet* versus *pheet*); in such cases, we default to the spelling that we believe is easier for the English-language reader.

4. Both Van Esterik (2000) and Costa and Matzner (2007) emphasize the importance of *kalatesa* to Thai identity and interactions. Costa and Matzner (2007, 141) define *kalatesa* as "a Thai noun that means proper, suitable, or balanced according to the dictionary definitions, and politeness, appropriateness, or context according to Thai informants." Given the importance of *kalatesa* to our analysis of spatiotemporal embodied relations of genders and sexualities, we quote a description at length here, in which Costa and Matzner draw on Van Esterik (Costa and Matzner 2007, 141–142):

> [*Kalatesa*] explains how events and persons come together appropriately in time and space. Knowing *kalatesa* results in orderliness in social relations, *khwam riabroi* (Van Esterik 2000: 36). [Van Esterik] is careful to point out that "*kalatesa* is not identical to the English meaning of context . . . but to the coming together of immediate circumstances in time and space in a certain fashion" (Van Esterik 2000: 40). Using the metaphor of a kaleidoscope, Van Esterik emphasizes that people and events come into relationship with one another in a certain way at a certain moment in time, dependent on an individual's social location and personal characteristics. Any slight adjustment results in another time-space conjunction that changes experience and, thus, identity. Van Esterik further states that *kalatesa* is crucial for its ability to focus attention on

"the importance of understanding surfaces, appearances, face, masks, and disguise as important cultural strategies of interaction" (Van Esterik 2000: 40).

5. Please see Thai glossary at the end of the chapter for more detailed definitions of Thai terms.

6. "BoySpace," like the names we provide for individual clubbers and cabaret performers, is a pseudonym. We have not changed the names of streets, regions, or other geographical markers.

7. We use the term *phuying praphet song* to refer to "men, who, to varying degrees, present themselves as women" (Costa and Matzner 2007, 157). Costa and Matzner explain why *sao praphet song* or *phuying praphet song* is a more appropriate term than *kathoey* or "lady boy": "*Sao braphet song* are more commonly known in Thailand and the West by the terms '*kathoey*' and 'lady boy' . . . we use the term *sao braphet song* because various Thai we spoke with felt that this term was more polite than *kathoey*. Since the term *kathoey* is ambiguous, i.e., it can have positive or negative connotations depending on the context and position of the speaker and can be interpreted as a slur, we decided to use the more neutral *sao braphet song*" (1). They also explain why using "lady boy" is problematic, writing: "For example, scholar Peter Jackson has contributed the most to our understanding of nonnormative sexual behavior and identity in Thailand. He typically employs the terms *kathoey* (e.g., 1995a, 1997a) and *lady boy* (Jackson and Sullivan 1999) when referring to biological men who transgress normative gender boundaries and appear 'effeminate.' The main problem with the term *lady boy* is that it is frequently used by non-Thai to refer to cross-dressing prostitutes" (157).

8. Danielle's proclamation here reflects local gay Thai clubbers' preoccupation with "male genitalia" as a desirable and essential aspect of gay Thai masculinity. The authors are nonetheless aware that gender identity is not dependent upon the possession of any particular type of genitals or other anatomical attributes.

9. As a U.S. citizen who was typically read in this space as "white" and non-Thai, the first author is acutely aware of her privilege relative to local and nonlocal patrons of BoySpace. Nonetheless, over the course of her fieldwork, Danielle observed that while at BoySpace, she (along with other feminine patrons both non-Thai and Thai) was not treated in ways that reflected the privilege she experienced outside of the club. It's worth noting that on the night described above, she was "promoted" to the very *temporary* position of "man" by local and nonlocal men who did occupy tiers of desirability within the sexual field of BoySpace. Future work will further explore how this temporary position intersected with her non-Thai status.

Cardoso, Fernando L. 2009. "Similar Faces of Same-Sex Sexual Behavior: A Comparative Ethnographical Study of Brazil, Turkey, and Thailand." *Journal of Homosexuality* 59 (4): 457–484.

Connell, Raewyn W. 1995. *Masculinities*. Berkeley: University of California Press.

Costa, Leeray M., and Andrew J. Matzner. 2007. *Male Bodies, Women's Souls: Personal Narratives of Thailand's Transgendered Youth*. New York: Haworth Press.

Garber, Marjorie. 1992. *Vested Interests: Cross-Dressing and Cultural Anxiety*. New York: Routledge.

Green, Adam Isaiah. 2008a. "The Social Organization of Desire: The Sexual Fields Approach." *Sociological Theory* 26 (1): 25–50.

Green, Adam Isaiah. 2008b. "Erotic Habitus: Toward a Sociology of Desire." *Theory & Society* 37: 597–626.

Jackson, Peter A. 1989. *Male Homosexuality in Thailand: An Interpretation of Contemporary Thai Sources.* New York: Global Academic.

———. 1995. *Dear Uncle Go: Male Homosexuality in Thailand.* Bangkok: Bua Luang Books.

———. 1997. "Kathoey >< Gay >< Man: The Historical Emergence of Gay Male Identity in Thailand." In *Sites of Desire, Economies of Pleasure: Sexualities in Asia and the Pacific,* edited by Lenore Manderson and Margaret Jolly, pp. 166–190. Chicago: University of Chicago Press.

———. 2000. "An Explosion of Thai Identities: Global Queering and Re-Imagining Queer Theory." *Culture, Health & Sexuality: An International Journal for Research, Intervention and Care* 2 (4): 405–424.

———. 2001. "Pre-Gay, Post-Queer: Thai Perspectives on Proliferating Gender/Sex Diversity in Asia." *Journal of Homosexuality* 40 (3–4): 1–25.

Käng, Dredge B. 2014. "Conceptualizing Thai Genderscapes: Transformation and Continuity in the Thai Sex/Gender System." In *Contemporary Socio-Cultural and Political Perspectives in Thailand,* edited by Pranee Liamputtong, pp. 409–429. New York: Springer.

Kempadoo, Kamala. 2011. "Women of Color and the Global Sex Trade: Transnational Feminist Perspectives." *Meridians: Feminism, Race, Transnationalism* 1 (2): 28–51.

Kitiarsa, Pattana. 2005. " 'Lives of Hunting Dogs': *Muai Thai* and the Politics of Thai Masculinities." *South East Asia Research* 13 (1): 57–90.

Knodel, John, Mark VanLandingham, Chanpen Saengtienchai, and Anthony Pramualratana. 1996. "Thai Views of Sexuality and Sexual Behavior." *Health Transition Review* 6 (2): 179–201.

Lindberg Falk, Monica. 2007. *Making Fields of Merit: Buddhist Female Ascetics and Gendered Orders in Thailand.* Seattle: University of Washington Press.

Loos, Tamara. 2006. *Subject Siam: Family, Law, and Colonial Modernity in Thailand.* Ithaca, NY: Cornell University Press.

Malam, Linda. 2008. "Bodies, Beaches, and Bars: Negotiating Heterosexual Masculinity in Southern Thailand's Tourism Industry." *Gender, Place and Culture: A Journal of Feminist Geography* 15 (6): 581–594.

Morris, Rosalind C. 1994. "Three Sexes and Four Sexualities: Redressing the Discourses on Gender and Sexuality in Contemporary Thailand." *Positions* 2 (1): 15–43.

Newton, Esther. 1972. *Mother Camp: Female Impersonators in America.* Chicago: University of Chicago Press.

Ocha, Witchayanee. 2012. "Transsexual Emergence: Gender Variant Identities in Thailand." *Culture, Health & Sexuality: An International Journal for Research, Intervention and Care* 14 (5): 563–575.

Olien, Jessica. 2010. "What Happens to Thailand's Sex Tourism During the Riots? It Takes a Lot of Violence to Drive the Sexpats Away." *Slate,* June 3. http://www.slate.com/id /2255294.

Rupp, Leila J., and Verta Taylor. 2003. *Drag Queens at the 801 Cabaret.* Chicago: University of Chicago Press.

Sanders, Erin. 2010. "One Night in Bangkok: Western Women's Interactions with Sexualized Spaces in Thailand." PhD thesis, University of Nottingham.

Schippers, Mimi. 2007. "Recovering the Feminine Other: Femininity, Masculinity, and Gender Hegemony." *Theory and Society* 36 (1): 85–102.

Sinnott, Megan. 2004. *Toms and Dees: Transgender Identity and Female Same-Sex Relationships in Thailand*. Honolulu: University of Hawai'i Press.

Sullivan, Gerard, and Peter A. Jackson. 1999. "Introduction: Ethnic Minorities and the Lesbian and Gay Community." *Journal of Homosexuality* 36 (3–4): 1–28.

Van Esterik, Penny. 2000. *Materializing Thailand*. New York: Berg.

West, Candace, and Don H. Zimmerman. 1987. "Doing Gender." *Gender & Society* 1 (2): 125–151.

Wilson, Ara. 2004. *The Intimate Economies of Bangkok: Tomboys, Tycoons, and Avon Ladies in the Global City*. Berkeley: University of California Press.

CHAPTER FOUR

Feeling like a "Man"

Managing Gender, Sexuality, and Corporate Life in After-Hours Tokyo

NANA OKURA GAGNÉ

Defining Terms: Hostess Clubs in Contemporary Japan

The term "hostess club" means different things depending on the social context, as well as within changing historical and economic milieus. The ambiguities of this label have served both to confuse scholars and to deliberately mask businesses around the world that cater to hidden prostitution and exploitation. Nonetheless, hostess clubs as social institutions are always embedded within the particular social, economic, and gendered contexts of a particular society, and thus despite the similarly gendered services, the "hostess club" label as well as the human dynamics and implications of gender and sexuality operating within these establishments can connote different things in different locales.

Hostess clubs take a variety of forms across Asia. In China, they are referred to as "karaoke bars," a legacy of being originally introduced by Japanese businessmen. They contain individual booths and offer services including drinks, dancing and singing, and prostitution (Zheng 2009). Following China's economic liberalization, the consumption of sex in this space simultaneously signifies "the embrace of a western-oriented model of modernity" and acts as "a rejection of artificial restraints imposed by a puritanical Confucian-socialist system" (Zheng 2006, 162). Tiantian Zheng (2006, 175) reveals how political and business elites became complicit in using their consumption of sex to "assess each other's moral qualities and business competence" and to facilitate mutual trust.

In Korea, hostess clubs including high-end "room salons" and lower-end *tallanjujom* ("karaokes") and brothels also tend to offer sexual services as a matter of course. They primarily cater to male cohorts of university graduates, workplace colleagues, or military personnel (Cheng 2000; Lie 1995).[1] Sea-Ling Cheng (2000, 42) identifies how Korean men struggle with different expressions of masculinity that emerge from "three powerful but competing discourses on sexuality and masculinity in Korea": Confucianism, Christianity, and the military. While excessive virility and sexual consumption are denigrated by Confucian and Christian ideals at home and in broader society, collective consumption of sexual services has become a key measure of group solidarity and trust among male cohorts. Thus the Korean case highlights how such spaces can be sites of *ambivalent transgression* of social norms for men (Cheng 2000). In both the Chinese and Korean contexts, then, hostess clubs in the form of private booths with sexual services provide explicit sexual intimacy, and the performance of a particular masculinity through the transgression of the normative gender ideologies is the primary method and motivation for constructing trust relations.

In the after-work leisure spaces of hostess clubs in Japan, however, customers pay for expensive drinks and snacks and conversations with hostesses but no sexual service is offered on site. Even though customers pay high prices for drinking and the space is exclusive (based on trust-bound membership), there is little privacy within the space and there are no individual booths. What marks the business of hostess clubs in Japan from that in other societies is the particular construction of trust and the particular "medium of service," which is "primarily talk" (Allison 1994, 8).[2] In this safe, bracketed space, verbal interactions on a variety of topics that can be considered taboo in other contexts are encouraged. This is because in this space the usual inhibitions and judgments regarding certain topics and behaviors, including business-related conversations and sexual or even lewd conversations, are suspended. While there are also tacit rules of conduct, this is a space for the *suspension* of normative gender ideologies circumscribed by work and home, not a space for their *transgression*. Therefore, hostess clubs in Japan ambiguously occupy the space between the spheres of corporate life and family life—an ambiguity which has made them the target of both criticism and admiration.

In analyzing these gendered spaces, one common issue raised by scholars and social critics is masculinity, in particular hegemonic masculinity. At first glance when trying to understand hostess clubs' role in the practice of corporate drinking, male customers at hostess clubs seem to perpetuate the image of "salarymen doxa" (Roberson and Suzuki 2003). By wielding economic capital to purchase the companionship of women at these clubs they promote corporate ideology and "salarymen masculinity" through conspicuous corporate consumption. In this reading, hostess clubs are thus the front stage for the reinforcement and presentation of corporatized masculine prerogative.

Alternatively, when considering individual hostesses and the male patrons who use hostess clubs, a second issue that is frequently raised is exploitation through the commodification of emotion or intimacy. Hostesses are forced to embody a "false self" and perform "emotional labor" (Hochschild 1983).[3] Likewise male customers could be seen as being manipulated into a false consciousness through commodified sexuality. In this reading, hostess clubs are thus the back stage where modern capitalist logic penetrates all of the actors involved by manipulating their emotions and playing on their desires. This co-opts them into perpetuating the commodification and marketization of all human social relations while deflecting their attention from the realities of exploitation that lie behind the global political economy.

In both of these readings, both hostesses and their customers are seen as caught up within a capitalist system of commodification, alienation, and exploitation, with little agency of their own. Yet, exploring the experiences of male customers and female servers challenges exclusively materialist readings and yields important insights into the complex management of emotions, intimacies, and masculinities operating and operationalized in this space. Rather than seeing hostess clubs as a front stage for the display of masculine power or a back stage for the manipulative choreography of commodified intimacy, hostess clubs might best be characterized as the "dressing room" that lies behind the practices and performances of both work and family life in contemporary Japan. Here we can catch a glimpse of "real" emotions, desires, and dreams that are hidden both in the workplace and at home. Hostess clubs in Japan are places where corporate customers open up to each other outside of work and reveal their "true selves"—the "human" side of themselves, while noncorporate individual customers try on the costumes of romanticized men with romantic and sexual desires vis-à-vis the hostesses, expressing themselves as "an individual man" in a safely managed fantasy away from home.

Drawing from fieldwork in three hostess clubs in Ginza, Tokyo, during 2006 and 2007 and from follow-up research in 2010 and 2014, this chapter focuses on the motivations and interactions of male and female participants and analyzes the particular constructions and articulations of trust and gendered desire in the space. From the perspective of hostess clubs' embeddedness in the broader political economy, the expressions of gender and sexuality in hostess clubs in Japan can be distinguished from conventional articulations of gender and gendered service industries in other countries. Specifically, in many societies the success of hostess clubs is rooted in their transgression of gendered ideologies and masculinity, which facilitate political and economic relations. In Japan, what undergirds the popularity and sustainability of hostess clubs is the creation of a moment of *suspension* of inhibitions—a space suspended from normative gendered ideologies and masculinity at work and home. This in turn reveals the resilience of gender ideologies outside such spaces for men and women today, despite the growing precarity of men's social roles as "corporate warrior" or "primary breadwinner" in postbubble Japan. Importantly, understanding the meanings of these spaces requires historical and ethnographic scrutiny of the interplay of gender, sexuality, and corporate life for individuals and Japanese society in general.

The Business of Leisure in Historical Perspective: From Edo to Tokyo

In Japan, business and leisure have long thrived hand in hand. Just as the development of vibrant commercial activities blossomed in the protocapitalism of the Edo period (1603–1868), Japan also had a vibrant mass culture of consumption available for ordinary citizens in the forms of *rakugo,* Noh, Kabuki, and most famously the leisure quarter, Yoshiwara (Seigle 1993; Teruoka 1989). Yoshiwara was the largest licensed leisure quarter in Edo (the old name for Tokyo), and it became the symbol of a "dream world" for many male individuals over its three-hundred-year history. Leisure quarters like Yoshiwara were strictly managed and boasted a range of establishments that catered to diverse individual patrons of different classes and offered a space for a range of intimate encounters with women (Watanabe 2004).

Thus while the commercialization of emotion or intimacy and sophisticated service are often framed as something new in postindustrial society, the idea and practice of complementary exchanges of emotion, money, and services in a commodified fantasy space are not so revolutionary in Japan (e.g., Nagai 1991; Watanabe 2004). This is not to say that the "floating world" of Japanese nightlife in the 2010s is a mirror of the socioeconomic relations of the Edo period. Indeed, despite the similar forms of fantasy, the permeation of the modern capitalist economy and modern family forms raises new needs for emotional release and the humanizing of social relations. In Japan today, the rise of the service economy has come with an intense focus on emotion management at work (Raz 2002). At the same time, the democratization of family forms also reinforces a different kind of emotion management at home. Together, these developments reinforce the importance of a space where customers can be released from emotion management at work and at home.

During the bubble period in the 1980s, corporate consumption facilitated business relations beyond strict corporate contexts. As a complement to business meetings, corporate drinking and corporate golfing were notable *social* dimensions to facilitate Japanese business relations (e.g., Allison 1994; Ben-Ari 1998). Crucial to this system was the creation and maintenance of "good human relations" (*ii ningen kankei*) at work (Gagné 2010; Matsuda 2008). One of the characteristics that mark the socioeconomic structure of Japanese society is the construction of long-term corporate relationships that emerged out of Japan's postwar growth. By the 1960s, Japan had come to be known as a "corporate-centered society," a way of describing the particular configuration of Japanese capitalism whereby the livelihood of employees was guaranteed by corporations (Gordon

1998). In this model, new gendered ideologies emerged (Vogel 1963). Japanese employees were known for their long-term dedication to their companies as corporate warriors and thus were able to support their family as primary breadwinner for their household. Japanese corporations reciprocated by offering various benefits, including employment protection, comprehensive health insurance, housing support, and various leisure and entertainment services. It was in this context that corporate drinking was integrated with employees' work lives in exclusive business contexts, and that other leisure activities and welfare for workers and their families became notable dimensions of Japanese business and family life.

The wave of this corporate-centered work and family lifestyle crested and then crashed in the late 1980s, along with Japan's bubble economy. After two decades of economic recession that began in 1989, the long-term economic downturn and the subsequent neoliberal economic reforms have spurred various restructurings. These included reducing full-time employment and job security, introducing competitive merit systems, and vast cuts to corporate expenses (Matanle 2003; McCann, Hassard, and Morris 2006). This not only shook employees' security as workers and breadwinners, but also cut corporate leisure and excursions to places like high-end restaurants, bars, and hostess clubs.

While these structural changes made employee dynamics in corporations tenser and diverted the flow of money away from the business of leisure, they *did not* negate the importance and social functioning of after-hours outings. Neither did they undermine the "intimate interactions" that gendered leisure spaces provide as intermediary spaces between work and home. In fact, there has been a relative increase in individual customers who come to drink for personal reasons. As a resilient space for gendered exchange that predates the rise of both corporate-centered relations and neoliberalism as an ideological and economic force, the continued success of hostess clubs highlights their important place vis-à-vis the ideologies of work and home in contemporary Japan.

Managing Corporate Intimacy through *Bureikō* and Social Drinking

When corporate customers come to hostess clubs with their coworkers, subordinates, bosses, clients, suppliers, and business associates, they usually come after a formal or semiformal business dinner. These men (and sometimes women) are often called "company expense-account people" (*shayō-zoku*) and the purpose could be to facilitate business relations with clients, to celebrate a promotion, achievement, transfer, or farewell, or to mark the year's end or New Year. Or, if sales are stagnating, a boss might bring his or her subordinates to raise the morale and spirits of the workers and to encourage them by drinking together. These multiple motivations underlie the practice of "social drinking" (Lebra 1976) that follows a "ladder" (*hashigo*) process in which customers visit more than one place as the night wears on, often starting with light dinner at a restaurant and later moving to bars, karaoke, or other entertainment spaces like hostess clubs.

Hostess clubs usually occupy the last rung in this ladder process of corporate outings. After a long day of business meetings and an evening of treating clients to restaurants and bars, corporate hosts use hostess clubs to relieve pressure and entertain their clients. Kiyomi-san, an experienced hostess, explained:

> In the case of business entertainment, the customers [who are hosting] are already tired after hosting their clients all evening. As business people cannot take their coworkers or clients to their home, then, we are useful for them as we will take over their part in hosting their clients. For our long-term trust relationship, we try our best to serve their clients and entertain them.

Corporate entertainment is thus a delicate process that involves balancing the various dynamics between seniors and juniors, among male and female employees, and, most importantly, between companies and their clients. Arranging a night out for one's coworkers and especially for an important client requires considerable planning and careful management. When I asked customers what was most important during corporate entertainment at hostess clubs, some answered, "a comfortable and pleasant drinking experience." Others mentioned the club's "atmosphere" including the aesthetics of the club, décor, food and drink, the physical appearance and mannerisms of the hostesses, and the attitude of the club's Mama-san (the head of the club and most experienced hostess). In this respect, hostesses' primary role is as "surrogate business experts" to lubricate after-hours alcohol-fueled sociality (*nomunication*).

This tendency of customers to rely on the Mama-san and the hostesses for the rest of the evening's hosting was highlighted for me one night when Minagawa-san, a regular customer, visited the hostess club alone. He thanked the Mama-san for his last visit and told me about what happened:

> Last time, I brought a bunch of my colleagues and subordinates after the year-end party. I was so drunk and terribly tired, so I left everything to Mama-san, and left for home. I did not know what happened after that, but my junior later called me and told me they all had a good time.

As in cases like Minagawa-san's, hostess clubs facilitate a spatial and temporal moment of release among coworkers. This has the function of breaking from rank and seniority and any sort of formality, which are still powerfully embedded in many Japanese institutions. This practice, known as *bureikō,* creates an egalitarian atmosphere and enables working men and women to drink and carouse together by breaking down barriers among employees and between customers and their clients. In such contexts, some bosses deliberately act like an equal while others pay the tab in advance and leave early so that their juniors can enjoy themselves fully without their boss around.

The combination of alcohol, hostesses, and *bureikō* may convey the idea that one can do anything when drunk. However, there are tacit rules of behavior in these clubs, and I never encountered particularly surprising or outrageous behavior, or any sort of masculine aggression or competition among the regular patrons. If the conversation was rude or sexual, no one seemed to be offended as participants took it lightly. Even if a man got upset about something, many people, including hostesses and other men, would attempt to soothe him and defuse the situation. In this sense, the interactions within hostess clubs were also important for managing the sometimes sensitive emotions of male customers.

An important reason for the relative absence of extreme behavior by male customers lies in the particular kind of "humanistic intimacy" pursued by corporate customers in these spaces as a part of the ladder process of social outings. One customer, Komuro-san, explained that it was difficult to figure out what another man thinks "deep down in his gut" (*hara no naka no kimochi*). So for him, taking his coworkers and clients to different spaces including hostess clubs allows them to witness aspects of each other that are hidden in other contexts. Another customer, Fujiyama-san, told me that if he has drunk with his clients before and something goes wrong in their business relations, the client is more likely to be understanding as they know each other "as humans" (*ningen-dōshi*) beyond strictly work relations. In the increasingly competitive Japanese corporate world, ascending the ladder of an evening's events together across different contexts helps to expose the multiple sides and deeper personality of each participant, which can facilitate and humanize the "corporate intimacy" involved in major monetary transactions.

This humanizing is a carefully constructed yet structurally loose process for revealing what Anne Allison (1994, 14) calls one's "humanness" (*ningenmi*)—what is often hidden in regular business or strictly formal contexts. One can see slight transformations in behavior among Japanese men as they drink, and as the night wears on one might hear "inner feelings" (*honne*) and "improper" speech, or watch men grow teary and sentimental or intoxicated with alcohol and the women in the clubs. Takie Lebra (1976, 116) calls Japanese men's public display of vulnerability "social nudity," noting that otherwise socially respected men can be "stripped of all face or social mask" and engage in "boisterousness, crying, indulgent postures, falling asleep in front of others," and other behaviors that violate conventional norms—actions that she notes would be inconceivable in similar foreign contexts. This exchange of mutual self-exposure serves to bind customers together beyond the lighthearted banter or lewd sexual talk that marks the surface-level interactions at hostess clubs (Gagné 2010, 42). This might seem surprising in a context where high-powered male corporate executives entertain their clients and employees by "buying" women's services—what might easily be read as a form of domineering masculine control. However, this gendered service and the customers' intentions in participating in corporate entertainment in Japan facilitate "interdependence" through mutual disclosure of their "human" sides, rather than independence through displaying competitiveness or hypermasculinity.

Rethinking Hegemonic Masculinity through Hostess Clubs

The particular construction of trust and mutual management of interdependence in Japanese hostess clubs is best understood in contrast with the gender dynamics of corporate and leisure contexts in other societies. In the business contexts of the United States, for example, any display of seeming weakness or vulnerability, including complaining and consulting, drunkenness and sleepiness, may appear as disingenuous or lacking in professionalism, and thus may undermine the fundamental character of the person (Gagné 2010, 42). This is not limited to business contexts, as even in leisure spaces American men still try to maintain a hegemonic masculinity (see, e.g., Ericksen 2011).

Likewise, in the context of corporate entertainment in China, Zheng (2009, 105, 109) shows how when political cadres and business elites come to drink, sing, and buy sex in karaoke bars in the city of Dalian, dominant masculinity or sex consumption serves to ensure social trust and signal the moral strength of a man. In a complete inversion of the display of humanness in Japanese business contexts, "it is precarious to show a sign of succumbing to an emotional involvement with hostesses." As powerful men are "identified as those who could emotionally and physically control the hostesses, exploit them freely, and then abandon them" (10), male customers are expected to keep their distance from hostesses emotionally but consume them sexually. This becomes the form of assessment of trust relationships between clients that coconstruct economic and state power among Chinese elites. The Chinese case thus reveals a competitive masculine prerogative and dominating virility for enhancing men's status, power, and trustworthiness through the capitalist logic of consumption, and customers confidently engage in sex consumption as a "weapon against the socialist morality and socialist state" (Zheng 2006, 182).

The case of men's patronage of gendered leisure services in Korea highlights how such spaces can be sites of *ambivalent transgression* of social norms for men. In her study of men's use of prostitution in Korea, Cheng (2000) identifies how social solidarity and mutual trust among men is built upon the knowing transgression of social norms through the collective violation of sexual mores. In the "rituals of commensality and the collective drunkenness" (62) that mark all-male socializing among university friends, workplace colleagues, and most intensely military cohorts, Cheng notes that visits are effectively compulsory, structured by the hierarchy of junior-senior relations enforced within the military and mirrored within corporate Korea. Thus participation is not a matter of individual choice but of collective compulsion and the flexing of masculinist authority. Notwithstanding the collective pressures for participation, however, these men wrestle with the guilt that such sexual exploits are in fact a violation of the sexual mores of Korean society. As men navigate these various spheres of masculinity they are confronted with zones of friction which impel them to transgress the "dominant moral code" operative in broader Korean society in order to express their masculinity vis-à-vis other men and thus to gain the trust of their colleagues (44).

Despite the differences in personal intentions, collective goals, and embeddedness in broader social mores of sexuality and solidarity between the Chinese and Korean contexts, these studies reveal how the construction and articulation of trust among men in both contexts are inextricably motivated by the expression of certain kinds of masculinity. In this way, the goals of being serviced by women (sexually or otherwise) in Chinese and Korean contexts is directly linked to enhancing one's masculinity vis-à-vis other men, be it in competition or in solidarity. Moreover, their consumption is seen as a transgression of their respective normative gender ideologies and morality. The interplay of masculinity within these spaces vis-à-vis broader society also reveals how such spaces are tied into other social spheres through a consistent moral logic in which such spaces facilitate the violation of social mores.

In my own fieldwork I encountered many instances when male customers became so drunk they exhibited a high degree of vulnerability to other men and could not even actively participate in entertaining their clients.[4] Even within the permissive space of Korean outings, where men are allowed to "abandon the demands of 'manly pride' and propriety, and [can] cry, sing, dance, or get vulgar and rowdy," losing control and vomiting, falling asleep, or becoming otherwise incapacitated is grounds for ridicule and rejection (Cheng 2000, 63). In Japanese hostess clubs, however, other men dialectically recognize this kind of behavior and even act protectively toward such men. Suspended from the rules of propriety of other social contexts, the club becomes an insulated space for release in which otherwise taboo conversations or behaviors *do not carry over* into other spheres, but remain suspended from moral judgments as part of the "dream world" of after-hours sociality.

In short, in Japanese hostess clubs showing one's vulnerability toward other men or hostesses does not necessarily lead to distrust, nor does it undermine the quality of a person as it might in other business contexts; it actually *enhances* trust and often facilitates relations between customers and clients as well as among co-workers and hostesses and customers. Indeed, male customers are also lauded by other customers and hostesses if they fall for the Mama-san or hostesses or treat them graciously. According to my informants, this is because the fact that they can show their "human sides" means that they trust each other well enough to show the private sides of who they really are. This self-exposure or social nudity is often interpreted positively by the customers themselves as well as by the Mama-san and hostesses as a dialectical process whereby showing one's vulnerable and embarrassing sides allows the other to recognize that he is gaining more trust. Within the hostess club, then, men's displays of drunkenness, sentiment, and fatigue, or falling for a particular hostess become the means by which structural power dynamics are ambiguated or temporarily transcended in the Japanese corporate world while simultaneously facilitating Japanese economic relations—not through virility and hegemonic masculinity, but through a kind of "humanistic intimacy" (see also Gagné 2010, 43).

Structuring Romantic Intimacy: Maintaining Limits in the Club

If customers come to a hostess club as part of corporate outings or with clients, their goals are clearly social and economic and bound up with long-term corporate relations. If customers come privately, however, their intentions are obviously more personal. Such individual customers are mostly top executives, company managers, or men who save money for a special night out. Other individual customers include owners of small or medium companies, independent entrepreneurs, and independent professionals including financial analysts, lawyers, tax accountants, and doctors and dentists who can spend money on their own pleasure. These customers often come to see their favorite hostess, to visit the Mama-san if they are close friends with her, or simply to distract themselves from their loneliness.

The actual relationships between hostesses and male customers are often ambiguous, but both hostesses and customers are aware that they are usually structured *within* and *limited to* the context of the club. For instance, Saki-san, a young, upbeat hostess, was the most popular among customers and was frequently invited for "accompaniment" (*dōhan*)—going out to a restaurant together with a customer before coming to the club. When I asked what happened if the customer wanted to stay longer outside the club, she explained, "They know our business rule. They know it is my duty [to return to the club]." She added that while the Mama-san and some hostesses are invited to corporate golf outings and corporate parties, as well as to personal weddings, birthday parties, and concerts, she never saw her customers outside of her work relations with the club. She explained this boundary by saying, "Both parties think that it would probably result in some complicated issues." Saki-san also told me that nothing troublesome had happened to her despite the fact that she had many customers.

Nonetheless, such limits may not be clear to outsiders unfamiliar with the space. One night, a man from Hong Kong was brought to a club by Japanese customers. From the moment he entered the club, it was clear that he felt he had entered a male paradise where he was free to do anything. He began trying to aggressively touch the hostesses and urging them to drink more and more. At first the hostesses and other customers tolerated his behavior, but soon his antics escalated beyond what was acceptable, and the entire group was kicked out on the Mama-san's orders. As the relieved looks on the hostesses' faces and the approving looks from the other customers revealed, the man had clearly crossed the line of acceptable behavior observed by other customers in the club.

On another occasion an American hostess named Lia was working at an international hostess club. Lia was a college student in the United States but every summer she came to Japan to work in hostess clubs, like many other foreign hostesses who come to Japan for short stays to make quick cash. Foreign hostesses I met often talked about their experience working in Japan positively. Many explained that they preferred to work as hostesses in Japan because unlike in Korea, China, Eastern Europe, or the United States, they "can make a lot of money just by talking and singing with customers"; hosting in other countries often requires sexual services.

While Lia was popular among customers, many hostesses did not like her because they thought she was too aggressive. Lia seemed to think of the place as being more directly romantic and sexual, and she often dressed in a revealing manner and drank a lot. The Filipina Mama-san at this club did not comment on her dress or her drinking behavior at first. However, Lia's dress got shorter and shorter and her drinking escalated, and she began touching men when she got drunk. She would put her hands all over the men's laps and arms and became overly loud in her speech and singing, occasionally disrupting other customers. Ironically, Lia's boisterous behavior was taken positively as "being American" by some customers, but other hostesses complained to me that her behavior was lewd or "unfair," as it crossed the boundaries that other hostesses strictly maintained.

At one point a regular middle-aged male customer who enjoyed talking to Lia in English felt he could touch her back, since she was touching him. Upon feeling his hand on her back, Lia (who was drunk) grew upset and punched him directly in the face. Shocked and upset, the man rose angrily and insisted on calling the police, but the Mama-san apologized profusely and dissuaded him. The Mama-san suspended Lia from work for a week and ordered her never to drink again in the club, threatening to fire her if she did. The incident became a big story in the club, and it also served to highlight the fine line between acceptable and unacceptable behavior by both customers *and* hostesses.

As I came to learn more about the space, I realized that there were a range of tacit but explicit rules that served to maintain the space as a "managed" *safe* space for both customers and hostesses. Along these lines, the Mama-san and experienced hostesses often told me that the key for hostesses was "to be supportive and wanted by male customers, yet not to the extent that unprofessional interactions or situations could result." This was for both ethical and business reasons, as one hostess told me that "once a hostess has a real relationship with a man, he would never come back to the club."

Feeling like a Man through the Pursuit of Women: Glamour and Sexuality in Hostess Clubs

> First of all, for Japanese men, real romance or sex itself is not the primary goal [of going to hostess clubs]. We men tend to gain courage and positive energy by interacting with women, whether the woman is a wife or mother, or somebody else. The hostess club is not a place where we feel something sexual (*seiteki na mono*), but most people feel something similar to it.
>
> *(Married customer in his fifties)*

Hostesses at high-end clubs in Japan are by definition the embodiment of a particular kind of romantic femininity, glamour, and sexuality. For those seeking intimate encounters in commercial leisure spaces, one of the key attractions of the gendered interactions in these spaces is "quasi-romance" (*giji ren'ai*). This is usually seen as romantic and sexual enticement that is *not quite real romance* and does not involve *sexual consummation*. Quasi-romance is a carefully constructed performance that requires the subtle management of boundaries between the teasingly sensuous and the overtly sexual. Hostesses attend to individual customers by talking with them and singing songs together, creating a personal, intimate encounter that makes men feel like desirable companions.

Hostesses distinguish themselves by capitalizing on their strengths—singing ability, conversational skills, or physical appearance—in order to attract customers. And yet, they also work to maintain a glamorousness that always remains just out of reach. Sakamoto-san, a customer in his early thirties, revealed his ambiguous feelings regarding the hostess club:

> Men know that hostess clubs are an unrealistic space. In other words, hostesses are like a "non-fruit-bearing flower" (*ada bana*). This flower is seen as beautiful and gorgeous, but it will never produce fruit and does not have any substance in reality. But maybe because of that, it is beautiful. So I do not have money to pursue it frequently, but I long for it.

Whether they were married or not, many individual customers told me that they felt particular longing for glamorous hostesses or Mama-sans. Since nothing really happened between themselves and the hostesses, some men felt that their actions were legitimate and acknowledged that such longing was missing at home. Most men I interviewed, as well as their wives, said that while they married out of love, after a while it became unrealistic to feel romantic about their relationships. Moreover, in the clubs many men jokingly talked about the lack of romantic feelings for or sexual relations with their wives, although they added that losing romance or sexual relations did not mean that their relationship was problematic.

Sawada-san, a regular customer who managed a multinational consulting company, used to work at a large Japanese trading company and lived in New York for several years as a Japanese expatriate. He drew on his experience with American relationships in describing Japanese marital life, explaining that romance is elusive in Japanese couples' lives:

> For my generation, we do not even show any romantic feeling. We don't even hug or hold hands in public. Even at home, we do not. Wives of my generation don't even put on makeup and don't care about fashion at home. So after fifteen years of being together as a husband, something romantic is completely relegated to second priority.

To further make his point, he compared Japanese and American wives:

For Westerners, though, women are often the object of sexuality. In the U.S., American wives try to be "sexy" even at home. I mean, "being sexy" is a compliment there. They call their husbands by their first names and with sweet terms. For American men, wives are simultaneously business and life partners and the object of sexuality. But in Japan, wives are ambiguous. Japanese wives call their husband "Papa." And other than going golfing or fishing, husbands often lay around all day at home, like large pieces of garbage. Then, I think Japanese husbands and wives in general are the *least* attractive. But in Ginza, there are women called hostesses, who are nicely dressed and attractive. These women give men some yearning (*akogare*) and let us experience femaleness (*josei rashisa*) and something close to sensuality.

For the regular customer Kaneko-san, the club was like a space for comfort even though it was highly commercialized. He explained:

While people say that men come for dreams (*yume*), it is not really like a dream in the sense of ambition or some kind of achievable goal. In Japan, *yume* means nothing but a situation or context that is different from reality. This place is just not realistic, that is all. . . . Nonetheless, people still come. Even though it is expensive, I still come, as it is a sort of comfort (*iyashi*) for me. It is a self-centered comfort, as each man feels differently in the club.

From men like Kaneko-san I often heard that home was not really a place where they felt comforted or romantic. But this does not mean that home and family were not important to them. Indeed, talking to customers also revealed that in addition to the emotional work that permeates their workplace obligations, they felt heavy obligations at home, and thus they felt the need for an additional space for naked emotion and desire.

Hostesses were also aware of this need. One experienced hostess, Yuri-san, usually spoke highly of Japanese wives. But when it came to issues of men's "sense of belonging" (*ibasho*) at home, she became very critical of women. She believed that for many Japanese men home is not a place for relaxation, as they tend to be ridiculed by wives and daughters. She often told me how Japanese men are tired from work, and once when a man fell asleep at the club, she even made a small place for him to rest on the sofa, using her shawls as a blanket to cover him. Yuri-san said, "Their wives do not even try to understand their work and simply criticize them. Many men almost give up, as confronting or fighting with them is also too much trouble."

Men's desires for emotional or sexual intimacy with a female companion can take other forms as well. One frequent customer, Fuwa-san, was a former member of a large corporation, but his lifestyle changed drastically after being laid off during corporate restructuring in the early 2000s. He no longer pursued his corporate-driven lifestyle, but he maintained one practice—going to drink and talk to women at hostess clubs. He explained:

> To be honest with you, as I am now self-employed, while I sometimes use the excuse of doing corporate entertainment with clients, it is more like a pretense because I am also going there to distract my loneliness. We humans are all different. So we drink with many different feelings. But if there is a woman next to me, being kind to me, I feel temporarily comforted, and I feel like I can use that as a motive power to try to work hard the next day! I think humans are all like that; we need to gain some motive power from something, whether it is from Ginza, from home, or from other hobbies.

In short, for individual customers hostess clubs are a space for yearning, quasi-romance, comfort, sexuality and sensuality, and rejuvenation. Crucially, the recognition and attentive care from hostesses and the Mama-san enables men to indulge in a different sense of self and desire that in fact rejuvenates them by enabling them to feel like a "man." In other words, rather than cultivating an independent and aggressive masculinity that is projected *against* women, these men can project a different kind of masculinity and desire—the pursuit of women—by continuously coming to receive the glamorous attention and care from hostesses. Ultimately, the satisfaction and comfort of this experience becomes directed toward their everyday lives outside of the clubs, as a way to gain energy and to work hard with renewed vigor.

Conclusion: Feeling like a "Man" in Postbubble and Neoliberalizing Japan

This brings us back to one of the major questions regarding gender and sexuality raised in the introduction: If hostess clubs are not a site for reproducing hegemonic gender norms or manipulating individuals into a false consciousness through commodified sexuality, how are these spaces situated within the broader political economy of work and home in contemporary Japan? Whether it is corporate drinking or personal visits, men tend to act with less inhibition in after-hours leisure spaces like hostess clubs. They can be openly verbal and emotional with each other, as well as with hostesses. Certainly this is funded by capitalist economic flows, shaped by gendered desires and dynamics, and charged with sexual/sensual excitement. However, at the same time it is managed, channeled, and contained within a space that is neither a front stage for the display of hegemonic masculine aggression nor a back stage for the coercive manipulation of emotion through dehumanizing capitalist market logic. Instead, whether customers come for corporate or personal reasons, hostess clubs are a "dressing room" for revealing their "human" side of vulnerability and emotionality as well as for slipping into and out of masculine costumes of idealized selves and desires "as a man." It is a space for men to be released from the emotional work of corporate and domestic contexts, and through this choreography of emotion men are able to openly display a social nudity that they must cover up both at work and at home.

Despite the stereotypes of hostess clubs as a modern capitalist crystallization of commodity fetishism and commodified intimacy, through the coconstruction of "interdependent relations" among coworkers and clients or between men and hostesses, hostess clubs are one of the few places where men are released from the dominant gender ideology that binds them to work and family. Here, a man can be a "man"—a human and a male—through displaying naked emotions and desires that are often hidden under the demands of gender ideologies in their corporate and domestic lives. Corporate customers are able to build trust through revealing various "human" sides because hostess clubs suspend the dominant ideology of the "corporate warrior" and "salaryman masculinity." On the other hand, individual customers can reveal their romantic and sexual desire through the suspension of the dominant ideology of the "primary breadwinner" or "central pillar" of the household.

In other words, customers can be released from inhibitions in the other spheres of their lives, thus enabling them to use the hostess club space creatively to serve diverse motivations and desires without transgressing the dominant gender ideologies that constrict their public and private lives. Intriguingly, Japanese hostess clubs inhabit a space that neither affirms or challenges broader social norms, a space *suspended from* masculine expectations stemming from the professionalization of men's roles as husbands, fathers, and workers.

Notes and References

1. High-end hostess clubs called "room salons" emerged from establishments that served the Choson Dynasty (1392–1910) aristocracy and which were later adapted to serve elites from home and abroad by emulating Japanese hostess clubs. Lower-end brothels cater to poor customers, while *tallunjujom* developed to serve mid-range customers, including Korean and American military personnel.

2. In the Korean hostess clubs in Osaka studied by Haeng-ja Chung, the majority of hostesses were Korean women who performed regular services such as serving drinks. Along with the superintendent, director, and executive director, there are usually a chef, waiters, piano accompanist, and showgirls who dance onstage. Apart from the hostesses and the head of the club (the Mama-san), Chung found that there were also "hidden women" called "soldiers" (*heitai*), who were hired specifically for sexual services (Chung 2010, personal communication).

3. Hochschild (1983) uses the term "emotional labor" to mean the management of emotion that can add exchange value in the service industry, and "emotional work" to mean the management of emotion that has use value in the private sphere.

4. Allison (1994, 178) compares Japanese businessmen's gendered desire to American men's sexual domination and consummation, showing how Japanese men in hostess clubs expect to *lose* control of themselves and rely on hostesses to make them "feel like men." During my fieldwork, not only men but also women expressed to me how they like to be cared for by the other sex, as this is the sign that they are recognized and valued.

Allison, Anne. 1994. *Night Work: Sexuality, Pleasure, and Corporate Masculinity in a Tokyo Hostess Club.* Chicago: University of Chicago Press.

Ben-Ari, Eyal. 1998. "Golf, Organization, and 'Body Projects': Japanese Business Executives in Singapore." In *The Culture of Japan as Seen through Its Leisure*, edited by S. Linhart and S. Fruhstuck, pp. 139–161. Albany: State University of New York Press.

Cheng, Sea-Ling. 2000. "Assuming Manhood: Prostitution and Patriotic Passions in Korea." *East Asia* 18 (4): 40–78.

Ericksen, Julia. 2011. *Dance with Me: Ballroom Dance and the Promise of Instant Intimacy.* New York: New York University Press.

Gagné, Nana Okura. 2010. "The Business of Leisure, the Leisure of Business: Rethinking Hegemonic Masculinity through Gendered Service in Tokyo Hostess Clubs." *Asian Anthropology* 9 (1): 29–55.

Gordon, Andrew. 1998. *The Wages of Affluence: Labor and Management in Postwar Japan.* Cambridge, MA: Harvard University Press.

Hochschild, Arlie. 1983. *The Managed Heart: Commercialization of Human Feeling.* Berkeley: University California Press.

Lebra, Takie Sugiyama. 1976. *Japanese Patterns of Behavior.* Honolulu: University of Hawai'i Press.

Lie, John. 1995. "The Transformation of Sexual Work in 20th-Century Korea." *Gender and Society* 9 (3): 310–327.

Matanle, Peter. 2003. *Japanese Capitalism and Modernity in a Global Era: Re-Fabricating Lifetime Employment Relations.* London: RoutledgeCurzon.

Matsuda, Saori. 2008. "*Hosutesutachi wa nani o uru?* [What do hostesses sell?]" In *Seiyoku no bunkashi* [A cultural history of sexual desire], edited by S. Inoue, pp. 183–216. Tokyo: Kōdansha.

McCann, Leo, John Hassard, and Jonathan Morris. 2006. "Hard Times for Salarymen: Corporate Restructuring and Middle Managers' Working Lives." In *Perspectives on Work, Employment and Society in Japan,* edited by P. Matanle and W. Lunsing, pp. 98–116. Basingstoke, UK: Palgrave Macmillan.

Nagai, Yoshikazu. 1991. *Shakō dansu to nihonjin* [Ballroom dance and the Japanese]. Tokyo: Shōbunsha.

Raz, Aviad. 2002. *Emotions at Work: Normative Control, Organizations, and Culture in Japan and America.* Cambridge, MA: Harvard University Asia Center.

Roberson, James, and Nobue Suzuki. 2003. "Introduction." In *Men and Masculinities in Contemporary Japan: Dislocating the Salaryman Doxa,* edited by J. E. Roberson and N. Suzuki, pp. 1–19. London: Routledge.

Seigel, Cecilia Sagawa. 1993. *Yoshiwara: The Glittering World of the Japanese Courtesan.* Honolulu: University of Hawai'i Press.

Teruoka, Yasutaka. 1989. "The Pleasure Quarters and Tokugawa Culture." In *18th Century Japan,* edited by A. Gerstle, pp. 3–32. Sydney: Allen and Unwin.

Vogel, Ezra. 1963. *Japan's New Middle Class: the Salary Man and His Family in a Tokyo Suburb.* Berkeley: University of California Press.

Watanabe, Kenji. 2004. *Edo sanbyaku-nen Yoshiwara no shikitari* [Edo 300 years: Rules of Yoshiwara]. Tokyo: Seishun Shuppansha.

Zheng, Tiantian. 2006. "Cool Masculinity: Male Clients' Sex Consumption and Business Alliance in Urban Chana's Sex Industry." *Journal of Contemporary China* 15 (46): 161–182.

———. 2009. *Red Lights: The Lives of Sex Workers in Postsocialist China.* Minneapolis: University of Minnesota Press.

CHAPTER FIVE

Mobilizing the Masses to Change Something Intimate

The Process of Desexualization in China's
Family Planning Campaign

DANNING WANG

Introduction

Scholars of the Cultural Revolution (1966–1976) have remapped the issue of sexuality in modern China in ways that evoke Foucault's (1977) theories regarding the Panopticon. However, an examination of the social and political discourses surrounding sexuality and family planning in China reveals a relationship between the state and the individual that is more complex than top-down coercion (Hershatter 1996; Larson 1999). For example, one study has shown that among sent-down Chinese youth in the 1960s and 1970s, sexuality was not a taboo topic; instead, it was part of daily life and an active arena within which power and opportunities were articulated and negotiated (Honig 2003). In the cities, even though sexuality was handled more discreetly and unobtrusively and discussion of the issue was often camouflaged, urban youths did not lack the opportunity to express their sexuality. In Everett Zhang's (2005) precise analysis and presentation, urban youths found creative methods of sexual expression.

In this chapter, I intend to show how the state and society successfully separated the issue of contraception and birth planning from the topic of sexuality to set up boundaries and discursive models that remained in effect for the next four decades in governing Chinese people's reproductive lives. This process, which I call "desexualization," remained so successful that, even today, birth planning is framed strictly in terms of demography, reproductive health, and mother-child relationships rather than conjugal intimacy, romance, and love affairs (Greenhalgh and Winkler 2005; White 2006).

The desexualization process refers to two parallel propaganda efforts that had the same effect of eliminating the issue of sex and sexuality from public discourse. Neither of these two campaigns was designed by the state for the particular purpose of promoting family planning. They were, in fact, imbedded in the state's general policy of promoting gender equality and marriage law while restructuring China's class hierarchy according to Marxist ideology. By associating the issue of sex and sexuality with bourgeoisie class and consumption, the state's construction of working-class women (*funv* 妇女) emphasized the productive side and the working-class nature of women's participation in the labor force, and connected consumption, as well as sexual attraction, with the exploitation of nature. As a result of this inherent politicization, sex and sexuality became a critical tool in regulating Chinese urbanites' daily behaviors.

The first propaganda effort mainly targeted unmarried young adults. By advocating the idea of "freedom of love" (*ziyou lianai* 自由恋爱), the state encouraged young men and women to participate in public life and to gain autonomy in their love lives. In reality, however, all organized public events followed strict asexual rules in the name of creating a "healthy and spirited" public atmosphere. From dress codes to public behavior patterns and dating rules, this asexual standard governed all aspects of the freedom of love.

The second propaganda effort involved the association of "democratic families" with gender equality. By emphasizing mothers' sacred role in contributing to the modernization of the state and the country, this campaign shifted the focus from women's sexuality in the domain of reproduction to their capacity to nurture the second generation of the revolution.

The social and political consequences of this desexualization process were magnified during the 1960s when the state actively promoted its family planning program and, in the process, introduced to the Chinese populace the concepts of birth planning/family planning, late marriage, elective sterilization, and modern midwifery. The medicalization of the reproductive aspects of Chinese life is of critical importance and has been recorded and analyzed by many scholars (e.g., Evans 1997; Greenhalgh 2005; White 2006). What I focus on in this chapter is the contribution to this process of the state's desexualized social propaganda and the state's administrative efforts in organizing this social campaign. In doing so, I argue that these discourses legitimized the state's control over personal affairs. Even today, the birth of children in China is not about the mother's body, but rather is framed in terms of relevance to the nation's economic prosperity.

The Desexualization Process in Family Life

Communist China's unique ways of promoting gender equality should be understood in relation to the party-state's nation-building process and its concern to redefine class relationships and the state-family relationship. Tani Barlow (1994) incisively pointed out that, in its construction of the concept of working-class women the communist state, from its beginning, established its authority to represent the ones who were exploited by the "three mountains" (imperialism, feudalism, and bureaucrat capitalism) and needed liberation. Therefore, from the beginning, the political subject of *funv* had a connection to the working class in terms of social status and cultural features. Unlike the term "new female" (*xin nvx-ing* 新女性) which emerged from the May Fourth/New Culture Movement and conveyed a middle-class intellectual image, the domestic and public roles of working-class women needed to be defined, taught, and nurtured by the party-state. The personal feelings and emotional needs of working-class women were determined by their class affiliation. In the party's effort to transform "feudal families" into "democratic families," specific political agendas were designed to teach working-class women how to "upgrade" their social status to be the real masters of their families. In the course of this upgrading process, women learned they could gain equal footing with their husbands by working outside the home as productive laborers. Meanwhile, their mothering role was also emphasized. As Barlow (1994) argues, it was via such a process that the state finally seized control of family life through the education of women.

I want to further develop Barlow's idea by showing that, by making the mother's role sacred and desexualizing working-class women's family lives, the state did not merely control family life, but also paved the way for further class struggles in society. While the state desexualized the conjugal relationship, it also elevated the mother's position in the family. Through teaching mothers to be heads of their households, the state created subjects for family control, in the mold of the Jiangxi experience that Barlow (1994) spelled out. Through these two processes, the state utilized sexuality to construct a set of political symbols while redrawing class boundaries and organizing various social movements to reconfirm class stratifications. One's sexual identity and activity came to signify, alongside birth origin, occupation, and property ownership, a political standpoint within the class struggle.

Sex and Class

The association of sexual appeal with the class concept of the bourgeoisie was accomplished by yoking the concept of sexiness to that of overconsumption on the part of the bourgeoisie. The image of sexuality thus came to stand for the opposite of the productive images associated with the working class.

In 1957, the state started to prepare for the next stage of its socialist reconstruction of the country, with the aim of empowering the country's economy. Policies in the domain of family and gender that served this national agenda were presented in the form of the "Dual Diligent Movement" (*shuangqin yundong* 双勤运动).[1] By linking the fostering of the national economy with the diligent management of the

Table: Binary class features constructed by state propagandists

Proletarian	Bourgeoisie
Production	Consumption
Productive	Parasitic
Diligent	Lazy
Frugal	Luxury
Public	Private
Collectivism	Individualism
Plain/healthy/spirited	Sexy/show-off/slutty

household economy (*qinjian jianguo qinjian chijia* 勤俭建国 勤俭持家), the Dual Diligent Movement linked the national interest with that of the family. The state promoted the ideal working-class family by criticizing the bourgeoisie family and advocating for its reform. Consumption style became a political issue and accordingly determined the future of the family and its members. This political rationale persisted through the 1960s. After Great Chinese Famine (1959–1961), the Dual Diligent Movement returned. As time went on, this rhetorical logic grew to encompass the class struggle embodied by the Cultural Revolution.

The core of this rhetorical logic was a set of binary associations constructed by the state propagandists, pitting the working class against the bourgeoisie. These class features not only described styles of consumption of food, clothes, and other products, but also went a long way toward determining a citizen's future and political life (see Table).

In the 1950s and 1960s, sex remained a public taboo and these political associations turned "being sexual" into an effective boundary marker between the bourgeoisie and the working class. By associating sexual desire and the notion of being sexy with the bourgeoisie and petty bourgeoisie during the Cultural Revolution, the state imbued sexuality with political implications; anyone pronounced "sexy" could immediately become the target for political machinations and repeated public criticism and humiliation through various social movements. A prominent example is that of the first lady Ms. Wang Guangmei, who was publicly denounced by the Red Guards at Qinghua University during the Cultural Revolution. One way of humiliating her was putting a chain of ping pong balls over her neck and hanging a pair of broken shoes on top of that. The chain of ping pong balls was an exaggerated image of the pearl necklace she wore while visiting foreign countries with her husband, China's chairman Mr. Liu Shaoqi. The pair of broken shoes was the local symbol for "slut." Forcing her to wear this costume was the worst punishment the Red Guard could level against her.

Unfortunately, these groundless accusations and the resulting public humiliations were merely one instance of a popular strategy of political attack during the Cultural Revolution.

During my fieldwork in Tianjin Municipality in 1997 and 2008, members of the intellectual families recollected that such accusations that women who were "careless," indiscreet, and engaged in slutty (*bu jiandian* 不检点) pastimes in their private lives formed the bulk of the content of big-character posters (*dazi bao* 大字报). The notion of a "careless" private life was a broad concept encompassing many different activities, from indulging in decorating one's self with cosmetic products and fashionable attire to going on multiple dates or having extramarital affairs. The political implications of living carelessly included seeking an easy life, indulging in comfort, being gluttonous and lazy, and, overall, intending to exploit others' labor in a bourgeois way. People with such daily habits and aesthetic preferences were described as parasites with unhealthy thoughts and bourgeois lifestyles. On the other hand, those willing to sacrifice for the revolution were healthy with progressive spirits and lived frugal, natural, and unpretentious lives. Politically, these were the people who would be willing to selflessly devote themselves to the ambitions of the party-state and sacrifice their own best interests for the state's grand goals.

Because of this boundary between classes, sexuality and the notion of sexiness became irrelevant to the working-class women who were treated as the vanguard of the socialist era. This boundary created a series of binary categories: production vs. consumption; working class vs. bourgeoisie; frugal vs. luxury; productive vs. parasitic. These categories later developed political significance. However, one can tell from reading local newspapers of the time that life was not as strictly defined as these political boundaries would suggest. Stable urban life and reliable working conditions nurtured a number of "luxury" lifestyles among workers. These workers "stained" themselves with "decayed" bourgeoisie thoughts by indulging in hunting, fishing, and picnicking, activities that did not match their class background.

Meanwhile, female consumption, excessive decoration, and a charismatic outlook all corresponded to the image of "sexy," with potential political implications. Publicly showing off a lifestyle characterized by consumption could easily push individuals across this boundary and put one in a politically problematic position (Sun 2009).

Freedom of Love

At the social level, the negative images of sex and sexy were also utilized to protect monogamy. Scholarly research shows that embracing the advocated ideology of freedom of love and the abandonment of the requirement for arranged marriages catalyzed the younger generation's support for the new party-state (Hershatter 2011).

However, in reality, this freedom of love was highly regulated by the state and its propaganda teams in an asexual way. First of all, interactions among urban youth could happen only in the course of conducting "healthy" social activities such as sports and entertainment. Excessive squandering and luxury consumption was not to be a part of these relationships. In the mass media, the issue of sex was discussed only in the context of monogamy. Premarital sex and extramarital affairs remained taboo; simultaneous multiple dating was considered indiscreet; publicly announcing a loving relationship was tantamount to confirming an engagement. In other words, the freedom of love was publicly defined as nonsexual with no sexual seduction.

As a result, premarital sexual conduct was eliminated from the discourse. Such conduct implied the political sense of "messing up the sexual relationship" (乱搞男女关系 luangao nannv guanxi). The sexual conduct of both men and women was contextualized in the family setting and closely supervised either in the work units or in the neighborhoods. Searching for sexual pleasure was shameful, improper, and dangerous. For young men and women, "healthy" sports and entertainment were encouraged in public fields. At the same time, however, men and women enjoyed new public spaces for socializing. The factories hosted sports competitions, Peking opera singing, night schools, and dancing parties, providing limited but precious opportunities for young men and women to express themselves and appreciate one another.

Mr. Wang[2] was an amateur Peking opera singer and photographer. He met his future wife at his factory when he spotted her coming to the opera concerts all the time. Mrs. Wang grew up in a courtyard in Tianjin where one of her neighbors was a famous opera singer. During outings organized by the factory, Mr. Wang took many pictures of Mrs. Wang and presented them to her as presents. In those pictures, Mr. Wang captured the young woman's smile, her round face, full chin, and healthy hair. The photos are full of the spirit of health, happiness, and hope. There is nothing sexual in these pictures, but anyone could tell how much the photographer appreciated the young lady. They flirted using ancient Chinese and lines from opera. Even fifty years later, Mrs. Wang remembered how quick her man could move on the stage with his flexible "kung fu" body, and Mr. Wang remembered his wife's white teeth and beautiful smile.

In such a sociocultural environment, the propagandists behind the family planning program had no fear of inciting promiscuity. From the beginning, the introduction of contraception happened only within the context of the family, and it was strictly about family and birth. The campaign target was birth in the setting of legal marriage, not births out of wedlock or extramarital births. Sex belonged only within marriage for the sole purposes of reproduction. Other than that, any aesthetic, literary, or social perspectives on sex were meaningless.

Late Marriage and the Nuclearization of Family

The second propaganda effort that followed the desexualization line promoted late marriage and "democratic families." The typical conjugal relationship in the state's rhetoric was not defined intimately. Married couples became the center of an extended family relationship, the nexus of intergenerational relations who coordinated with each other in handling both filial services and parenthood, while at the same time dealing with both their private and public lives. In this state version of new family life, a couple's asexual comradeship and partnership were intensified by the narration that having too many children would disrupt their harmonious intimate relations.

Late marriage was treated as a priority in family planning implementation. In March 1963, the state republished the Marriage Law, within which marriage eligibility ages had been set at twenty for males and eighteen for females. However, in July 1963, the city government of Tianjin issued regulations promoting late marriages: without violating the Marriage Law, the regulations targeted the distributing of continuous schooling opportunities, working opportunities, and job assignments. These regulations were designed to discourage people from getting married early.[3] For example, starting in the summer of 1963, universities, professional schools, and high schools were discouraged from enrolling married students. The labor department was directed to give unmarried candidates priority when allocating jobs. Those who were married could not co-reside on campus. In the department issuing marriage certificates, cadres were responsible for dissuading those who were younger than twenty-five.

A series of propagandist dramas and shows were developed to promote late marriage. In these shows, early marriage and numerous children led to domestic chaos and directly affected the harmonious relationship between couples.[4] Unlike the Western portrait of love affairs between the sperm and egg, these shows demonstrated that, when family size became a problem, it also created trouble for the couple's relationship. Therefore, sterilization became an option. The only hint of romance in these performances was that couples were supposed to see a show together. Other than that, the dating couple were supposed to spend time in the parks with their peers to play. Private times and conversations were minimized to the extreme. There were no conversations about the pain or any side effects that women might experience from the sterilization process. None of these shows mentioned negotiation of these issues between husband and wife; the basic assumption was that women were the ones who should undergo sterilization due to their role in reproduction. Some men with what the state considered an advanced, positive outlook on life would volunteer for the surgery. Sterilization was characterized as the final solution to a chaotic domestic life caused by having too many children. Couples were promised that life would become orderly again after adopting these solutions.

Not surprisingly, most of these themes were later adopted in the 1979 movie *Sweet Business* (甜蜜的事业), which targeted the rural audience for the same purpose. In the movie, the female cadres reduced the "proper" number of children from six to five, to three, and then one! Such a simplified numerical calculation deleted all of the cultural and symbolic meanings of reproduction and reduced the family issue to a simplified number game and an easy procedure.

The Scientific/Medical Side of Contraception

Family planning as a public campaign and social movement emerged in early 1963 in Tianjin. Tianjin was picked as the first city to go through the process so that the state could accumulate experience for its subsequent efforts in the other cities (*Tianjin Jianzhi* 天津简志 [A brief history of Tianjin] 1991, 1183–1188). In response to prompting from the central government, Tianjin's leaders prepared the campaign to begin after the Chinese New Year. Through the ten agenda items that the family planning bureau issued in February, the tone of the campaign was set: the targeted population was everyone in the city. Within the administrative hierarchies, specific offices and personnel were developed to oversee the issue.[5] In other words, it was a massive social campaign organized along with an administrative hierarchy to oversee the state's propaganda mechanism. Each year, the campaign was to be administered two to three times through the organization of the following activities: identifying role models and broadcasting their experiences to convince the population at large how well family planning worked at the level of the individual household; providing free sterilization and abortion to whoever requested them; guaranteeing a ready supply of contraceptive devices to satisfy demand; standardizing surgical sterilization procedures; increasing the number of hospital beds for sterilization operations; and replacing previous policies that encouraged birth with the ones that advocated family planning and birth control.[6]

The family planning office also drafted documents for the purpose of publicly promoting family planning. The draft included three sections: why family planning was necessary; how to properly understand family planning; and some basic procedures to promote family planning. Among these procedures, contraception (with a focus on spacing of births) was listed alongside late marriage, sterilization, and abortion.

Medicalization of the Family Planning Campaign

The public discourse of family planning gave legitimacy to a normally taboo topic by using the language of technology and science. It deleted subjective aesthetic appraisal and expanded the scope of one's relationship with one's genitalia through medical objectivity. Beyond reproduction, sex organs were still not discussed in daily conversation. Harriet Evans (1997) has pointed out how the state relied on medical knowledge to reconstruct the female sexual body with the direct result of controlling it. The powerful code of silence concerning female sexual body parts can be understood in the light of Foucault's (1978) insight concerning the proliferation of sex talk and the incitement to discourse resulting from sexual repression.

Women's reproductive organs have been subject to a process of social construction in China. Presenting a single organ in the medical discourse is a technique of "objectification." The ultimate sites of sexual pleasure are never publicly mentioned with any reference to an intimate relationship. During the family planning campaign, three medical procedures—IUD implantation, sterilization, and abortion—were viewed as scientific, convenient, and beneficial for health.[7] According to the city's propaganda and the deputy mayor's public pronouncements, the scientific aspect of family planning was divided into natural science and social science. The natural science part was rooted in the medical components of the program and the medical professionals were organized to deliver seminars to the propaganda cadres and political models in the work units.[8] The social science part came from the idea of economic planning. As part of the holistic socialist planned economy, population growth needed to be controlled and planned. By stressing the numbers involved in family planning, it became legitimate to compare the program's results cross-regionally. For example, by the end of 1963, the Tianjin government concluded there had been only 9,000 cases of abortions in the city compared to 60,000 in Shanghai. As a result, internal, local targets for sterilization, abortion, and IUD implanting were set up. In general, the following year's campaign focused on increasing the incidence of sterilization and abortion.[9]

As Mary Douglas (1966) reminded us, discipline and regulation of the body can also be achieved through definitions of purity and danger. Relating cleanliness and bodily pollution to the attending of certain cultural and political events highlights how Chinese society established and maintained convention and order by regulating people's bodies. According to the local historical record, many women believed their bodies to be a burden. Sex organs were dangerous and vulnerable and made them feel out of control. Compared to the genitals, breasts were distinct—a positive in terms of human reproduction and the nurturing of children, but subjected to negative appraisal. It was politically unacceptable to be sexually attractive and fashionable by putting on facial makeup. Women generally adhered to this socially required self-discipline out of fear of reducing their political advantage and losing proletarian status and being relegated to the status of a petty bourgeoisie. These women needed to guard themselves in order to remain chaste. Few women dared to wear clothing that was revealing and many chose to wear their bulky uniforms even after work so that they would not be criticized.

Menstrual blood was dirty, and good women never exposed it in public, even to other women. For years women shared the same public toilet, but they were taught by their mothers and colleagues how to wrap the tissues so as to make their menstrual debris neat and tidy. In addition, pregnant women were not considered "lucky" and were encouraged to avoid being seen by others. Female workers reported that they wore large work uniforms to hide the bumps of their pregnant bellies so that their male colleagues would not see them. Pregnant women were not supposed to walk in the middle of a road, as bumping into a pregnant woman was still treated as something "unlucky." It was unimaginable for a pregnant woman to "show off" her pregnancy.

Forming a Social Campaign to Change the Behavior Pattern

By the mid-1950s, the party-state had already accomplished the unification of social management in the urban setting. Both work units and neighborhood committees were utilized to organize grassroots political campaigns so that the state's ideological propaganda could be broadcast and its policies could be implemented (Zhang 2004). To implement family planning policies at the local level, the state relied on the same social structure it had used to carry out its longest-running social campaign, which started in 1963.

Yang Nianqun's (2001) study shows how the training of modern midwives in Peking in the 1930s replaced local practices with institutionalized state control by reconfiguring urban space in regulating medical institutions. The medicalization of birth and delivery served the purpose of urban control in the nation-building process. The state's deliberate control of the whole process by regulating police and midwifery procedures later became an effective tool in urban management. In this process, Foucault's (1977) idea of archiving citizens and Gidden's (1995) idea of reconfiguring time and space could be used to analyze the socialist era when the new state intended to regulate the urban population. Both the

Republic and the People's Republic regimes relied on the reconceptualization, or medicalization, of women's reproductive bodies to manage the populations of modern cites. As Julia Strauss (2006) emphasized, the two regimes were connected.

Tina Philips Johnson (2011) pointed out that, in the name of empowering the nation, childbirth in urban China became "scientific" and "modern" with the abandonment of traditional midwifery. Chinese medical specialists were cautious about the "Western" practice of medicalizing childbirth. However, childbirth eventually became so thoroughly medicalized that the cesarean rate in China skyrocketed.

Whereas the Republic era had focused on replacing traditional practice with a systematic medical system, the new round of urban control relied on the *danwei* and *jiedao* systems in implementing the state's policy. With the additional layers of political control assisted by the medical system, the state administrative system successfully reconfigured the protocols of urban control and governed the urban population in a new format.

In July 1963, the deputy major of Tianjin announced a citywide campaign and social movement: the Communist Party would work on this program at all levels, and all administration levels would be involved in promoting family planning. A family planning committee would be organized. In addition to increasing the production of contraceptive devices and pills, numerical goals for the city for fertility rates, the total number of late marriages, the number of individuals who adopted contraception or sterilization, and the number of abortions were set.[10]

The deputy mayor's talk was delivered to the city's propaganda cadres. After the talk, these cadres started to design detailed materials for the mass campaign that was carried out along two lines: the *danwei* system and the district residential areas. For the district of Heping, a propaganda team organized exhibitions and seminars.[11] They asked the work units to train "backbone" (*gu gan* 骨干) activists while cadres and their leaders set up ideal models for the masses. The district government called each work unit and neighborhoods to set up cadres to document the records of individual families. Cadres and backbone activists would concentrate their "persuasion" efforts on "difficult cases." In order to avoid public humiliation, there would be no competition, no challenge, no public criticism. When broadcasting information related to contraceptive methods, there would be no joking or teasing.

The Ideal Models: Shifting the Boundary between Public and Private

Within the context of the state's policy, the penetration of the boundary between the public and private remained problematic. Facilitating the ideal model design required two major steps: the selection and training of the backbone activists and the scheduling of the family planning agenda to coincide with work and other social campaigns.

In selecting and training the model backbones, four rules were followed. Candidates needed to be well respected among employees and willing to help others. They also needed to practice family planning methods and be willing to share their experiences in public.

After selecting suitable candidates, the work units invited doctors and midwives to hold seminars to teach employees about contraceptive methods and then relied on the models to spread the message. Model candidates could be warmhearted mothers who already had multiple children and were willing to go through the sterilization process. After they underwent the procedure, they would explain the process to the others. Also, married women were encouraged to talk about private issues such as postnatal contraceptive methods, holiday contraception, and how to effectively space births among themselves. Normally, women were recruited for such roles, but some male cadres were also recruited to become backbones. These models' personal social networks became critical for the transmission of this private knowledge. Because of the efforts of the models and activists, the state was confident the official agenda could be effectively delivered to the mass population.

To make sure the implementation of the policy would not be interrupted, officials in charge of the model system also tried to coordinate the family planning agenda with production schedules and other social campaigns. These efforts included organizing seminars at the peak of production seasons. In the "Socialist Education" campaign, while comparing female workers' productive/reproductive experiences in the new and the old societies, local cadres were instructed to insert the family planning idea in their presentations to demonstrate the advantages of the new society. During the summer, in the flooding season when the male employees were organized to work in the countryside to help fix the river banks, the work units reminded women to remember family planning when their husbands returned.

The work units also had the right to remind employees of the impact of adopting contraception in the process of adjusting workers' salaries. The basic assumption was that employees had a responsibility to manage an orderly family economic life and they should not rely on their work unit to carry the extra financial burdens imposed by a large family. Finally, the city government started to organize competitions in defining model work units. Detailed regulations were issued to encourage late marriage, reduce family sizes, and eliminate reliance on the state's financial support. With the addition of these criteria, all work units began to pay serious attention to the issue of family planning.

Conclusion: Women, Family, and the State

The year 1963 was critical. After the three-year famine and low birth rates during the food-crisis years, Tianjin's total fertility rate had dramatically increased. At the end of 1962, the state readopted the family planning policy and required locals to implement it as a major priority.

However, by November 1963, in the annual review of the city's work in this domain the city government was not satisfied with the outcomes. The birth rate for the year had surged. More education needed to be conducted with the urban youths. Also, compared to Shanghai, the number of urban couples who underwent sterilization and abortion was too low. In order to make sure the city's fertility rate could be reduced in 1964, the deputy mayor called upon the local cadres in the work units and the neighborhoods to work harder on the procedures and policies developed in 1963.

When we review the procedures and patterns developed in 1963, the party-state followed lines similar to those it had utilized since the Jiangxi Soviet era in promoting gender equality. The state held ultimate power in social campaigns. With superior medical/scientific knowledge, the state claimed the right to teach the masses how to adopt a better lifestyle. By redefining family in terms of its relationship with the state, the state relied on the image of working-class women to reconfigure the public vs. private dichotomy. In a generally desexualized social environment, such a pattern of urban population control set the basic tone for the forthcoming one-child family planning campaign that would emerge in the late 1970s.

Notes and References

1. On September 9, 1957, at the third national meeting of All-China Women's Federation, the central government advocated for women to participate in the Dual Diligent Movement (*Qinjian jianguo qinjian chijia, wei jianshe shehui zhuyi er fendou—zai zhongguo funv di sanci quanguo daibiao dahui shang de gongzuo baogao* 勤俭建国, 勤俭持家, 为建设社会主义而奋斗—在中国妇女第三次全国代表大会上的工作报告 [The third national meeting of All-China Women's Federation, the central government's advocacy for women to participate in the Dual Diligent Movement: Diligently constructing the country and diligently managing the domestic life to fight for the construction of the socialism], http://www.china.com.cn/aboutchina/zhuanti/zgfn/2008–10/06/content_16572566.htm).

2. All informants' names are changed in this chapter to hide their identities.

3. On July 15, 1963, Tianjin Municipality Government issued *Several Regulations by Tianjin People's Committee on Promoting Late Marriage and Planned Birth* (天津市人民委员会关于提倡"晚婚"和推行计划生育有关几项办法的规定; Tianjin Municipality Government 1963c).

4. Three play scripts are stored in the Tianjin Archive Collections. They are: *Late Marriage Is Good* (小演唱 《还是晚婚好》No. c-153–32, pp. 114–119), *What a Weekend* (快板剧 《过星期》No. c-153–32, pp. 120–128), and *Birth Planning Is Good* (话剧 《还是计划生育好》No. c-153–32, pp. 129–140).

5. Two official documents were issued on February 21 and 29, 1963. The first one was the *Plan of Implementing the Central and Municipality Governments' Directions on Enhancing the Work of Birth Planning* (关于贯彻中央及市委指示精神加强计划生育工作的实施方案; Tianjin Municipality Government 1963a) and the second *Propaganda Agenda on Advocating Birth Planning* (关于认真提倡计划生育的宣传提纲; Tianjin Municipality Government 1963b).

6. Tianjin Municipality Government 1963a; Tianjin Municipality Government 1963b.

7. According to the published documents based on the working experience of the Tianjin Domestic Trading Bureau, in its process of promoting late marriage and birth planning among the employees, these three operations (三术) were the core of the education project (Tianjin Archive Collections, *Domestic Trading Bureau Experience on Birth Planning* (内贸系统计划生育经验之一), No. y-140–32, pp. 118–142).

8. Deputy Mayor Yang Zhenya delivered a public speech on July 17, 1963, to all of the propaganda cadres of Tianjin to promote birth planning.

9. On November 21, 1963, Deputy Mayor Yang Zhenya concluded the annual performance of the city's effort in promoting birth planning. In this speech, he set up the following year's goal. On December 5, 1963, the deputy head of the city's propaganda bureau, Li Mai, repeated the same strategy in his own concluding speech.

10. Ibid.

11. The relevant propaganda material of Heping District is stored in the Tianjin Archive Collections, No. y-140–32, pp. 86–92.

Barlow, Tani E. 1994. "Theorizing Women: Funv, Guojia, Jiating." In *Body Subject and Power in China,* edited by Angela Zito and Tani E. Barlow, pp. 253–290. Chicago: University of Chicago Press.

Dirlik, Arif. 1975. "The Ideological Foundations of the New Life Movement: A Study in Counterrevolution." *Journal of Asian Studies* 34 (4): 945–980.

Douglas, Mary. 1966. *Purity and Danger: An Analysis of Concepts of Pollution and Taboo.* New York: Praeger.

Evans, Harriet. 1997. *Women and Sexuality in China: Dominant Discourse of Sexuality and Gender since 1949.* Cambridge, UK: Polity Press.

Foucault, Michel. 1977. *Discipline and Punish: The Birth of the Prison.* Translated by Alan Sheridan. New York: Pantheon.

———. 1978. *History of Sexuality.* Vol. 1. Translated by Robert Hurley. New York: Pantheon.

Giddens, Anthony. 1995. *A Contemporary Critique of Historical Materialism.* Basingstoke, UK: Macmillan.

Greenhalgh, Susan, and Edwin A. Winckler. 2005. *Governing China's Population: From Leninist to Neoliberal Biopolitics.* Stanford, CA: Stanford University Press.

Hershatter, Gail. 1996. "Sexing Modern China." In *Remapping China: Fissures in Historical Terrain,* edited by Gail Hershatter, Emily Honig, Jonathan N. Lipman, and Randall Stross, pp. 77–96. Stanford, CA: Stanford University Press.

———. 2011. *The Gender of Memory: Rural Women and China's Collective Past.* Berkeley: University of California Press.

Honig, Emily. 2003. "Socialist Sex: The Cultural Revolution Revisited." *Modern China* 29 (2): 143–175.

Johnson, Tina Phillips. 2011. *Childbirth in Republican China: Delivering Modernity.* Lanham, MD: Lexington Books.

Kohama Masako 小滨正子. 2009. "Jihua shengyu de kaiduan—1950–1960 niandai de Shanghai 计划生育的开端—1950–1960 年代的上海 [The beginning of the family planning—Shanghai in the 1950s]." *Zhongyang jianjiuyuan jindaishi yanjiusuo jikan* 68: 97–142.

———. 2011. "Zhongguo nongcun jihua shengyu de puji–yi 1960–1970 niandai Q cun weili 中国农村计划生育的普及–以 1960–1970 年代 Q 村 为例 [The spread of the family planning in rural China—with the example of Q Village in the 1960s]." *Jindai zhongguo funvshi yanjiu* 19: 173–214.

Larson, Wendy. 1999. "Never This Wild: Sexing the Cultural Revolution." *Modern China* 25 (4): 423–450.

Lu Fangshang 吕芳上. 2004. "Geren jueze huo guojia zhengce: jindai zhongguo jieyu de fansi—cong 1920s <funv zazhi> chuban chaner zhixian zhuanhao shuoqi 个人抉择或国家政策： 近代中国节育的反思—从 1920 年代《妇女杂志》出版产儿制限专号说起 [Personal choice or the state's policy: Reflection of the contraception in contemporary China—From the publication of the special issues of <Women Magazine> on the new born]." *Jindai zhongguo funvshi yanjiu* 12: 195–230.

Qinjian jianguo qinjian chijia, wei jianshe shehui zhuyi er fendou—zai zhongguo funv di sanci quanguo daibiao dahui shang de gongzuo baogao 勤俭建国， 勤俭持家， 为建设社会主义而奋斗—在中国妇女第三次全国代表大会上的工作报告 [The third national meeting of All-China Women's Federation, the central government's advocacy for women to participate in the Dual Diligent Movement: Diligently constructing the country and diligently managing the domestic life to fight for the construction of the socialism]. September 9, 1957. http://www.china.com.cn/aboutchina/zhuanti/zgfn/2008-10/06/content_16572566.htm.

Scheper-Hughes, Nancy, and Margaret M. Lock. 1987. "The Mindful Body: A Prolegomenon to Future Work in Medical Anthropology." *Medical Anthropology Quarterly* n.s. 1 (1): 6–41.

Song Shaopeng 宋少鹏. 2011. "Gongzhong zhi si—guanyu jiating laodong de guojia huayu, 1949–1966 公中之私—关于家庭劳动的国家话语, 1949–1966 [The privacy within the public—the state's discourse on domestic work, 1949–1966]." *Jindai zhongguo funvshi yanjiu* 19: 131–172.

Strauss, Julia. 2006. "Morality, Coercion and State Building by Campaign in the Early PRC: Regime Consolidation and After, 1949–1956." *China Quarterly* 188 (December): 891–912.

Sun, Peidong 孙沛东. 2013. "Kujiao shang de jieji douzheng—'wenge' shiqi Guangdong de 'qizhuang yifu' yu guojia guixun 裤脚上的阶级斗争—'文革' 时期广东的 '奇装异服'与国家规训 [The class struggle on the bottom end of a trouser leg: The 'deviant' clothes in Guangdong during the Cultural Revolution and the state's discipline]." *Jingji shehui*: 84–101.

Tianjin Jianzhi 天津简志 [A brief history of Tianjin]. 1991. *Tianjin shi defang zhi bianxiu weiyuanhui bian* 天津市地方志编修委员会 编 [Edited by the Editing Committee of Tianjin's Local History]. Tianjin: Tianjin People's Publisher.

Tianjin Municipality Government. 1963a. *Guanyu guanche ZhongYang ji shiwei zhishi jing-shen jiaqiang Jihua Shengyu gongzuo de shishi fangan* 关于贯彻中央及市委指示精神加强计划生育工作的实施方案 [The plan of implementing the central and municipality governments' directions on enhancing the work of birth planning]. February 21.

Tianjin Municipality Government. 1963b. *Guanyu renzhen tichang Jihua Shengyu de xu-anchuan tigang* 关于认真提倡计划生育的宣传提纲 [The propaganda agenda on advocating birth planning]. February 29.

Tianjin Municipality Government. 1963c. *Tianjin shi renmin weiyuanhui guanyu tichang "wanhun" he tuixing jihua shengyu youguan jixiang banfa de guiding* 天津市人民委员会关于提倡"晚婚"和推行计划生育有关几项办法的规定 [Several regulations by Tianjin People's Committee on promoting late marriage and planned birth]. July 15.

White, Tyrene. 2006. *China's Longest Campaign: Birth Planning in the People's Republic 1949–2005*. Ithaca, NY: Cornell University Press.

Yan, Yuxiang. 2010. "The Chinese Path to Individualization." *British Journal of Sociology* 61 (3): 489–512.

Yang Nianqun 杨念群. 2001. "Minguo chunian Beijing de shengsi kongzhi yu kongjian zhuanhuan 民国初年北京的生死控制与空间转换 [The regulations of birth and death and the change of time/space in Beijing during the early years of the republic]." In *Yang Nianqun (zhubian) <kongjian, jiyi, shehui zhuanxing: "xin shehui shi"yanjiu lun-wen jingxuan ji>* 杨念群（主编）《空间，记忆，社会转型："新社会史" 研究论文精选集》[In Time/Space, Memories, and Social Transformation: "New Social History," edited by Yang Nianqun], pp. 131–207. Shanghai: Shanghai People's Publisher.

Zhang, Everett Yuehong. 2005. "Rethinking Sexual Repression in Maoist China: Ideology, Structure and the Ownership of the Body." *Body and Society* 11 (3): 1–25.

Zhang Jishun 张济顺. 2004. "Shanghai lining: jiceng zhengzhi dongyuan yu guojia shehui yitihua zouxiang, 1950–1955 上海里弄： 基层政治动员与国家社会一体化走向，1950–1955 [Shanghai allies: The grassroot political mobilization and the direction of the unification of the state and the society, 1950–1955.]" *Zhongguo shehui kexue* 2: 178–188.

Zhong, Xueping. 2011. "Women Can Hold Up Half the Sky." In *Words and Their Stories: Essays on the Language of the Chinese Revolution*, edited by Ban Wang, pp. 227–248. Boston: Brill.

Zhou, Yongming. 1999. *Anti-Drug Crusades in Twentieth-Century China: Nationalism, History, and State Building*. New York: Rowman and Littlefield.

CHAPTER SIX

Pleasure, Patronage, and Responsibility

Sexuality and Status among New Rich Men
in Contemporary China

JOHN OSBURG

In the domains of gender relations and sexuality, many urban Chinese characterize the present as a time of "opening" (*kaifang*) after the prohibitions of the Maoist years, invoking the familiar narrative of sexual repression. They praise the present as a time when romance and marriage can finally be rooted in private emotions rather than be the product of political, familial, or financial pressures (see Farquhar 2002, chap. 4). However, instead of the final realization of companionate marriage based on mutual affection between equals and sexual equality for women, which have been goals of Chinese reformers since the May Fourth Movement, the reform period has been marked by the rise of hierarchical, patron-client forms of sexuality, especially among the elite. Mistresses, multiple wives, and extramarital affairs are the norm among wealthy entrepreneurs and government officials, and the sex industry has developed in pace with the rest of China's economy and become an integral part of nightlife for China's newly rich men.

Some observers see the explosion in divorce and extramarital affairs, and the rise of the sex industry in China, as the result of a hypermasculinity now surging forth after decades of suppression. Meanwhile, the Chinese state is eager to blame these phenomena on "spiritual pollution" originating from the West, which it views as a by-product of China's opening to the outside world. Examination of the sexual practices of elite men in China, however, suggests that this is not just another instance of "men gone wild," fueled by a potent mix of new wealth and hormones, of a "castrated" generation of men reclaiming their lost virility, or of a conservative sexual culture succumbing to Western-inspired sexual freedom. While the retreat of the state from the domain of private life in China has no doubt opened up the possibility for new forms of sexual expression, the emergent forms of masculinity and femininity and their corresponding sexualities are not unmediated reflections of pent-up private desires (Farquhar 2002). Rather, masculinity and femininity in post-Mao China have been actively constructed and reconstructed during the reform period in dialogue with economic changes, global influences, and reimagined and reinvented traditional gender forms (see, e.g.,

Brownell 2001; Evans 2002; Rofel 1999, 2007; Schein 2000; Yang 1999; Zheng 2009).

In the early 2000s I conducted three years of ethnographic research with a group of wealthy, predominately male entrepreneurs from a variety of industries in Chengdu, China. This research examined the role their social networks play in organizing their business ventures and orienting their personal values and ethical commitments. China's economic reforms notwithstanding, state agents still control access to capital, business licenses, and land. Entrepreneurs court government officials in order to win government contracts, obtain tax breaks and regulatory flexibility, and negotiate shifts in policy (Wank 1999). Through their ties to entrepreneurs, state agents both generate revenue for local government agencies and obtain illicit income for themselves through bribes or kickbacks that often dwarfs their official salaries.

My research specifically examined these state-business networks as gendered social formations. They are gendered in two aspects. First, entrepreneurs, state enterprise managers, and government officials alike increasingly aspire to a similar masculine "boss" ideal: they aim to become dispensers of favors and opportunities, people who can command the assistance of powerful individuals with just a phone call. Participation in these networks as both patron and client is not only fundamental to post-Mao ideologies of masculinity; these networks provide access to business and career opportunities essential to maintaining elite status in China. Second, although some of these networks are based on ties of kinship and native-place, the bulk of the relationships of which these networks are composed are forged and maintained through ritualized "masculine" forms of leisure—experiences of shared pleasure in venues catering to the desires and enjoyments of elite men. These venues include high-end restaurants, karaoke clubs (KTVs), foot massage parlors (*xijaofang*), saunas, and teahouses. My research subjects (and I) spent most nights and many afternoons in these venues cultivating business ties or maintaining existing ones. Rather than view their interactions as part of a "supposedly universal psychology of male bonding" (Kipnis 2002, 92n.16), as they are often understood in the West, a starting point of my analysis is that masculinity is not a universal essence or biological impulse, but a culturally and historically variable construction that requires constant maintenance through performances (Butler 1999 [1990]; Connell 1995). By drinking, singing, and being flattered by female companions in nightclubs, men are both creating and enacting a particular version of masculinity associated with being a man of status and wealth in post-Mao China. They are at the same time seeking to forge homosocial ties crucial to their career success and financial futures. In these venues, women as hostesses, sex workers, or mistresses play a key role in mediating relationships between entrepreneurs and government officials and in mirroring men's social status (Liu 2002; Zhang 2001; Zheng 2006). This chapter examines wealthy men's various sexual relationships, which include wives, mistresses, and sex workers encountered during their ritualized socializing. I analyze the different feelings, pleasures, and material transactions understood to inhere in each type of relationship.

Sexualized Entertainment and Alliance Building in China

Unlike the competitive "scoring" model of masculine sexuality, with its attendant victories and defeats familiar to American youth and portrayed in countless beer and body spray commercials, the businessmen I knew in Chengdu operated according to a different underlying equation of sexuality, status, and masculinity. In the American model, heterosexual men accrue status through the sheer number and diversity of their sexual conquests, but in China, only certain types of sexual relationships with particular kinds of women were understood to project status onto elite Chinese men.

Many entrepreneurs I knew asked me about the competitive "pickup" culture that they saw depicted in Hollywood films and witnessed at Chengdu bars popular with foreigners. While they understood the logic of the "open market" sexuality of the bar and dance floor, they were ambivalent about this type of masculine performance. They assumed that any unaccompanied women in these establishments were most likely either sex workers or in some way morally tainted and physically unattractive. Otherwise, my friends assumed, these women wouldn't be there in the first place. Because of the presumed low status of the women who frequented pickup bars, my Chinese informant friends did not view seducing women in these establishments as in any way confirming their virility, sexual attractiveness, or status (unless, that is, they succeeded in seducing foreign women, which is an issue too complex to be dealt with briefly here). Furthermore, for business-oriented entertaining this risk-laden field of "scoring" would be highly detrimental to building relationships with other men. Hosts would never dare risk the potential humiliation and loss of face to their guests (often older government officials) by leaving them to their own charms and devices on the dance floor or sitting at a bar. This would generate a hierarchy of winners and losers that would threaten the group's solidarity.

During instrumental, business-oriented entertaining, referred to as *yingchou* in Chinese, hosts make every effort to ensure that their guests receive their choice of women and that they are provided with whatever sexual services they require.

Thus, business entertaining is organized to guarantee control over sexual outcomes. This control is essential to ensuring that status hierarchies are adequately respected, guests are satisfied, and no one's masculinity is called into question. Properly orchestrated, an evening in a KTV nightclub or sauna renders fellow businessmen deserving of their status as elite men and capable of enjoying the same pleasures and luxuries.

Given the role of young women in forging ties between men, elite entertainment on the surface resembles a classic case of the "traffic in women," in which men form alliances through the exchange of objectified women.[1] As Gayle Rubin (1975, 179) argues in her classic essay, gender roles and conventions of sexuality are "constituted by the imperatives" of a system of social organization. Similarly, in business entertaining, men attempt to harness and appropriate women's sexuality as a way of enhancing their own status and building ties with other men. However, as will be shown below, this particular traffic in women depends on the women being recognized as subjects with their own desires rather than as objects to be exchanged or transparently purchased. While nearly all of the men I worked with paid for sexual services, and sex workers played a key role in entertaining, paid sex ranked lowest among their many different kinds of sexual relationships. Some well-established bosses I knew insisted that they never paid for sex and that young women were attracted to them for their power and reputation (see also Zheng 2006).

In her ethnography of Tokyo hostess clubs, Ann Allison (1994, 22) outlines a dynamic that is in many ways similar to that of Chinese KTVs. She argues that Japanese hostesses project an idealized masculinity onto their clients. This "ego massage" helps smooth relations between coworkers and gives clients an exaggerated sense of masculinity, which is then sutured to their jobs. Through flattery, pouring drinks, and attentive listening, these hostesses serve as mediums through which men can construct themselves as ideal male subjects. What the companies of these businessmen ultimately pay for is the recognition provided by the hostesses to their male employees that they are attractive, virile, and masculine. According to Allison, this results in a kind of subjectivity that makes for good and committed workers—self-assured and, crucially, with their ego oriented more toward work than toward home (202). Hostesses in KTVs employ many of the same techniques to project an idealized masculinity onto their clients. They flatter them with compliments about their singing and appearance and pretend to enjoy the endless dice games that often accompany drinking. They address their clients either as "husband" (*laogong*) or as "handsome guy" (*shuaige*). While hostess clubs in Japan help ease tensions generated by workplace hierarchies, for entrepreneurs in China, hostesses help to secure the enjoyment and pleasure of their clients, thereby helping to cultivate affection for the evening's host. Just as bonds are formed over the shared enjoyment of good food and booze, these men are drawn closer over the shared pleasure of "illicit" sex, and this "shared transgression" and mutual enjoyment provide the basis for their intimacy (Cameron and Kulick 2003). These embodied memories of shared enjoyment lay the foundation for affective ties between business associates.

Despite the potential for shared pleasure and intimacy, the performance of elite masculinity required in KTVs generates its own set of anxieties. In her history of prostitution in Shanghai, Gail Hershatter (1997, 8) notes that prerevolutionary men's guidebooks were filled with advice on how to avoid being taken advantage of by wily courtesans. These guides, which Hershatter refers to as "primers for the production of elite masculinity," spoke to what appears to have been a profound anxiety on the part of men that they would either be duped out of their money or engage in behavior that would call into question their elite status. In the contemporary context, Tiantian Zheng (2006) echoes this point, interpreting entrepreneurs' interactions with hostesses as above all a test of their sophistication and emotional control. Hershatter (1997) argues that in early twentieth-century Shanghai the ultimate goal of many of the men who patronized courtesans was not sex, but, through their own sophistication and status displays, to mold themselves into a courtesan's object of affection and reverse the vector of desire.

Similarly, many of my research subjects understood the ability to attract beautiful women, without directly and transparently paying, as the ultimate confirmation of their virility and status. They hoped to transform a relationship founded on money into one rooted in mutual affection. Many elite men framed payments to mistresses or hostesses as gifts—as tokens of a concern for their well-being and happiness rather than as payments for time and services rendered. According to this imaginary, only country bumpkins or old, ugly men actually needed to compensate women to overcome their "natural" lack of charm and desirability.

Among well-established and successful entrepreneurs, paid hostesses were a convenient means of securing a client's enjoyment, but they were not the preferred means. Men who only cavorted with paid hostesses and sex workers were often suspected of being nouveau-riche bumpkins new to the world of elite entertainment. Many well-established men of means instead called on networks of younger women who were not professional hostesses or sex workers to accompany them in KTVs. These networks included mistresses' friends and classmates, junior employees of their companies, and occasionally female business associates.

In fact, one strategy for securing a meeting or winning the favor of a hard-to-reach official or businessman was to promise to introduce him to an attractive young woman who might potentially serve as his girlfriend or mistress. Simply paying a hostess to sleep with a client or official, while often seen as necessary to ensure that he enjoyed himself fully, implied a distance in the relationship and generated less *ganqing* (sentiment) than organizing a date with a "beauty" (*meinü*). If one of these introductions succeeded, then the official would be "indebted" to the entrepreneur. My informants took obvious pleasure in pointing out the mistress-patron relationships in which they had played matchmaker. But even the introduction alone already enhances the official's or client's status by implying that he is the kind of man capable of attracting and associating with beautiful women.

Among Chengdu men, the qualities of women who conferred the most status on their male companions were well established and almost universally recognized. They included youth (under thirty at least, under twenty-five preferred), purity (evidenced by virginity or a perceived small number of previous sexual partners), beauty, artistic cultivation (singing or dancing ability), education, and high "quality" (*suzhi*), which was often indicated by a combination of educational level, perceived morality, urban upbringing, and family background. The most available women—hostesses—were usually the least desirable because of their low levels of education, perceived "dirtiness," and rural backgrounds. Hostesses, however, were well aware of this ideology and often played into customers' desires by claiming to be down-on-their-luck university students temporarily forced to work in KTVs and by disguising or denying their rural backgrounds. Ironically, real university students and women from wealthy families were more inclined to demonstrate their sophistication by wearing revealing clothes and exhibiting a more open sexuality. Chengdu men often joked that in Chengdu all the proper girls (*liangjiafunü*) dressed like prostitutes and all the prostitutes dressed like university students.

Nearly all of the male entrepreneurs I worked with were married, and virtually all of them engaged in some form of extramarital sex. Nearly all patronized saunas that offered sexual services and slept with hostesses, and the majority also had girlfriends on the side. They often differentiated between the types of emotions, desires, and financial transactions specific to their different sexual relationships (Zelizer 2005). Lovers (*qingren*), girlfriends (*nüpengyou*), and mistresses (*qingfu*) were the most idealized objects of desire.[2] Lovers, more than wives, were seen to reflect a man's current status and the state of his finances. By examining entrepreneurs' different typologies of women and their corresponding sexual relationships, we can understand the different value attached to each type of relationship and the role status, sexuality, and money play in each.

Wives

The gendering of space associated with traditional Chinese society can be summarized by the phrase "men control the outside; women manage the inside" (*nan zhu wai; nü zhu nei*). A similar gendered separation undergirded the lives of the elite men I worked with in Chengdu. While they were expected to perform certain normative roles associated with the domestic sphere—father, son, husband—and the failure to fulfill these roles could result in condemnation by their families and peers, the bulk of their time and energy was devoted to relationships associated with the "outside" world of career and business, which was the primary source of an elite man's status (Uretsky 2007, 127).

Like the *sarariiman* studied by Allison (1994, 199) in *Nightwork,* over time the identities, desires, and relationships associated with the outside world of society came to overshadow my informants' domestic selves, often leading to a sense of estrangement from home. In her study of masculine sexual culture in Yunnan, Elanah Uretsky (2007, 128) notes that both female and male informants emphasized to her that "an unsuccessful man goes home after work, mildly successful men go home after carousing, while the most successful rarely go home." In this context, sexual relationships associated with the outside world were far more important to men's status and the construction of elite masculinity than their relationships with their wives.

Many entrepreneurs who had married before their rise to prosperity viewed their wives as relics of the past and representative of a poorer and less sophisticated period both in their lives and in China as a whole. The derogatory phrase for older wives, "coarse grain wives" (*zaokangzhiqi*), indicated both the harsher times they had suffered through with their wives and their "coarser" appearance. In fact, many Chinese I interviewed interpreted extramarital affairs as the product of a temporal disconnect between successful entrepreneurs and their wives. According to this interpretation, while entrepreneurs spent most of their time in the outside world of society (*waimian*) "developing" with the times, their wives were confined to the domestic sphere (*jiali*), limiting the scope of their knowledge and concerns to children and household chores. Thus wives were often understood to be incapable of understanding the complex social world navigated by their husbands and to lack the social graces and cultural sophistication to accompany their husbands while entertaining. Few of the entrepreneurs' wives worked, especially if they were younger and thereby more at risk of seduction and pollution in the "outside" world of business.

Regardless of whether they worked outside the home, wives were almost never present during evenings of entertaining. After dinner one evening, Mr. Liao once apologized to me profusely in front of his wife for her insistence on coming along with us to a KTV.[3] "I'm so sorry you won't be able to have any fun," he told me repeatedly. Even at banquets or teahouses and other forms of entertainment that did not involve hostesses, girlfriends and mistresses were the preferred companions. Several entrepreneurs told me they would have felt embarrassed to bring their wife along to an evening of *yingchou,* especially if all of their peers were accompanied by mistresses or hostesses.

Entrepreneurs often deliberately kept their business lives and connections separate from their wives and their wives' social circles. On the few occasions in which I met my informants' wives they often remarked how rarely they had a chance to meet their husbands' friends. Entrepreneurs also exploited their wives' apparent ignorance of their business ventures to hide their other romantic activities. "Taking care of a client" (*pei kehu*) and *yingchou* were the most common excuses for late nights out or even vacations with girlfriends or mistresses.

For these men, the domestic sphere was a realm of responsibility. But this responsibility was measured not by "quality time" and fidelity, but by the conditions their families lived under—such as their houses, their children's schools, and their wives' cars. They felt that once their financial obligations to their families were satisfied, as evidenced by the material comfort in which they lived, they had a license to enjoy the fruits of their labor and the pleasures offered in the outside world of business entertaining. According to their logic, the more time they spent in the outside world of society cultivating relationships, the better their chances of business success and thus the better they could provide for their families and thus fulfill their responsibilities. Besides, they told me, successful men have a stressful life (*huode henlei*) and deserve to enjoy themselves every now and then. This ideology of enjoying the pleasures of the outside, while keeping their domestic relationships intact, is best summarized by a saying frequently quoted to me: "Outside flags of many colors flutter about, but at home the red flag is never taken down" (*Waimian caiqi piaopiao; jiali hongqi budao*).

Mistresses and Lovers

Local interpretations of Valentine's Day reflected the division between wives and lovers. In Chinese, Valentine's Day is rendered as "Lover's Day" (*Qingren Jie*), and many older, less cosmopolitan entrepreneurs interpreted this holiday quite literally. They understood it as the day to treat their mistresses and girlfriends (not their wives) to dinner, shower them with gifts, and be seen out with them in upscale Western-style restaurants. (Many young people, who were more familiar with the significance of Valentine's Day in America, found this local interpretation of the holiday rather amusing.) When I asked one older businessman if his wife got upset if he didn't take her out on Lover's Day, he replied that she probably only had a vague idea that such a holiday even existed. Whether this was true or not, it reflected the strong division between the domestic realm of responsibility and the outside world of romance and pleasure, from which their wives were mostly excluded.

Christmas was another Western holiday (*yangjie*) in which it was important to be seen out with a young, attractive lover in an upscale restaurant, hotel, or bar. Jealous, cash-strapped male university students complained to me that on Christmas Eve Mercedes Benzes and BMWs of rich men lined up at their school gates to pick up female students for Christmas dates. While entrepreneurs' wives accompanied them for any traditional Chinese holidays, such as the family reunion dinners (*tuanyuanfan*) around Chinese New Year, mistresses were seen as the only suitable partners for the new "Western" holidays promoted by high-end leisure establishments.

The most highly desired mistresses were those with backgrounds in the arts and entertainment, preferably with some nascent fame. In practice, however, mistresses were frequently drawn from the ranks of entrepreneurs' own companies. Secretaries were often expected to sleep with bosses and would risk being fired by refusing their bosses' advances. Lovers were also plucked from the staff of elite entertainment venues and other businesses that catered to the new rich.

In the late 1990s, the foreign and domestic press abounded with stories of so-called second wives (*ernai*) in the more economically robust areas of China, and in Guangdong in particular. Ethnic Chinese businessmen from Hong Kong, Taiwan, and Singapore were the first to seek de facto second wives in areas where they were doing business. They took advantage of the stark contrast in wages and living standards between overseas Chinese and mainlanders at the time to attract young women with limited avenues for success in the new market economy. Cities such as Guangzhou and Shenzhen, which attracted many investors from Hong Kong and Taiwan, even saw the rise of "second-wife villages" (*ernai cun*) in areas of the city. By 2004, however, most of my informants in Chengdu viewed the institution of *ernai* with disdain. They understood taking a second wife to be a more "feudal" (*fengjian*) mode of expressing elite male status more appropriate to newly rich peasants (*baofahu*) than to sophisticated, urban entrepreneurs.

A favorite topic of conversation among my male research subjects involved quoting the monthly rates to "keep" (*bao*) current female models, actresses, or pop stars and speculating on the rates that up-and-coming stars could fetch. Presumably all one needed to *bao* someone was the right amount of cash. The price paid however, was not only a reflection of the value of the mistress; that is, her youth, purity, beauty, or fame. Older, less attractive, and less cultured elite men were expected to pay more. Just as beautiful, cultivated women fetched a higher price, ugly, old, and uncultured men were "fined" for their unappealing qualities. Thus to *bao* a woman was seen by many entrepreneurs I knew as a technique of necessity for the newly wealthy and presumably old, fat, ugly, and uncouth as well. It was assumed that men who resorted to these transactional relationships lacked the charm, sophistication, status, and reputation to elicit "authentic" affection and desire in women.

My informants used a different verb, *yang,* to categorize their relationship with girlfriends and mistresses.[4] *Yang* means "to provide for or take care of," and is most commonly used to describe parents' care for their children and later, children's care for their parents in old age. For wealthy businessmen, caring for their mistresses meant providing them with a monthly stipend, an apartment, and, if they were truly wealthy, a car as well, but it also involved caring for their general well-being and helping them solve any difficulties they faced. An entrepreneur might provide other forms of support depending on his mistress's circumstances. For example, I encountered several female university students in Chengdu who had their tuition and living expenses paid by wealthy, older male patrons. He might help her start a business or find work for her friends and relatives.

Despite the apparent material foundations of the relationship, my informant friends often spoke of their lovers in idealized romantic terms and understood their relationships to be primarily composed of affect. A journalist I interviewed from a popular Chengdu newspaper understood mistresses as providing over-stressed businessmen with an emotional and spiritual confidant: "You foreigners can go to church, but in China a rich man has only his mistress to pour his heart out to" (*qingsu*). Several informants echoed this notion that mistresses served as spiritual and emotional confidants in ways that wives could not. Mistresses were purported to understand the pressures faced by an entrepreneur because they were part of the outside world of social relationships and deal making, unlike wives, who only understood domestic affairs.

In an interview I asked Mr. Wu what compensation he provided for his mistresses and whether the material interest of young women bothered him. I explained that many Americans felt that material interest tainted the emotional purity of a romantic relationship. Rich men in the West sometimes worried that women "were only after their money" as represented by the popular figure of the young female gold digger. Mr. Wu replied that it did not bother him that women were initially attracted by his money: "I think it's normal for them to be like that. In fact, I hope that they put money first. That makes it easier for people like me." (Mr. Wu considered himself to be overweight and ugly and thus only able to attract beautiful women because he had money.) I explained that Americans felt that material interest did not provide a very solid foundation for a relationship. He responded that if two people are together for long enough, affection (*ganqing*) will develop naturally between them, especially if they take care of each other.

In fact, providing tangible evidence of one's feelings in the form of comfortable apartments and nice clothes was seen as a more effective demonstration of affection than mere romantic rhetoric.[5] Young women even criticized men who made declarations of feelings and romantic gestures without backing them up with tangible actions and gifts. Mr. Wu understood providing for his mistresses as the foundation of their affection for him, but not its only basis. Similarly, many elite entrepreneurs in Chengdu, along with their mistresses, wives, and subordinates, understood human relationships, be they between husband and wife, parent and child, or patron and client, to be composed of varying degrees of interest and affect. But for them this was no "dirty secret" that induced anxiety or denial.

While entrepreneurs idealized their relationships in terms of taking care of dependent young women, both entrepreneurs and their lovers manipulated this social field to achieve more limited social, economic, and sexual goals. The men promised cars, jobs, apartments, and all the perks of full-fledged mistress status to their lovers, but these more substantial items seldom materialized. Most of my informants would string along young women with gifts of mobile phones and Louis Vuitton handbags until, from their perspective, the woman became too demanding of goods, money, or favors, or their relationship evolved into one of increasingly plausible authentic affection. Relationships also ended when mistresses were deemed too old, which generally meant over thirty, or when they pushed too hard for marriage. Some entrepreneurs do divorce their wives to marry their mistresses but this was not common among the entrepreneurs I knew in Chengdu, who mostly subscribed to the "colored flag, red flag" ideology mentioned above.

Mistress affairs sometimes ended with a "buyout," whereby a wealthy patron would provide his mistress with an apartment, a lump sum of money, or a business to run to guarantee her long-term income. Young women often singled out and praised men who "took responsibility" (*fuzeren*) in their extramarital affairs. One well-known real estate developer in Chengdu was often commended as a model patron. He was known to have provided each of his past mistresses with a villa (*bieshu*) of her own before he moved on to a new, younger mistress.

Just as in their relationships with other men, wealthy men and government officials strive to cultivate relationships of patronage with their mistresses and lovers. Elite men gain status from being the provider for multiple dependents, be they aspiring entrepreneurs or college coeds. And just as officials hand out capital and licenses that guarantee success for entrepreneurs, elite men provide the easy street to enjoyment of the fruits of the market economy for young women.

For elite men, status derives above all from being able to deliver the goods—favors and connections, houses and handbags—to grateful dependents.

Paid and Unpaid Sex

Entrepreneurs understood sex workers and hostesses as good for little more than enjoying oneself, entertaining clients, and for providing a sexual release. Several informant friends, both male and female, understood the role of sex workers to be merely that of "solving the problem" (*jiejue wenti*); that is, taking care of men's basic physical needs (*nanren shentishangde xuyao*).

For an entrepreneur, falling for a sex worker or even a hostess not normally available for sex would likely incur the ridicule of his peers, for these women lacked most of the qualities desired by a man of status—high *suzhi,* purity, and artistic cultivation. Similarly, men who let their affairs go too far were also criticized. While divorce was understood and rarely condemned, divorce of a proper and decent wife merely for a younger, more attractive woman of dubious moral character was usually criticized as revealing a lack of responsibility (*zerengan*) to one's family.

Allison (1994), in her study of Japanese hostess clubs, found that the ability to pay for sex directly corresponded to a man's status; but among the groups of entrepreneurs I knew in Chengdu, sex with sex workers occupied a more precarious position. Paid sex was often described as highly pleasurable and sometimes contrasted with sex with mistresses (who, because of their perceived purity, were often characterized as inexperienced and lacking in technique) and with wives (who were viewed as beyond their sexual prime and almost desexualized). But commercial sex even in the most high-end saunas did little to enhance men's status. Instead it was viewed as an essential component of entertaining and an occasional necessity to help them take a break from the pressures of business. Some elite men even expressed an aversion to any form of blatant commercial sex. Others portrayed themselves as being forced to pay for sex because they were unable to attract women with their looks and charm. When I asked a married entrepreneur, Mr. Zhang, about his love life, he responded, "Not so good. No girlfriends, only prostitutes."

The first night I met Brother Fatty, a local boss of a mafia-like brotherhood (*heishehui*), he insisted to me that he never pays money for sex: "I refuse to pay money, and I don't need to pay." His ideal sex partners were those who, in recognition of his greatness and power, willingly offered themselves to him (or at least demonstrated their sincerity and lack of venality convincingly). As evidence of the type of beauty he could attract without paying, he dropped the names of several second-tier actresses who (he claimed) were his former mistresses.

Although he would offer his guests their choice of hostesses at his nightclub, I rarely witnessed him interacting with hostesses at his club or at others. Instead he surrounded himself with young female students, actresses, and dancers introduced to him by his business associates.

Never paying reflected Fatty's self-understanding as a man with enough face (*mianzi*) to transcend commodified relationships, and it was a principle that he extended to many other facets of his life. He understood that the power of his relationships and reputation allowed him to transcend most crude transactions. Twice (once at a car wash, and once at a restaurant) at establishments run by associates who were under his protection he was mistakenly given the bill. Somewhat embarrassed by their lack of deference to him in my presence, he told the clueless cashiers, "I don't have to pay here."

Given his wealth, power, and extensive network of influential friends, businessmen and underlings frequently sought to win Fatty's favor by introducing him to younger women. In negotiating these offers he was concerned first about the women's features—their age and the quality of their skin in particular—but above all he was interested in their motives for wanting to be with him. Once while I was riding in his Mercedes he received a call from an acquaintance offering to introduce him to a "virgin" university student who was eager to meet him. Fatty was very interested, but he was concerned that the girl was only after money or gifts, and asked his friend, "Are you sure that she just doesn't want a mobile phone?" He was uninterested in women looking for a mobile phone or a shopping spree; he wanted women to want him and for their desire to spring from an awareness and recognition of his fame and power. Only these authentic forms of desire effectively confirmed and reflected his status.

Conclusion: Sexuality, Status, and Alliances among the New Rich

Elite men in Chengdu clearly preferred meeting and forming relationships with women who most closely possessed the qualities described above—youth, purity, beauty, and class. They would often sweeten their dinner invitations to colleagues and officials with the promise of an introduction to a "beauty" (*meinü*). Some entrepreneurs used such promises to secure a meeting with a hard-to-meet high-ranking official or businessman. It was assumed that men who already possessed significant amounts of money and power could still be tempted by sex, especially less blatantly commercial forms.

Many entrepreneurs I worked with encouraged their girlfriends to bring their friends along during evenings of entertaining to provide potential dates for their associates. From a distance, this behavior quite closely resembles a "traffic in women" in which men seek to secure alliances with each other through the "exchange" of young women. However, the effectiveness of this exchange depends on an understanding of the women involved as not objects, but as subjects, with their own motivations and desires that men can only hope to influence. In fact, it is the noncommodifiable and autonomous nature of these women's desire that served as the source of their value in mirroring men's status and mediating relationships between men. This process resembles objectification less than exploitation in the Marxist sense—the extraction and appropriation of the value produced (or performed) by young women's desire for the purpose of building ties and mirroring status among elite men.

Furthermore, seldom did this traffic take the form of a reciprocal exchange but was instead bound to the hierarchy of host-guest and patron-client relationships. Introductions to beauties were most often understood as prestations (obligatory gifts or payments) to powerful men that reflected (or enhanced) the men's status and virility. These prestations were most effective when the woman being introduced seemed to harbor an authentic desire for the official or client. Simply treating a client or official to sexual services often reflected a distance in the relationship between the two men, and nothing augmented an elite man's masculinity more than having a young beauty fall for him (or at least give a convincing performance of falling for him). This outcome, however, depended on the desires of young beauties, which entrepreneurs attempted to influence with stipends, apartments, and gifts but disavowed "purchasing" entirely. Despite their fantasies of control, they could only hope that the young women they called upon to aid in their alliance making succumbed to the temptations of luxury and opted to "take the shortcut" (*zou jiejing*) by serving as the mistress to a wealthy man.[6] For elite men in Chengdu, merely paying for sex or to *bao* a second wife represented lowerstatus forms of sex consumption. More successful and wealthy men such as Fatty felt that real status was indicated not by the price paid but by less transparently commodified forms of value—their fame, connections, and reputation. The possession of these qualities was confirmed by the authenticity of the affections of their high-class girlfriends and the depth of their ties to other elite men.

Elite nightlife constitutes the primary arena in which entrepreneurs' consumption, social networks, and sexualities are on display to their peers, but male play in KTVs is not merely a gendered performance. Here relationships between men are made that structure politics and business. Whether for the more instrumental purposes of *yingchou* or simply a night carousing with friends, the subjectivities generated and the networks produced in these encounters cannot be reduced to a "hypermasculinity" surging forth after decades of repression. Instead they create networks governed by their own codes of honor (*yiqi*), face, and brotherhood. These networks constitute powerful, "informal" institutions that transcend state, society, and market in China.

Notes and References

1. My argument here differs from Sedgwick's (1985) model of homosociality. Sedgwick examines the "erotic triangles" that help orient the "homosocial continuum" of relationships between men. In the examples she analyzes, men are bound together through their rivalry for the same woman. In KTV clubs it seems rather that men are bonded through a parallel structure—participants are all figured as men who enjoy, deserve, and can afford the same luxuries.

2. These three terms were used to refer to essentially the same type of relationship—one that occupied the gray area between formal spouse and paid sex worker.

3. Pseudonyms are used in this chapter to protect the identities of my informants.

4. There is also a verb that combines these two terms: *baoyang*. *Baoyang* is a more a general term for supporting a mistress or second wife often found in formal spoken and written contexts; it was seldom used by my informants. Thus, despite the equation of *bao* with *yang* in formal contexts, I maintain that there is an evolving distinction between *bao* and *yang* among my informants.

5. See Kipnis (1997) and Yan (2003) for discussions of the relationship between feelings, speech, and actions in Chinese familial and romantic relationships.

6. This is not to suggest that mistresses of wealthy men never develop "real" affection for their lovers, but rather that the convincing performance of authentic emotion and desire through linguistic and sexual practices is what authenticates the relationship. As Cameron and Kulick (2003, 115) argue, intimacy is an "interactional achievement."

Allison, Anne. 1994. *Nightwork: Sexuality, Pleasure, and Corporate Masculinity in a Tokyo Hostess Club.* Chicago: University of Chicago Press.

Brownell, Susan. 2001. "Making Dream Bodies in Beijing: Athletes, Fashion Models, and Urban Mystique in China." In *China Urban: Ethnographies of Contemporary Culture,* edited by Nancy Chen, Suzanne Clark, and Lyn Jeffrey, pp. 123–142. Durham, NC: Duke University Press.

Butler, Judith. 1999 [1990]. *Gender Trouble: Feminism and the Subversion of Identity.* New York: Routledge.

Cameron, Deborah, and Kulick, Don. 2003. *Language and Sexuality.* New York: Cambridge University Press.

Connell, R. W. 1995. *Masculinities: Knowledge, Power, and Social Change.* Berkeley: University of California Press.

Evans, Harriet. 2002. "Past, Perfect, or Imperfect: Changing Images of the Ideal Wife." In *Chinese Femininities, Chinese Masculinities: A Reader,* edited by Susan Brownell and Jeffrey N. Wasserstrom, pp. 335–360. Berkeley: University of California Press.

Farquhar, Judith. 2002. *Appetites: Food and Sex in Post-Socialist China.* Durham, NC: Duke University Press.

Hershatter, Gail. 1997. *Dangerous Pleasures: Prostitution and Modernity in Twentieth Century Shanghai.* Berkeley: University of California Press.

Kipnis, Andrew. 1997. *Producing Guanxi: Sentiment, Self, and Subculture in a North China Village.* Durham, NC: Duke University Press.

———. 2001. "Zouping Christianity as Gendered Critique? An Ethnography of Political Potentials." *Anthropology and Humanism* 27 (1): 80–96.

Liu, Xin. 2002. *The Otherness of Self: A Genealogy of the Self in Contemporary China.* Ann Arbor: University of Michigan Press.

Rofel, Lisa. 1999. *Other Modernities: Gendered Yearnings in China after Socialism.* Berkeley: University of California Press.

———. 2007. *Desiring China: Experiments in Neoliberalism, Sexuality, and Public Culture.* Durham, NC: Duke University Press.

Rubin, Gayle. 1975. "The Traffic in Women." In *Toward an Anthropology of Women,* edited by Rita Rayner, pp. 157–210. New York: Monthly Review Press.

Schein, Louisa. 2000. *Minority Rules: The Miao and the Feminine in China's Cultural Politics.* Durham, NC: Duke University Press.

Sedgwick, Eve, Kosofsky. 1985. *Between Men: English Literature and Male Homosocial Desire.* New York: Columbia University Press.

Uretsky, Elanah. 2007. "Mixing Business with Pleasure: Masculinity and Male Sexual Culture in Urban China in the Era of HIV/AIDS." PhD diss., Columbia University.

Wank, David. 1999. *Commodifying Communism: Business, Trust, and Politics in a Chinese City.* New York: Cambridge University Press.

Yan, Yunxiang. 2003. *Private Life under Socialism: Love, Intimacy, and Family Change in a Chinese Village 1949–1999.* Stanford, CA: Stanford University Press.

Yang, Mayfair Mei-hui. 1999. "From Gender Erasure to Gender Difference: State Feminism, Consumer Sexuality, and Women's Public Sphere in China." In *Spaces of Their Own: Women's Public Sphere in Transnational China,* edited by Mayfair Mei-hui Yang, pp. 35–67. Minneapolis: University of Minnesota Press.

Zelizer, Viviana. 2005. *The Purchase of Intimacy.* Princeton, NJ: Princeton University Press.

Zhang, Everett Yuehong. 2001. "Goudui and the State: Constructing Entrepreneurial Masculinity in Two Cosmopolitan Areas of Post-Socialist China." In *Gendered Modernities: Ethnographic Perspectives,* edited by Dorothy L. Hodgson, pp. 235–266. New York: Palgrave.

Zheng, Tiantian. 2006. "Cool Masculinity: Male Clients' Sex Consumption and Business Alliance in Urban China's Sex Industry." *Journal of Contemporary China* 15 (46): 161–182.

———. 2009. *Red Lights: The Lives of Sex Workers in Postsocialist China.* Minneapolis: University of Minnesota Press.

CHAPTER SEVEN

Labor, Masculinity, and History

Bangbang Men in Chongqing, China

XIA ZHANG

Introduction

In the year 2007, on a hot and humid summer afternoon in Chongqing in southwest China, I was grocery shopping with a female relative in a local farmer's market. The temperature was above 100 Fahrenheit and the market was crowded. As we walked purchasing food, our shopping bags were getting heavier and heavier. My companion wanted to buy a big watermelon. I reminded her that we were far from the nearest bus or taxi station, and we could not possibly carry all our stuff in the hot weather for more than five minutes. Agreeing, she suggested that we hire a *bangbang,* the local appellation for rural migrant men who work as professional porter or carrier, to solve our problem. We went to the entrance of the market, where we saw more than ten *bangbang* across the street waiting for clients. Each of them held or sat on a bamboo pole and a bunch of greenish plastic ropes, the tools that they used to carry goods. My relative went ahead, shouting "*bangbang,*" which was the local way to indicate to the thus named that someone needed his services. Immediately, all the waiting *bangbang* ran to us, competing for the opportunity. After a few minutes of bargaining, my companion picked the one who had asked for the lowest pay—five yuan (about $0.80). For this, he promised to deliver the over twenty pounds of goods by foot to my place, an apartment about a twenty-minute walk away. As usual, we did not pay him until we arrived.

While we walked with the *bangbang* man back home, my relative watched his movements closely, continually warning him not to knock her goods onto the wall and urging him to walk faster. The *bangbang* tried his best to follow these instructions, but could not make her happy. When we reached my place and it was time to pay, my relative reduced the payment to 4.5 yuan (around $0.70), saying that he had not provided satisfactory service. The man argued. My relative became upset and said, "Why don't you *bangbang* behave like real men? Look at you, bargaining a few cents like a woman!" The man answered, "Only rich men don't bargain. Why don't you ask one of them next time to carry your watermelon?"

During my fifteen months of ethnographic fieldwork in Chongqing City among the *bangbang* men in the summer of 2004 and between 2006 and 2007, I witnessed many scenes similar to this one, in which the men's masculinity was challenged, questioned, or ridiculed by their clients, many of them members of the newly emergent middle class. The *bangbang* men usually responded to this gender discrimination by developing their own understanding of what it means to be a man. This understanding overlaps in some ways with but also differs significantly from the urban middle-class notion of masculinity. This chapter examines how *bangbang* men draw on historical and changing ideals of masculinity to deal with the "double oppression" (by class and gender) to which they are subject as rural migrant men in the rapidly developing metropolis of Chongqing.

Masculinity, as many scholars have suggested, "encompasses norms, standards or models to which men in a culture are expected to conform if they wish to interact appropriately and acceptably with others" (Song 2004, 3). Kenneth Clatterbaugh (1990, 3) argues that three components are crucial for the social construction of masculinity: masculine gender roles, stereotypes of masculinity, and gender ideals. Following Clatterbaugh, Geng Song (2004, 3–4) defines masculine gender roles as what men are, masculine stereotypes as what people think men are, and masculine gender ideals as what people think men should be. These three components of socially defined masculinity interact with each other. Thus, Song claims that the notion of masculinity is "a dialectical combination of the three [components]" (4). In this chapter, I focus mainly on the dominant gender ideals in Chinese society and examine their historical transformations in relation to the hierarchical division of labor as well as their impact on *bangbang* men's gendered experiences in post-Mao China. Due to the extremely diversified meanings of masculinity in Chinese society today (Song and Hird 2013), I have coined the term "dominant gender ideal" to refer to the widely held and popular notion of masculinity in mainstream Chinese society that determines what the appropriate gender roles for men should be, a term that recalls Clatterbaugh's (1990) "gender ideal."

Contemporary ethnographic research on labor and gender has focused on global economic inequalities and the diverse practices that have produced a gendered global labor force. This scholarship offers insights into how workers' lived experiences of work and migration are shaped by gender and labor inequalities (e.g., Constable 1997, 2014; Mills 2003; Parrenas 2000; Pun 2005). Much of this literature discusses women, given their underprivileged position in a gendered economy. Ethnographers are just beginning to pay attention to the fluid and complex relations between the material conditions of labor and the configuration of masculine identity, focusing on transnational migration. Research has been done to examine how, in various cultural contexts, hegemonic masculinity intersects with complex politics of class, sexuality, and power to shape individual migrant men's subjectivity and experiences. Jane Margold (1995) examines how late capitalist control over migrant labor often denies migrant men not only their masculinity but also their humanity. Other scholars argue that overseas male workers are better able to claim a fully adult masculine status at home through their work in high-status sites of globalization (Nonini 1997; Osella & Osella 2000). Some ethnographers are also concerned with how a crisis of masculinity has resulted from economic restructuring and localized globalization (e.g., Gamburd 2000; George 2000; Goldring 2001; Levitt 2001; McDowell 2000; Newman 1999). Recent research shows that even within one receiving country, the male gender strategies used by immigrant men to cope with their crises of masculinity vary immensely, depending on factors such as individual sources and the political economy of the receiving country (Donaldson and Hibbins 2009). Overall, these academic writings provide valuable insights about the significance of work and economic power for men's sense of masculine pride.

The studies of men and masculinity in China have been mainly conducted by both literature critics and anthropologists. Literature critics (e.g., Hinsch 2013; Louie 2002; Song 2004; Zhong 2000) approach the question of Chinese masculinity through in-depth cultural analysis of literary texts and visual products, such as novels and films. Among these scholars, Kam Louie's (2002) pioneering work *Theorizing Chinese Masculinity* is of particular importance in that it insightfully points out how the intersection of class and labor contributes to the historical changes of Chinese masculinity ideals—the *wen-wu* (scholarly talent-martial valor) dyad. Following Louie's approach, Hinsch's (2013) work on Chinese masculinity covers the full span of Chinese history and examines how nationalism, imperialism, capitalism, modernization, revolution and reforms help transform the meaning of Chinese masculinity both in history and in contemporary China. Literary critics' groundbreaking works provide rich material and valuable perspective to my study of masculinity. However, their research is not based on ethnographic fieldwork and thus leaves out the question of how individual Chinese men today understand, appropriate, and contest the meanings of masculinity in a rapidly changing Chinese society.

Anthropologists' work on Chinese masculinity, on the other hand, is mainly concerned with how localized entrepreneurial models of masculinity are based on representations of gender hierarchy in the global economy (E. Y. Zhang 2001; L. Zhang 2001; Zheng 2007, 2009). This scholarship highlights the fact that masculinity in post-Mao China is primarily defined by wealth and social status, but also points out that the construction of Chinese masculinity is conditioned by socialist legacies. For example, Tiantian Zheng's (2007) research found that the male entrepreneurs' consumption of the sex services of the nightclub hostesses in Dalian, China, is more than proving their sexual competency and potency; it is a "business ritual" that they carry out to select business partners, to maintain mutual trust and male bonding, and to contest socialist morality and state. Everett Zhang (2003) argues that wealth is not enough to bring masculinized power; the fact that male entrepreneurs must for business purposes go through *goudui* (activities such as banquets, mahjong, nightclub entertainment, and saunas) with government officials exposes how the party-state can easily emasculate wealthy men with its power. Except for the works of a few scholars (e.g., Lin 2013a; E. Y. Zhang 2001; Zheng 2009, 2007, 2012), scant attention has been paid to the competing meanings of Chinese masculinity and the historical basis of these constructions. Meanwhile, anthropologists have just started to pay attention to the issues of labor and class when discussing masculinity in China (Lin 2013a, 2013b; Song and Hird 2013).

In the case of migrant workers, among whom male rural migrants are the majority, the factor of class and the politics of labor are essential to developing a more thorough understanding of these men's gender experience. I argue that masculinity in China does not revolve around a single or uniform concept (such as the notion of machismo in Latin America [Gutmann 2006]), but involves many diverse and conflicting meanings in relation to class, work, and the rural-urban division. I also argue that this inconsistency in the meaning of masculinity in contemporary China reflects the changes in dominant masculinity ideals over the course of Chinese history. Two key factors have led to changes in Chinese ideals of masculinity: (1) rural-urban inequalities that render rural men less masculine than their urban counterparts and rural migrant men more masculine than impoverished nonmigrant rural men in post-reform China; (2) persistent shifts in national and public discourses about the value of manual vs. mental labor during the presocialist (before 1949), socialist (1949–1978), and postsocialist (after 1978) eras in China. My purpose in tracing these historical shifts is not to provide a monolithic picture of "the history" of Chinese masculinity but to point out the importance of developing a paradigm of Chinese masculinity from within a Chinese context, and to describe the intricate relationships between historical constructions and contemporary expressions of gender ideology in China. In a nutshell, this research attempts to not only provide a current and ethnographically grounded analysis of Chinese migrant men's gendered experiences, which has been largely ignored by Chinese migration studies, but also highlight the intersection between changing political economy and the changes in the social construction of masculinity norms in China.

Historical Transformations of Chinese Masculine Ideals

Kam Louie, through a close reading of works of literature and films from major Chinese historical junctures, points out that the dominant masculinity ideal in China before the 1850s was conceptualized in terms of the *wen-wu* dyad. He further points out that a balance of *wen* and *wu* was regarded as the ideal expression of masculinity in traditional Chinese culture. According to Louie, Confucianism and its rise to dominance in premodern China played a major role in shaping the ideal of Chinese masculinity. The Confucian preference for *wen* over *wu* prevailed during most of Chinese history, placing scholarly men above those who do manual labor. According to Geng Song, Mencius says that "there are two kinds of people in the world. Those of one kind work with their minds and the other with their strength, and 'those who work with their minds rule others; those who work with their strength are ruled by others'" (Song 2004, 80). Farming, as manual labor, was less valued than intellectual work during much of the premodern era.

China began the process of modernization under Western imperialism and martial penetration after the First Opium War (1840–1842). In a strategy of self-strengthening, the Qing government abolished the civil service examination in 1905, resulting in the rapid decline of the social status of Confucian scholars. As the society was rapidly transformed, the Chinese ideals of masculinity were increasingly constructed in relation to the newly emerging nationalism and capitalism, and in response to China's semicolonial status at the time (Hinsch 2013). Increasingly, a man's manliness was connected to his value and usefulness to the nation either as a tool of national renovation, an embodiment of material prosperity and the entrepreneurial ethos, or an enthusiastic advocate of physical fitness and mass sporting activities. With the advent of the New Cultural Movement (1915–1923), many urban intellectuals (mainly men) began to search for a new identity in a modernizing, industrializing society (Glosser 2002). Those who took the ideal of the "New Youth"[1] (Louie 2002, 23) as their model valued physical labor, business studies, and profitable activities that had been abhorred by the Confucians (133). These are attributes based on the Western entrepreneurial ethos and the republican spirit of individual liberty, rather than a Confucian indoctrination that neglects individual rights and autonomy in favor of a life of relationships. However, a strong class bias discouraged these elite educated men from taking jobs outside the literary and governmental sectors. The accomplishments of the traditional literati remained symbolically valuable in Chinese society, especially among the privileged urban elites who, as Cohen (1994, 154–155) suggests, constructed the peasantry "as a culturally distinct and alien 'other', passive, helpless, unenlightened, in the grip of ugly and fundamentally useless customs, desperately in need of education and cultural reform."

In the 1930s, the Chinese Communist Party (CCP) aimed to promote the values of manual workers and peasants. The virtues of rural life in contrast to the corruption of the city were extolled by Mao Zedong. With the establishment of the People's Republic of China in 1949, the CCP promoted workers, peasants, and soldiers (especially men) as heroes, although in practice peasants remained materially disadvantaged. State-promoted art and literature featured male revolutionary heroes who exhibited exaggerated physical strength and courage, rejected bourgeois lifestyles, and expressed devotion to communist ideals. The CCP also launched the Great Leap Forward (1958–1961) in order to tackle the differences between city and country, worker and peasant, and mental and manual labor (Hinton 1984, 207). Mayfair Yang's (1999) research points out that the state feminism promoted by the CCP during the Maoist period did not truly liberate Chinese women from patriarchal oppression and gender inequality. Instead, it was largely masculinized, and involved the adoration of militarized physical-labor-based masculinity. However, the official celebration of male manual work did not mean that the popular stereotype of manual laborers as poor, uneducated, and less preferable was completely eradicated. Despite the CCP's effort to move workers, peasants, and soldiers from the margin to the center in literary representations and on the stage, the traditional sense of *wen* masculinity still had an upper hand in daily life. As Yiyan Wang (2003, 46) suggests, CCP cadres (the majority of them men) were the modern literati in a sense. With their literacy and communist education, they played a dominant role in relation to the illiterate and uneducated masses of workers, peasants, and soldiers.

With the economic and social reforms of the post-Mao era (since 1978), China has become market-oriented and economically stratified. In an era of commodification and consumption, individual social positioning no longer depends solely on one's class of origin (*chushen*); it also depends in many ways on one's level of personal income. Those with high incomes enjoy high social status, and are often linked to a notion of global masculinity (although as Chinese men, they are often considered effeminate in comparison to the images of idealized man circulated in the Western media [Hinsch 2013, 156–157]), whereas people in labor-intensive occupations with low pay, including peasants, are often debased and their work undervalued in the popular discourse. With the widening rural-urban gap since the 1980s, the countryside and rural people have been stigmatized materially and symbolically as backward, ignorant, and despicable (Pun 2005; Yan 2003, 2008). Previously glorified images of masculine and powerful peasants have largely disappeared. Rural migrant workers, most of whom engage in manual labor in urban regions, elicit prejudice from more established urban residents. They are blamed for the rising crime rate in urban regions, though they are most often its victims (Zhang 2001), and it is often said that their "quality" (*suzhi*) is low (Anagnost 2004). In certain contexts, urban men are preferred by employers over rural men even for manual labor.

The turbulent social and cultural changes during the early 1980s, following upon China's opening up to the outside world, led to the emergence of a contradictory pattern of masculine ideals. One of these was promoted by Chinese women writers who were particularly disparaging about the perceived weakness of Chinese men and declared that there were no "real men" in China. The image of the tough guy, as exemplified for instance by the Japanese movie star Ken Takakura, became a new version of the masculine ideal in popular discourse. Consequently, a new style of fiction called *xungen* (roots-seeking) literature[2] emerged in an attempt to produce evidence to counter the accusation that China lacked real men. The tough guy in *xungen* literature has a cold, tough exterior and an indomitable spirit. The writers painstakingly show that these characteristics are innately Chinese and not imported from the West, suggesting a return to the notion of *wu* ideal. Along with the search for the "tough guy," postsocialist China has also witnessed the resurrection of a set of alternative images of ideal Chinese men—the lower-class hooligans (*liumang*) and punks (*pizi*) who use brotherly righteousness (*yiqi*) "to express masculine honor, and construct a contemporary version of the virile man" (Hinsch 2013, 158). Although rural migrant men such as the *bangbang* do not necessarily identify themselves with *liumang* or *pizi,* they do often express an appreciation of the ideals of brotherhood, toughness, and pugnacity, features embodied by the *liumang* and *pizi* who similarly come from the lowest rungs of society.

These changes in masculine ideals have resulted in the coexistence of competing meanings of Chinese masculinity, affecting individual rural migrant men's gendered experiences in complicated ways. Below I draw on the ethnographic data collected from my fieldwork in Chongqing to illustrate how the *bangbang* men appropriate, contest, and struggle with the conflicting discourses of masculinity in contemporary Chinese society, and to show the constitutive process of identity making and remaking.

Bangbang Men in Mountainous City

The recent movement of over 200 million people from rural to urban China is one of the most conspicuous changes of the post-1978 reform era, and may be the largest mass migration the world has ever seen. China's eastern coastal region and largest cities (e.g., Beijing and Shenzhen) were the initial destinations of most rural laborers, but the destinations now include large inland cities such as Chongqing. Because of its mountainous topography and rapid urbanization, Chongqing, as the pillar of heavy manufacturing industry and the largest port city in southwest China, has been in great need of low-skilled and unskilled transport-related heavy labor. There has been a surge of migrants into Chongqing since the start of the "Three Gorges" project in 1996 and the initiation of the "Go West" project in 2000. Chongqing was home to over 1.48 million rural migrants in 2000 (Liu 2001), and the number continues to grow. In Chongqing, *bangbang* refers to members of a group of over 200,000 porters who provide delivery service for low pay (20–40 yuan/day or $3–$7/day). They mainly work at the docks along the Yangtze and Jailing Rivers, in markets, commercial zones, and public transportation terminuses. Some of them also do temporary work as construction workers and scavengers. The occupation is dominated by economically disadvantaged rural migrant men who lack school education and connections and have nothing to rely on but their physical labor. They work for whoever can afford their labor, carrying almost anything using their hands, backs, and shoulders with the help of ropes and bamboo poles. They get paid in cash immediately after they finish the work. Most *bangbang* do not have long-term employers but are self-employed. In an effort to compete for work opportunities, *bangbang* often organize themselves into groups of more than five men who lay claim to certain commercial zones, and sometimes live together, pool their daily earnings, and thus collectively share the risks and benefits among them.

In Chongqing, *bangbang* often become the focal point of social attention. One reason is because in China, only Chongqing has such a huge population of male porters working in its urban center. In order to promote Chongqing's tourist industry, the local government made an ahistorical statement that the *bangbang* in contemporary Chongqing are doing the same job that the coolies did along the Yangtze River after Chongqing was forced to open its port to Western merchants in 1891. The government's goal is to create a glorious image of Chongqing as an economic center of the upstream Yangtze River, which has a long history of trade and business. Another reason is that *bangbang* are highly mobile, rural, adult men who often serve female customers with no supervision. The existence of a huge number of rural men in the urban region often gives rise to social debates over gender relations. In other words, in Chongqing, *bangbang* men are a local phenomenon. They are the subject of a popular national television series and several feature films, and have become a poignant symbol of China's displaced rural male workers. Whereas recent media reports tell of the multitude of difficulties faced by rural migrants, *bangbang* I met in my fieldwork often expressed deep pride in their work, and were widely considered successful at what they do by their peers. Whereas Chongqing's locals often regard *bangbang* as poor, unattractive rural men who are desperate for work, *bangbang* themselves contest these images, emphasizing their choice of this occupation, their strength and muscularity, their ability to support their families, and the superiority of their work over other types of manual labor.

Lao Liu, a forty-seven-year-old *bangbang* with a solid body, has worked in Chongqing for about ten years.[3] He recently helped his oldest son get a job at a local factory. His wife farms the family's fields in their home village. "I am the one who provides nearly everything for my wife and children," he said proudly. When I reminded him of his wife's contribution to the family, he laughed, "But during the busy season of harvesting, I go back to help her. Without me, she cannot even harvest the paddy," he said confidently. When I asked him about how urban people treated him, he said, "I know some urban people look down upon us *bangbang*. Some *bangbang* are afraid to offend them. I am not. Why should I be? Urban men's bodies have been ruined by an indulgent (urban) lifestyle, such as prostitution, mahjong playing, and banqueting. . . . They are easily beaten down, like women. I beat a punk urban kid until he begged me to let him go."

Big Brother Mo, a fifty-two–year-old *bangbang* and former quarryman, told me that he liked *bangbang* work and would never go back to the quarry where he had worked for ten years. I asked if it was because quarrying is more toilsome than *bangbang* work. He answered: "Both kinds of work require almost the same labor. But I get more *ziyou* (freedom) being a *bangbang*." I asked what *ziyou* he enjoyed from working as a *bangbang*. He seemed surprised that I asked this question but answered: "That's obvious. Don't you see us *bangbang* men have no bosses? I'm my own boss. I decide if I work today or not, when and where to work, whom I work for, how long to work, and whom I want to work with. No one has the right to order me around. Can quarrymen have such *ziyou*?" He then told me about his painful experience of working in a private quarry where the quarrymen had to obey the boss's orders. "My wage was in the boss's hand," he said, "what could I do? One time my son was in the hospital. I wanted to go take care of him, so I asked for a short-term leave. My boss said okay, but to come back to work as soon as possible or I would risk being fired. I'd just had enough of it. You know we rural men are not like urban workers, who are accustomed to obeying the discipline of the *danwei* (work unit)[4]; we never have a *danwei* and we've been accustomed to *ziyou*."

Though these two stories are far from enough to provide a comprehensive contour of *bangbang* men's conception of self and their masculinity—something this chapter does not intend to do—they present a snapshot of the diversity and multiple scripts of their sense of masculinity. *Bangbang,* as strangers in the city (Zhang 2001), are depicted by many urban locals as not "manly" enough due to the manual labor that they engage in and the low pay that they earn. Furthermore, the fact that *bangbang* men work in the highly female-predominated service industry (despite the fact that *bangbang* work is male-dominated) also contributes to the popular view that *bangbang* are not "manly." In local vernacular discourse, calling an urban middle-class adult man "*bangbang*" is particularly derogatory and insulting. When young urban women look for a marriage partner, *bangbang* are not an object of desire but rather the topics of jokes and condescension. In many ways, *bangbang* men's experience of gender resembles what Margold (1995) found among Filipino migrant male workers in Saudi Arabia. Margold points out that migratory experiences are degrading and humiliating, as Ilokano workers experience a disintegrating sense of self and masculinity. Whereas her research implies a consistent, monolithic masculine self that has been challenged and destroyed by the experience of migration, my research among the *bangbang* finds that the rural-urban migratory experience, while challenging these migrant men's masculine pride and integration in many ways, also provides opportunities in certain contexts for them to develop alternative masculine ideals and claim new urban masculine subjectivities.

In the urban context, *bangbang* men's solid bodies and the extraordinary strength that results from their manual labor have become a source of their masculine pride. Historically, China's failure in the First Opium War occasioned a discourse on Chinese masculinity in which an effeminate and weak body (the rhetoric of "The Sick Man of East Asia") was denigrated in the nationalist conception of China's painful history of being penetrated and dominated by Western imperialism, while a strong body denoted being masculine and modern. The *bangbang* neatly appropriate this discourse to mediate urban humiliation and marginalization. Lao Liu's narrative suggests that his extraordinary physical strength not only enables him to manage the heavy workload of a busy harvest season and thus secure his leading role at home, but also serves to bolster his claim to masculine superiority in relation to an idea of the urban male body that is feminized as "easily beaten down, like women," even while he recognizes that "urban people look down upon us *bangbang*." Although there are *bangbang* who lament their poor education and express their desire for "brain work," most whom I met regarded intellectual work as entailing physical weakness and a shameful state for men. *Bangbang* also adopt the "tough guy" ideal to justify the value of their manual labor. One day during my fieldwork, I was taking photo of a group of *bangbang* men. One *bangbang* onlooker yelled to those in front of my camera, "Are you scholars? You look so weak! You should all hold the poles in your hands and show off the masculine vigor of us Chongqing men!" All the *bangbang* in the picture agreed with this and acted in the way he suggested. This episode suggests that *bangbang* regard intellectual workers as physically weak and thus not masculine at all. For a man to be a *man,* he must be tough and strong. Thus, doing a manual job is understood as expressing the right way of being masculine.

Interestingly, almost all the *bangbang* I interviewed preferred working as *bangbang* to doing other manual work (even if they may temporarily take up other paid physical work), because *bangbang* work provided them with the valuable *ziyou* (flexibility in terms of body movement and work schedule) that other jobs rarely offer. *Ziyou* does not mean that the *bangbang* can do whatever they want, rather that they have more ability to choose. As Big Brother Mo's story suggests, labor relations between employers and employees in most rural men's manual work involves a high level of disciplinary pressure—low wages, harsh and unhealthy working conditions, long hours, and constant supervision. For rural men like Mo, what is most painful and unendurable is the bodily control that challenges his masculine pride, not only on the shop floor but also in his personal life. Even when he wanted to fulfill his obligations as a father, he had to ask his boss and was threatened with losing his job. In contrast, *bangbang* work seems to provide these working men more flexibility, dignity, and a sense of control. Elsewhere, I have argued that the notion of *ziyou,* which is also promoted by the state, should be understood as playing a significant role in facilitating rural migrants' subject formation, transforming them into self-reliant and enterprising laborers and thus making them vulnerable to fierce exploitation and job insecurity (Zhang 2008). In Lisa Hoffman's (2006, 553) words, "freedom is not indicative of the absence of power or governance but is a technique of governing where the regulation and management of subjects happens 'through freedom.'" While this argument stills remains true in the case of *bangbang,* the other side of the same story is also true—the nature of *bangbang* work is unique in that it somehow empowers the laborers in providing them flexibility and a sense of control. As Mo proudly announced, "I'm my own boss."

Interestingly, a relatively higher-income urban job did not sound attractive to Mo because it lacks *ziyou* (he would have to obey the "discipline of the *danwei*"). In my interviews with *bangbang,* many of them criticized urban office workers for their subordination to *danwei* cadres. One *bangbang* poignantly mocked: "They (the urban office workers) have to lick their cadres' boots to get promoted! I wouldn't do such a girlish thing!" His words imply that the self-employed nature of *bangbang* work suggests a sense of manliness, as opposed to urban office jobs that potentially compromise men's masculine power and pride. As C. T. Hsia (1968, 75–114) points out, historically, *wu* heroes such as Wu Song[5] are more likely to be peasants, and always had few restraints on their bodily control and discipline, while *wen* men were required to observe elaborate Confucian formalities. Although it may be far-fetched to reduce the *bangbang* men's prioritization of *ziyou* to this *wu* tradition of the prototypical rural men, I repeatedly heard *bangbang* talking about the *wu* heroes of the *All Men Are Brothers*-type stories, and gasping in admiration at the free will the heroes embody, which implies a possible influence of the *wu* ideal on rural men's imagining of *ziyou*. It is still unclear to what extent and in what ways the Western notion of independence and the self-made man may come into play in *bangbang* men's perception of *ziyou* and independence. However, with the gradual collapse of the job assignment system, the erosion of *danwei* culture, and the flourishing of the talent market[6] (*rencai shichang*) in contemporary China, the ideas of free will and independence have permeated urban culture.

However, it would be dangerous to overemphasize *bangbang* men's masculine confidence in their solid bodies, *ziyou,* and independence. In my interviews, some *bangbang* admitted that they dared not confront long-term employers and officials, even when these urban residents insulted them. One *bangbang* bitterly confessed: "I can easily beat them (annoying employers and officials) down, but how can I break my rice bowl (as a result of beating them)?" Some urban locals told me that *bangbang* men's *ziyou*, their seemingly uncontrolled free movement, worries them. A few urban residents I met attributed the rising urban crime rate to the free movement of *bangbang*. "Who can tell if they will kill somebody or rape an (urban) woman? They just run away!" I was told. During my stay in Chongqing, the local government launched several compelling programs to "put them [*bangbang*] straight," such as establishing a labor registration system in some supermarkets and organizing freelance *bangbang* into groups. However, most *bangbang* expressed their dissatisfaction with these governmental strategies. They felt they were further marginalized by the labor registration system because it not only injures their *ziyou,* but also makes them vulnerable to manipulation by urban supervisors.

Conclusion

This chapter argues that while historians have tried hard to incorporate gender and feminist scholarship into historical studies, it is also important for contemporary studies of gender to take history into account, especially the historical shifts of the meanings of gender ideals that contribute to individuals' gendered experiences. The coexistence of competing and incongruous meanings of Chinese masculinity that have been in historical flux has been appropriated, affirmed, reproduced, and contested by rural migrant men through their migratory experience, leading to the elaboration of new models of urban subjectivity. The *bangbang* men's sense of self is subject to various forms of urban degradation and disintegration due to their relatively unprivileged economic and social status and the type of work that they do. However, migration also provides opportunities for them to claim and reassert their masculine pride in manual labor and thus to contest the degrading urban discourse on rural migrant men. Adapting Martin Manalansan's (2003) argument concerning shifting Filipino gay identity in New York City, I argue that *bangbang* men's sense of self is not that of the sacrificing, contributing heroes in the story of Chinese urbanization, nor are they mere victims of perpetual displacement, marginalization, and oppression. They are culturally and socially constructed subjects influenced by class, gender, education, migration status, the rural-urban division, and the legacy of historical constructions of masculine ideals that they rework, reinvent, and appropriate within a contemporary context.

Notes and References

1. New Youth was an idea that served as a model for educated youth during the May Fourth Movement, in opposition to the traditional Confucian idea of youth. The New Youth understanding of the difference between the (superior) West and the East was that the West valued youth, whereas the East venerated age. Their mission was to get rid of the old and bring in the young.

2. The root-seeking literature movement was a literary trend during the mid-1980s in China. It was led by a group of fiction writers such as Han Shaogong, A Cheng, Mo Yan, and Zhang Chengzhi. These writers were influenced by the magical realism of Borges and Marquez, and thus explored local and traditional cultures to gain insights into the virtues of the present society and to redefine self-consciousness rooted in tradition. The use of magical realism and the affirmation of literary subjectivity sets root-seeking literature off from the previous realistic mode of writing. Many root-seeking literature works have allowed Chinese literature to re-entry world literature and cinema, notably Mo Yan's famous novel *Red Sorghum*.

3. In this chapter I have used pseudonyms in order to protect *bangbang* informants.

4. *Danwei*, normally translated as "work unit" in English, is an urban unit of production that emerged in the early years of the Maoist China. A *danwei* usually includes one or more walled compounds, protected by guards. A *danwei* can include workshops, residential buildings, clinics, bathhouses, child care centers, and even schools. *Danwei* of this sort was the institution around which most urban Chinese's daily lives were organized, and goods and materials were distributed, during the Maoist period. Post-Mao China's economic reforms in urban areas have led to the gradual collapse of the social institution of *danwei* (Harrell 2001, 144).

5. Wu Song is one of the protagonists in the classical Chinese novel, *All Men Are Brothers*, by Shi Nai'an and Luo Guanzhong, a story about 108 outlaw heroes (mainly men) who would take "a knife in the ribs for a mate" (Louie 2002, 79) and who live at the margins of Song soci-

ety (960–1127 AD). Wu Song is famous for his extraordinary physical strength and bravery. The most notorious episode that demonstrates his strength tells how he slew a tiger even after he had gotten drunk.

6. Talent markets are places where people with higher education and skills gather information, search for job opportunities, and meet with employers.

Anagnost, Ann. 2004. "The Corporal Politics of Quality (*Suzhi*)." *Public Culture* 16 (2): 189–208.

Cheng, Cliff. 1996. *Masculinities in Organizations.* Thousand Oaks, CA: Sage.

Clatterbaugh, Kenneth. 1990. *Contemporary Perspectives on Masculinity: Men, Women and Politics in Modern Society.* Boulder, CO: Westview Press.

Cohen, Myron L. 1994. "Cultural and Political Inventions in Modern China: The Case of the Chinese 'Peasant.'" *Daedalus* 122 (2): 151–170.

Constable, Nicole. 1997. *Maid to Order in Hong Kong: Stories of Filipina Workers.* Ithaca, NY: Cornell University Press.

———. 2014. *Born Out of Place: Migrant Mothers and the Politics of International Labor.* Berkeley: University of California Press.

Donaldson, Mike, and Raymond Hibbins, eds. 2009. *Migrant Men: Critical Studies of Masculinities and the Migration Experience.* London: Routledge.

Gamburd, Michele Ruth. 2000. *The Kitchen Spoon's Handle: Transnationalism and Sri Lanka's Migrant Housemaids.* Ithaca, NY: Cornell University Press.

George, Sheba. 2000. "'Dirty Nurses' and 'Men Who Play': Gender and Class in Transnational Migration." In *Global Ethnography: Forces, Connections and Imaginations in a Post Modern World,* edited by M. Burawoy et al., pp. 144–174. Berkeley: University of California Press.

Glosser, Susan L. 2002. "'The Truths I Have Learned': Nationalism, Family Reform, and Male Identity in China's New Culture Movement, 1915–1923." In *Chinese Femininities/Chinese Masculinities: A Reader,* edited by Susan Brownell and Jeffrey N. Wasserstrom, pp. 120–144. Berkeley: University of California Press.

Goldring, L. 2001. "The Gender and Geography of Citizenship in Mexico-U.S. Transnational Spaces." *Identities* 7: 501–537.

Gutmann, Matthew C. 2006. *The Meanings of Macho: Being a Man in Mexico City (Men and Masculinity).* 2nd ed. Berkeley: University of California Press.

Harrell, Stevan. 2001. "The Anthropology of Reform and the Reform of Anthropology: Anthropological Narratives of Recovery and Progress in China." *Annual Review of Anthropology* 30: 139–161.

Hinsch, Bret. 2013. *Masculinities in Chinese History.* New York: Rowman and Littlefield.

Hinton, William. 1983. *Shenfan.* New York: Random House.

Hoffman, Lisa. 2006. "Autonomous Choices and Patriotic Professionalism: On Governmentality in Late-Socialist China." *Economy and Society* 35: 550–570.

Hsia, C. T. 1968. *The Classic Chinese Novel.* New York: Columbia University Press.

Levitt, Peggy. 2001. *The Transnational Villagers.* Berkeley: University of California Press.

Lin Xiaodong. 2013a. *Gender, Modernity and Male Migrant Workers in China: Becoming a 'Modern' Man.* London: Routledge.

———. 2013b. "Chinese Male Peasant Workers and Shifting Masculine Identities in Urban Workspaces." *Gender, Work & Organization* 20 (5): 498–511.

Liu, Jianjin. 2001. "Report on the Employment and Mobility Status of the Chinese Rural Labor Force (1997–98)." In *Research Reports of Chinese Rural Development II*, pp. 103–118. Beijing: Press of Social Sciences Document.

Louie, Kam. 2002. *Theorising Chinese Masculinity: Society and Gender in China.* London: Cambridge University Press.

Manalansan, Martin F. IV. 2003. *Global Divas: Filipino Gay Men in the Diaspora.* Durham, NC: Duke University Press.

Margold, Jane A. 1995. "Narratives of Masculinity and Transnational Migration: Filipino Workers in the Middle East." In *Bewitching Women, Pious Men: Gender and Body Politics in Southeast Asia,* edited by A. Ong and M. G. Peletz, pp. 274–298. Berkeley: University of California Press.

McDowell L. 2000. "Learning to Serve? Employment Aspirations and Attitudes of Young Working-Class Men in an Era of Labour Market Restructuring." *Gender, Place & Culture* 7: 389–417.

Messerschmidt, James W. 1996. "Managing to Kill: Masculinities and the Space Shuttle Challenger Explosion." In *Masculinities in Organizations,* edited by C. Cheng, pp. 29–53. Thousand Oaks, CA: Sage.

Mills, Mary Beth. 2003. *Thai Women in the Global Labor Force: Consuming Desires, Contested Selves.* New Brunswick, NJ: Rutgers University Press.

Newman, Katherine S. 1999. *Falling from Grace: Downward Mobility in the Age of Affluence.* Berkeley: University of California Press.

Osella, Caroline, and F. Osella. 2000. "Migration, Money and Masculinity in Kerala." *Journal of the Royal Anthropological Institute* 6: 115–131.

Parrenas, Rhacel Salazar. 2000. *Servants of Globalization: Women, Migration and Domestic Work.* Stanford, CA: Stanford University Press.

Rofel, Lisa. 1999. *Other Modernities: Gendered Yearnings in China after Socialism.* Berkeley: University of California Press.

Pun, Ngai. 2005. *Made in China: Women Factory Workers in a Global Workplace.* Durham, NC: Duke University Press.

Song, Geng. 2004. *The Fragile Scholar: Power and Masculinity in Chinese Culture.* Hong Kong: Hong Kong University Press.

Song, Geng, and Derek Hird. 2013. *Men and Masculinities in Contemporary China.* Leiden, the Netherlands: Brill.

Wang, Yiyan. 2003. "Mr. Butterfly in Defunct Capital: 'Soft' Masculinity and (Mis)engendering China." In *Asian Masculinities: The Meaning and Practice of Manhood in China and Japan,* edited by Kam Louie and Morris Low, pp. 41–58. London: RoutledgeCurzon.

Yan, Hairong. 2003. "Spectralization of the Rural: Reinterpreting the Labor Mobility of Rural Young Women in Post-Mao China." *American Ethnologist* 30 (4): 578–619.

———. 2008. *New Masters, New Servants: Migration, Development, and Women Workers in China.* Durham, NC: Duke University Press.

Yang, Mayfair Meihui. 1999. "From Gender Erasure to Gender Differences: State Feminism, Consumer Sexuality, and Women's Public Sphere in China." In *Spaces of Their Own: Women's Public Sphere in Transnational China,* edited by Mayfair Meihui Yang, pp. 35–67. Minneapolis: University of Minnesota Press.

Zhang, Everette Yuehong. 2001. "Goudui and the State: Constructing Entrepreneurial Masculinity in Two Cosmopolitan Areas in Southwest China." In *Gendered Modernities: An Ethnographic Perspective,* edited by D. Hodgson, pp. 235–266. New York: Palgrave.

Zhang, Li. 2001. *Strangers in the City: Reconfigurations of Space, Power, and Social Networks within China's Floating Population.* Stanford, CA: Stanford University Press.

Zhang, Xia. 2008. "Ziyou (Freedom), Occupational Choice, and Labor: *Bangbang* in Chongqing, People's Republic of China." *International Labor and Working-Class History* 73: 65–84.

Zheng, Tiantian. 2006. "Cool Masculinity: Male Clients' Sex Consumption and Business Alliance in Urban China's Sex Industry." *Journal of Contemporary China* 15 (45): 161–182.

———. 2007. "Embodied Masculinity: Sex and Sport in a (Post) Colonial Chinese City." *China Quarterly* 190: 432–450.

———. 2009. *Red Lights: The Lives of Sex Workers in Post-Socialist China.* Minneapolis: University of Minnesota Press.

———. 2012. "Female Subjugation and Political Resistance: From Literati to Entrepreneurial Masculinity in the Globalizing Era of Post-socialist China." *Gender, Place & Culture* 19(5): 652–669.

Zhong, Xueping. 2000. *Masculinity Besieged? Issues of Modernity and Male Subjectivity in Chinese Literature of the Late Twentieth Century.* Durham, DC: Duke University Press.

CHAPTER EIGHT

Boyz II Men

Neighborhood Associations in Western India as the
Site of Masculine Identity

MADHURA LOHOKARE

In this chapter I elaborate upon local neighborhood associations (*mandals*) in Pune,[1] Western India, as crucial sites that mediate the performance of their young male members' class-, place-, and caste-specific masculine identities. In the light of the acute marginalization of working-class boys and young men from a rapidly neoliberalizing urban space, belonging to a *mandal* provides space for them to project a collective self-image that is geared toward upholding a class-based moral code. I demonstrate how this identity is consolidated not just via cultural activities of the *mandal,* but more importantly through the realm of local electoral politics, which has become an integral part of the terrain of *mandals* in the context of Pune.

Attempting to address a huge gap in our understanding of the making of gendered relations in South Asia, scholarly focus since the 2000s has sought to theorize construction of masculine identities through ethnographic documentation spanning arenas as diverse as work (De Neve 2004; Ray 2000), engagement with and representation in cinema (Mazumdar 2001; Osella and Osella 2004), migration (Osella and Osella 2006), caste and education (C. Jeffrey 2010; C. Jeffrey, P. Jeffrey, and R. Jeffery 2008; Rogers 2008), and politics (Hansen 2001; C. Jeffrey 2010). A large section of the above research in fact focuses on the lifeworlds of marginalized urban men, illustrating how their gendered self-making is circumscribed by formations of caste and class that are articulated in a grammar specific to the urban form as it continues to evolve in a rapidly neoliberalizing South Asia.

Locating the city as a space of anxiety and loss (of power/agency), a condition that has been exacerbated by the neoliberal policies that mark Indian cities today, the aforementioned body of research illustrates men's recuperative strategies via realms of consumption (Favero 2003; Lukose 2009), local politics (Hansen 2001; Roy 2008), sexuality (Srivastava 2004), or via developing city skills (McDuie-Ra 2014). I locate this chapter within this emergent literature as it seeks to trace the contours of a masculine identity that is produced and enacted in the class-specific practice of "publicness" in urban India. I contend that the masculine ideals extolled and aspired toward in the *mandals* need necessarily to be viewed through the ways they are articulated to the disempowerment of the *mandal* members in their class and caste contexts of neoliberal Pune. I illustrate the ways in which the realm of politics is enmeshed with formations of gender and class on the site of associational culture in the city of Pune to produce distinct contours of masculine identity for working-class men; I also demonstrate how this process of construction of masculinity is a response to the expectations and aspirations generated by globalization in urban India.

In the first section of the chapter I locate the *mandal* at the intersection of the spatial, political, civic, and religious axes of the city's life in order to situate my examination of the peculiar masculinity that is shaped in *mandal* spaces. I then introduce the context of the working-class neighborhood in the city of Pune. The three sections that follow present ethnographic data on discourses and activities of the *mandal* as a site of performance of a masculine identity for its male members. These sections focus on the marginalization of the young men from the city's social and economic life, and frame their recuperative strategies.

The *Mandal* and Its Historical Roots

The *mitra mandal* (or *mandal*), which is Marathi for "a collective of *male* friends," is a highly localized entity, which represents a spatially bounded community such as a residential cluster or an alley. Each neighborhood or slum in cities across western Maharashtra generally has one or more *mandals,* run exclusively by male members. The city of Pune has a strongly entrenched public culture of *mandals* organized by religious or community-specific groups, including Muslim and Dalit communities. The network of *mandals* is far denser in the poorer parts of the city as compared to their numbers in middle-class residential neighborhoods, suggesting the distinct class profile of this subculture.

The historical origin of *mandals* can be traced to the culture of voluntary associations that emerged in late-nineteenth-century colonial India. Initiated by the emergent indigenous bourgeoisie, these associations transformed the Hindu religious concept of giving (*dana*) via philanthropy and service (*seva*) into nation-building activities and provided youth with an important space to enter public life (Watt 2005). The notions of disinterested, selfless social service that underlay the associations' activities came to epitomize exemplary nationalist commitment, active citizenship, and civic engagement for its participants (Kidambi 2007; Watt 2005). Recent research confirms that the ideal of civic participation and citizenship and notions of the "public" in postindependence India continues to be mediated heavily by participation in religio-cultural activities (Copeman 2009; Hancock and Srinivas 2008; Waghorne 2004).

The *mandals* in Pune are located precisely within this discourse of "publicness"; an emphasis on apolitical selfless service to the community, the range of religio-cultural activities that constitute this service, and the moral capital credited to it continues to shape the identity and the activities of *mandals* in contemporary Pune. These activities include celebrating religious festivals and national holidays, feeding pilgrims, organizing blood donation camps, running a gymnasium/library, writing civic messages on notice boards, and organizing minor financial help for neighborhood members.

Despite the fact that *mandals* are highly localized entities, hitherto research has paid scant attention to the spatialized dimension of their activities. I contend that the *mandal*-neighborhood complex as a physical-moral space forms a significant basis for self-definition of the members of the *mandal* as well as of the neighborhood. Often residents of a neighborhood engage with and construct the temporal and spatial rhythms of their area via the medium of the *mandal* and its activities. For instance, buildings housing a *mandal's* temple, the adjoining sitting spaces, or gymnasium typically act as hubs for men of the neighborhood to get together in the evenings or for children to play around, and at times for women to hold their self-help group meetings. These everyday uses of *mandal* spaces often obliterate the physical distinction between the *mandal* and the neighborhood.

More crucially, the *mandal* and the neighborhood are fused in the residents' perceptions not just in spatial terms; the social value and moral capital earned by the *mandal* via its religious and social work is easily transferrable to the neighborhood as well. The upshot of this fluidity of boundaries between the *mandal* and the neighborhood is a scenario in which the *mandal* membership and its functioning are acutely enmeshed with the social relationships contained within the neighborhood and the caste/community alliances therein.

Last, *mandals,* as highly localized and integrated sociospatial entities, are crucial actors in local electoral politics in contemporary Pune, providing political parties with access to local caste-/religion-based constituencies, opportunities for networking, and an ideal platform for launching populist schemes and mobilizing youth in the city.[2]

To the extent that the *mandal* inhabits the domain of the "public," which in its historical, performative, and spatial context itself has been cast in masculine terms, it is primarily certain kinds of masculine forms of mobility and sociality that make possible the existence and functioning of a *mandal*. A *mandal* then is not merely an exclusively male space in the city's landscape; rather I contend that *mandals,* as sociospatial entities situated at the intersection of politics, locality, and religion, are profoundly *masculine* in their very structure and their self-definition. By implication then, the fact of belonging to a *mandal* itself bestows a masculine identity on its members, idealized in the image of the *mandal* and the nature of its work.

The following statement by a president of one Pune *mandal*, Naresh, reveals in most unequivocal terms how *mandal* members' identity is tightly enmeshed with the *vasti* (settlement or slum) space and the *mandal* as a masculine entity: "*Mandal* is us. *Mandal* is our area. If the *mandal*'s name gets tainted, by implication the reputation of boys here gets tainted. Hence the *mandal*'s reputation must stay unblemished." It is this relationship that frames my analysis of the masculine identity that is constructed in *mandal* spaces.

Location/s

This chapter is based upon fieldwork conducted over a period of eighteen months between January 2011 and June 2012 in Siddhartha *mandal*[3] which is located in the central-eastern part of the city. This part of the city is divided into wards traditionally called *peths,* which constituted the original urban core of the city as it developed in the eighteenth century. *Peths* were a complex mix of residential and commercial areas with a distinct caste-based geography: Brahmin-dominated residential *peths* in the west, and lower-caste, Muslim populations inhabiting central and eastern *peths,* which were also hubs of commercial activity and artisan workshops (Gokhale 1988; Kosambi 1989). Remarkably, contemporary *peth* organization retains roughly similar caste and economic geography, with narrow alleyways clogged by traffic and crowded in by haphazard, run-down buildings. *Peth* residents work in the retail and wholesale trades, as public sector employees, domestic laborers, petty traders, or self-employed skilled and unskilled workers (Benninger 1998).

The term *poorva bhag* ("eastern part," used to refer to the non-Brahminical *peths*) is still a loaded term: characterized as being *magaslela* (backward) or a slum area, the *poorva bhag* clearly indexes the lower-caste/working-class/Muslim profile of these *peths*. Siddhartha *mandal* encompassed a rather well-demarcated neighborhood largely referred to as Shelar *galli,*[4] in Moti Peth, consisting of approximately sixty households. A majority of the households in this *galli* were Matang, a Scheduled Caste,[5] and had migrated to Pune between the 1940s and the 1960s, driven by drought in the Solapur region in southeast Maharashtra.

Remarkably, at least one senior member from each of the households here held a permanent government job as a sweeper with the city's civic body. The younger men were mostly employed in unskilled minor jobs, like delivery boys, as salesmen in shops, or simply helped their parents with the sweeping. It was this group of men who were the members of Siddhartha *mandal* and were in charge of its activities, which mainly included celebration of the ten-day-long Ganesh festival and events like Independence Day and the birth anniversary of Annabhau Sathe (an important icon for Matangs across Maharashtra). Siddhartha *mandal* had twenty to twenty-five active members between the ages sixteen and thirty-five, all of whom were residents of Shelar *galli*.

Moral Masculinities

As I showed earlier, the *mandal* itself is identified with its members in insepara-ble ways. In this section I highlight how the discourse around a *mandal* in con-junction with the everyday practices of its members predicated on this discourse generated idealized images of masculine identity, undergirded by a fundamen-tally class- and caste-based morality. More specifically, the moral value of help-ing others and of being able to maintain unity among themselves constituted the bedrock of values supporting the *mandal.* I contend that these values produced a profoundly moral masculine ideal that all the members strived (or failed) to achieve through specific *mandal* activities and via their everyday social relation-ships in the *vasti.*

Most members of *mandals* were emphatic about the notion of helping others. For Kasbe *kaka* (a senior *mandal* member), running a *mandal* entailed looking after the basic needs of the people affiliated with the *mandal:* ensuring the basic level of amenities in the neighborhood, drainage lines, clean water, helping needy students, etc. "One should be conscious toward one's duty toward others in their times of joy and grief," he said. For Kartik, treasurer of the *mandal* at the time of my fieldwork, the primary objective of the *mandal* was to bring people together and consolidate their "relation." "If the *mandal* does not exist, no one will even bother about what is happening to others," he explained. The categories of *madat* (help) included helping the needy get to the hospital, minor financial help in cases of crisis, helping needy students to continue their education, and providing space/material help for family celebrations.

Remarkably, while describing how they put this ideal into practice, most men spoke passionately about extending selfless *madat* to those in a health crisis: Ra-tilal narrated an incident about the death of a HIV-positive woman in the *vasti* and his courageous role in taking care of her last rites when no one was even ready to touch her body. Atul spoke, not without pride, about his taking care of a badly burned man in his *vasti* and carrying another neighbor in his arms after the latter collapsed in the *vasti* due to a sudden paralytic stroke. Kiran told me how he drove down a busy main street in the city at breakneck speed, clearing the traffic ahead of him to make way for a speeding van carrying a neighbor who had tried to commit suicide, despite having had a conflict with him.

While these narratives represent deeply class-based understandings of *madat,* revealing the fundamental dependence of working-class lives on social networks of physical and financial support and communal resources, the self-image of the young men in extending this valued help was unmistakably heroic, with an element of drama to it.

In light of the moral value attached to *madat,* failure to extend it was judged harshly, especially as it showed a *mandal* in a poor light. The younger boys pointed out how people in the neighboring settlement or the neighboring Jaihind *mandal* never help each other; in fact it was their *mandal* boys who helped those in need there, they claimed. "Annabhau Sathe himself has made us like this, the way he fought for others." Here the notion of *madat* as a voluntary task of arbitration in local conflicts was transformed into a caste attribute, inculcated in the *mandal* members by the legacy of the most important icon for Matangs in Maharashtra, Annabhau Sathe.

The mental map of Moti Peth for most of the men consisted of the cluster of *mandals,* the caste/linguistic communities that they indexed, and their own performance on the helpful/uniting criteria. These *mandals* figured prominently in the members' attempts to establish their own caste identity as united or helpful or righteous. Thus Nadepalli settlement, populated mostly by Telugu-speaking weavers from the Sali caste, was a "selfish" community, where no one helped each other. Most members of the Tiranga *mandal,* associated with the Bairagi caste, engaged in petty theft and were cheats. Jaihind *mandal* in neighboring Ward 755 was particularly crucial in this spatial exercise of self-definition: it was also primarily a Matang *mandal,* but it was located in a much more destitute slum and was constantly highlighted as a den of vice and immorality, thus allowing other Matang *mandals* to claim moral superiority based on their lack of vices, addictions, and abusive language. Class, gender, place, and caste considerations were thus woven together to create an ideal of *madat,* which the boys internalized and learnt to respect and idealize in the physical and social context of the *mandal-vasti* complex.

The ability to maintain the *eki* (unity) of the *mandal* and stick by each other through hard times was another ideal that occupied a vital place in the moral world of members: "Our *mandal* boys may not attend each other's wedding, but they will definitely attend their funeral," went the axiom. The need to keep the *mandal* space free of personal conflicts/politics was an overwhelming concern that all the men I interviewed aired strongly. This, was however, more an ideal than a reality; the young men's consistent reference to this concern indexed precisely the fact that this ideal was not being fulfilled. Indeed, over the last decade, this *mandal* had been beleaguered by factions contesting ownership of land in the neighborhood. Nostalgia for the *mandal* as it was when they were growing up was common, a time that was characterized by unprecedented unity in the *mandal* and high-quality activities.

Despite the repeated assurances of the men on these matters, the intensity with which the failure to achieve *eki* was condemned was a striking indicator of the continued anxiety that factions aroused among all *mandal* members. Kartik gave his verdict while talking about the lack of unity in his *mandal:* "Our *mandal* is almost closed down now. It has just one objective, gambling and enjoyment. Let the work go to hell." The discourse of *eki* in the *mandal* and the reactions to its failure was telling. The constant refrain of keeping one's selfish interests out of the *mandal* implied that the *mandal* was indeed a site of a collective good and collective interest, central to life in the working-class context of Moti Peth. The *mandal* thus represented a concrete sense of "publicness," the failure to achieve which was often highlighted with morally suspect acts such as selfishness, drinking, or gambling.

This notion of the *mandal* as a public domain with a class-defined morality was also a gendered notion: the referents of the ideal *mandal* being defined by the starkly masculine roles of extending *madat* at all occasions and time, bringing together the neighborhood through their programs, and the ability to negotiate differences in the electoral political domain. Historical research has demonstrated the unmistakable masculine contours of an idea of the public that emerged in colonial India, where the discourses of cultural nationalism, citizenship and publicness itself were cast in terms of upper-caste, middle-class male ideals (Chakrabarty 1991; Chatterjee 1993; Das 2007; Hansen 1999). Thus the morality associated with the public domain of *mandals* is cast in masculine terms and becomes the yardstick for evaluating the performance of the members, on which their identity strongly hinges.

Chopra, Osella, and Osella (2004, 28) contend that the performance of masculinity is not always directed toward an audience of women, but in fact performed in the "evaluative presence other men." According to them, "The relations between men in all-male contexts are of critical importance to establish masculinity" (ibid.). In their efforts to demonstrate their successful upholding of the masculinized values of *madat* and *eki* underlying the *mandal* (often in comparison to the failure of others to do the same), members simultaneously referenced and shaped the contours of a masculine ideal in the *galli.* The values constituting the *mandal* were transformed into a site of contest and competition among an all-male audience, evocative of the shop floor competition among migrant workers in Delhi analyzed by Ramaswami (2006) or the competitive displays of "manly" skills in coffee houses elaborated in Herzfeld (1985) and de Almeida (1996). Based upon their evaluations of their own and others' performances of *eki* and *madat*, *mandal* members drew upon the existing gendered discourses in their larger context, thus defining for themselves the outline of an ideal manhood.

Doing Politics

Research in recent times has confirmed the value that "doing politics" has acquired in the lower-class, lower-caste context of contemporary India. C. Jeffrey et al. (2008) demonstrate how local, low-caste (male) youth in rural North India respond to unemployment by establishing themselves as *netas* (political leaders), engaging in local political brokering and networking, which provides the young men with a model of masculinity that incorporates the value of education, earning them respect. In the context of local politics, Roy (2008) points to similar "practices of patronage and mobilization" (107), cast in primarily masculinized idioms, thus leading to the *masculinization of politics* (106–118) in the context of urban India.

Lukose (2009) contends that the essentially masculine contours of political action in urban Kerala makes it an ideal site for the assertion of lower-class masculinity in a bid to resist the increasing predominance of middle-class activism in defining the "public." Similarly, Hansen (2001, 105–113) demonstrates how the militant right-wing party Shiv Sena, in order to establish their stronghold on the city, effectively harnessed the aspirations and hopes of boys from poorer backgrounds, for whom being a part of the political party was instrumental in gaining money, power, and status. While the above instances overlap in differing degrees with the notion of the "political society" (Chatterjee 2004), the acutely masculine terrain of this domain has given rise to a remarkable constellation of politics and masculine identity across various contexts in India.

Reflecting this trend, *mandals* in Pune over the last decade have consolidated a crucial position in the political society of Pune, serving as nodes for increasing party cadres and mobilizing large-scale support, based on their presence in specific caste- or religion-based neighborhoods. In this section I describe how celebrations of the *mandal* serve as sites par excellence for establishing and fine-tuning political alliances and what it means for the young men's gendered identities to be the active engineers of these alliances.

Contributions from political parties formed a chunk of funding for all the major celebrations conducted by the *mandal* and the pre-festival discussions around funding tended to be charged and contentious. A few weeks before a major celebration dedicated to Ganesh, one *mandal's* members had a passionate discussion about accepting a large amount of money from the local Congress Party. Interestingly, the hotly debated issue did not revolve around accepting the money but around accepting money from a single political party, which would require an explicit declaration of the *mandal's* allegiance to that party and openly canvassing for the party during the elections. In this regard, the *mandal* members took great pride in claiming that the *mandal* as a collective had never openly "sold" itself to one party. In Randhir's words, "No flag of one political party will ever fly on our *mandal* roof!"

In my interview with the younger members of the *mandal,* they admitted candidly to their election agenda of making maximum monetary profits from the well-established practice of buying and selling votes. But at the same time they vehemently denied any intention of the entire *mandal* to work for a single political party. According to them, "Tomorrow no one should turn around and say, you work under our control." The upshot of the negotiations was that the major celebrations of the *mandal* were all sponsored jointly by the political parties who had stakes in Moti Peth, as the young men negotiated in smaller groups with political parties in order to gain what they could during the elections.

The meetings between emissaries of political parties and *mandal* members were often arranged by a senior member; negotiating with party candidates required a certain level of experience and an astute sense of judgment on the part of the negotiators. The job of meeting with party candidates itself was taken as evidence that the men were in that position because of their well-established networks that they could harness and thus make a difference in the local political equation.

I witnessed one such meeting, between the *mandal* members and a female candidate of a rising political party; we crowded into her election headquarters late in the night to strike the final election deal, two days before the election. After an awkwardly silent few moments, Ravi, one of the senior members, spoke up: "Not a single vote from our area will betray you. We are not asking anything for ourselves, but the younger boys wish to take a trip." There was a cautionary tone in Ravi's voice as he warned the candidate that the emissaries from the rival party were constantly hovering around the *galli.* For me, this meeting condensed multiple facets of the basic grammar of the world of effective political bargaining. Ravi's brief speech included the right combination of an assurance of support, a disclaimer of selflessness, and a degree of pressure in the form of the cautionary intimation about the rival emissaries. It also clearly followed the internal hierarchy within the *mandal:* the senior members, projecting a more mature, disinterested front, were speaking on behalf of their younger brothers. The qualities of an astute political player at the level of the *mandal* that emerged from these instances were indistinguishable from an idealized manhood, given the exclusively male terrain of the *mandal.*

During the election period the *galli* provided a site for the *mandal* members to project and perform a persona that exuded knowledge, judgment, and expertise in the realm of politics in the *vasti,* as they described animatedly facts and trivia about the election. Opinions and critical evaluations were offered about certain wards in the city as strongholds of particular political parties, arch rivalries in specific wards, caste-specificities of different areas of the city, the variety of sops and money pumped into other wards, and so on. When viewed through the predictable and familiar idiom of wards and local political competition, the city itself became more *legible;* thus this projection and performance enabled a distinct sense of mastery over the grammar of a space that was not just limited to the *galli* or Moti Peth, but which temporarily took in the entire city in its spread. Their engagement with local politics via the *mandal* and its activities constructed for the men a space where they could project empowered (if only temporary) self-images as *mandal* members who could expertly navigate the fine nuances of local political equations.

Most of members admitted that it was precisely working in the *mandal* that had equipped them with the confidence and judgment necessary to deal with this "outside world" of politics. As Vivek put it: "Working in the *mandal* one learns how to behave with others, how to recognize people." In Vinit's words, "One gets recognition through *mandal* and also learns the whole package of good people with bad people."

I contend that the rhetoric of the *mandal* "not being under any outsider's thumb" was central for members because it represented a reconciliation between their desire to engage in a local politics that the hegemonic discourse had branded fundamentally corrupt and anti-democratic but which provided them with a strong sense of value and agency (even if it was in the temporary events of negotiating for votes or during celebrations and elections), and their imperative to preserve a sense of pride and self-respect (through the image of being incorruptible). In the light of their individual choices, it was important to derive a sense of the *mandal* as the site of their collective identity staying "clean" and incorruptible.

Recuperating Power, Seeking Dignity

For members of Siddhartha *mandal,* the need to preserve pride and self-respect was borne out of an acute sense of disempowerment and the realization of lack of respect from the world outside Moti Peth. In this section I illustrate how their inability to participate in the neoliberal ethos of consumption and aspiration was articulated by the *mandal* members in idioms of disempowerment and highlight how *mandal* activities served as a site to build a counternarrative to this sense of powerlessness.

Most of the *mandal's* members were school dropouts, having quit school due to poverty or lack of interest. Now underemployed in unskilled jobs or unemployed, there was an acute recognition of having missed the opportunities that education would have offered to them. Against the contemporary Indian context in which education is celebrated as a ticket to modernity and social mobility and proficiency in English is associated with enormous material and symbolic hegemony, their lack of English skills generated profound feelings of humiliation and inadequacy among the members. Kiran, himself educated till the tenth grade, described a scenario wherein the uneducated young men could order something to eat from a street vendor, but would be helpless in a Kentucky Fried Chicken (KFC) outlet, where the menu was written in English. Arun also underlined their inability to place an order in a mall and the resultant shame that his uneducated peers felt on account of their nonexistent English skills.

Their lack of education engendered an inability not just to *consume,* but also to participate in an aspirational ethos that increasingly rewarded only certain kinds of service-oriented labor as dignified and respectable. Several young members who would eventually inherit their parents' sweeping jobs faced the prospect of performing labor that was highly stigmatized: Prasad and Atul candidly admitted to me that they felt exposed and ashamed by having to sweep the streets in full view of upper-class girls or better-off peers. Satish termed such work "hard work" as opposed to the more respectable "smart work"; he emphasized that the young men in the *mandal* were unable to break into the world of smart work owing to their lack of education.

Lukose (2009) and Rogers (2008) both point toward the processes through which working-class and lower-caste youth in urban India experience intense pressure to conform to idealized images of fashionable, consuming white-collar workers/citizens, a direct consequence of the rapid political and economic changes accompanying India's globalization. The anxieties generated by their inability to consume (in KFC or a mall) and to participate in smart work for the *mandal* members are a clear testament to the centrality the realm of consumption has attained vis-à-vis discourses of social identity in contemporary India, and to their simultaneous failure to attain this ideal due to their entrenched caste and class disadvantages.

Mandal members' inability to see a future for themselves was a sobering indicator of their sense of disempowerment, notwithstanding their easy swagger and goofing around in the *vasti* spaces. Naresh and Satish enumerated their (lack of) choices to me: they could not muster the capital required for a business, they were unqualified for smart work, and they were scared to venture into illicit business. The possibilities of acquiring employment that would bestow respect, dignity, and "smartness" narrowed down progressively for the young men, perhaps articulated in Ravi's comment, "Our life itself is 'slow'!"

Most striking were members' responses to my question about leaving Moti Peth, if they even had an opportunity to do so. While all of them always fantasized about living in "standard" areas of the city, most of them responded that they would stay in Moti Peth. For Shailesh, leaving was not an option: "If Moti Peth does not develop soon, I will buy a flat somewhere outside, but will not leave Moti Peth," he said. Kartik's rationale for staying in the same area was that "once you go out you meet all sorts. But one's place of origin is always better because one knows everyone there." The reluctance to leave Moti Peth was not just tied to a definite sense of security from *olakh* (knowing everyone) and the assumed network of support that this provided, but also linked to a measure of control that being in the *galli* provided. There was perhaps a realization that Moti Peth is the only place to be for them in the context of the outside city, expressed poignantly in Ravi's comment: "Can we dream of doing outside what we can do in this *galli?* Would we able to talk back if someone were to question us outside?" It was evident that the young men's dreams of gaining a life of dignity and opportunity, and their notions of having a future and gaining respect, were constricted to the space of the *galli* within the cityscape and that their affective worlds were bound tightly to that space.

I argue that it was in this context of members' powerlessness outside of Moti Peth that the attributes of morality or political acumen encoded in *mandals'* activities served to restore a sense of masculine self. Consequently, the *mandal* space became a site for circulation of explicit narratives of power. In their enthusiastic post-Ganesh festival debriefing, tremendous admiration was reserved for the *mandal* run by a flamboyant Hindu right-wing politician, Neeraj Naik. Members admired how he was the only one who had dared to screen in public the Cricket World Cup match between India and Pakistan, when the police had specifically banned all public screenings due to possibility of tensions erupting. When I asked why they all looked up to him so much, Rama said, "He looks after his boys completely, right from their clothes, shoes, and meals." No wonder then that Naik just needed to signal to one of his boys and within a flash he would be surrounded by their protective ring, Anil noted.

Naik, with his impressive personality (*mandal* members said that he always wore a white *kurta* and a beard), was part of an extremely seductive narrative of working-class masculine power, one which commanded unflinching loyalty from the local young men and boys and had the courage to defy authorities. In another instance, the members were enthralled by the story of a Congress Party candidate in the neighboring ward who zoomed through the streets on his Ducati with his cronies in tow and carrying briefcases full of cash to be dispensed freely in order to buy votes. It was rumored that he had gifted six kilograms of silver to each mandal in his ward (a kilogram of silver costs between 57,000–59,000 rupees [$950]). In a ward in Karim nagar, the story went that if you promised to net ten votes for the candidate, the reward was a motorbike; if you promised twenty-five, the reward was a car. These stories acquired almost a mythical quality, as they circulated among an eager audience of young men in the *galli* during the election period. Narratives like these were not just about admiring a hypermasculine image, but deeply enmeshed with stories of consumption and the power of money, which was flaunted unabashedly, almost crassly. Such power was only accessible to the *mandal* members through these legends of obscene excess.

Conclusion: Articulating *Mandals* to Masculinity

This chapter has attempted to locate the recuperative practices of low-caste young men in urban India as they cope with loss of confidence and control, a cumulative consequence of their caste and class vulnerability and the neoliberal imaginaries of aspiration and consumption that saturate Indian cities today. The erosion of marginalized men's sense of masculinity can thus be situated at the intersection of political economic changes in a rapidly globalizing India and the new avenues of self-making that have evolved in the wake of these changes.

The *mandal,* via its historical legacy of religious and social work, becomes an appropriate space for projecting masculine ideals directed toward enhancing self-worth and respect for its members in a class-specific context. The porous boundaries between *mandals'* religious activities and local electoral politics further expand this space where members experience a temporary sense of power not just through their active involvement in political negotiations, but also via the narratives of power that circulate through *mandal* spaces across the city. These processes, through which *mandal* members respond to their marginalization, render visible to us the ways in which marginalized men negotiate their gender, caste, and class identities on the terrain of everyday practices of local politics and associational culture.

Notes and References

1. Pune, with a population of 4.5 million (Pune Municipal Corporation 2014), is located in the state of Maharashtra in Western India and is considered as the educational and cultural

center of the state. In the last two decades, the city's economy has embraced the postindustrial, knowledge- and service-oriented activities of multinational-owned information technology hubs and business process outsourcing companies. Similar to several cities in post-1991 India, Pune's physical landscape includes malls, upmarket restaurants, cafés, and multiplex theaters, located largely in the newly developed areas located on the outer fringes of the city.

2. See Hansen (2001) for an analysis of how the Hindu right-wing party Shiv Sena effectively harnessed neighborhood *mandals* to establish a strong grassroots base in Mumbai.

3. All names of people and places have been changed in order to protect the identity of the interlocutors. The only place name that has not been changed is that of the city of Pune. Names of political parties have been retained.

4. *Galli* in Marathi refers to a narrow alleyway. Most members of the *mandal* and local residents used *galli* and *vasti* interchangeably to refer to their neighborhood.

5. The term "Scheduled Caste" refers to what were formerly the untouchable castes. The Constitution of India guarantees protection of the rights of members of these castes in its first schedule and also lays down the rules for affirmative action for these castes.

Barnett, Marguerite Ross. 1976. "Competition, Control and Dependency: Urban Politics in Madras City." In *The City in Indian Politics,* edited by D. B. Rosenthal, pp. 94–116. Faridabad, India: Thomson Press.

Benninger, Christopher. 1998. "Pune: The Emergence of a Metropolis." In *Million Cities of India: Growth Dynamics, Internal Structure, Quality of Life and Planning Perspectives,* edited by R. P. Misra and Kamlesh Misra, pp. 236–253. New Delhi: Sustainable Development Foundation.

Chakrabarty, Dipesh. 1991. "Open Space/Public Space: Garbage, Modernity and India." *South Asia* 14 (1): 15–31.

Chatterjee, Partha. 2004. *The Politics of the Governed: Reflections on Popular Politics in Most of the World.* New York: Columbia University Press.

Chopra, Radhika. 2006. "Muted Masculinities: Introduction to the Special Issue on Contemporary Indian Ethnographies." *Men and Masculinities* 9 (2): 127–130.

Chopra, Radhika, Caroline Osella, and Filippo Osella, eds. 2004. *South Asian Masculinities: Context of Change, Sites of Continuity.* New Delhi: Kali for Women and Women Unlimited.

Copeman, Jacob. 2009. "Gathering Points: Blood Donation and the Scenography of 'National Integration' in India." *Body and Society* 15 (2): 71–99.

Das, Veena. 2007. *Life and Words: Violence and the Descent into the Ordinary.* Berkeley: University of California Press.

De Almeida, Miguel V. 1996. *The Hegemonic Male: Masculinity in a Portuguese Town.* Providence, NJ: Berghahn Books.

De Neve, Geert. 2004. "The Workplace and the Neighbourhood: Locating Masculinities in the South Indian Textile Industry." In *South Asian Masculinities: Context of Change, Sites of Continuity,* edited by Radhika Chopra, Caroline Osella, and Filippo Osella, pp. 60–95. New Delhi: Kali for Women and Women Unlimited.

Favero, Paolo. 2003. "Phantasms in a 'Starry' Place: Space and Identification in a Central New Delhi Market." *Cultural Anthropology* 18 (4): 551–584.

Gokhale, B. G. 1988. *Poona in the Eighteenth Century: An Urban History.* Oxford, UK: Oxford University Press.

Hancock, Mary E., and Smriti Srinivas. 2008. "Spaces of Modernity: Religion and the Urban in Asia and Africa." *International Journal of Urban and Regional Research* 32 (3): 617–630.

Hansen, Thomas Blom. 2001. *Wages of Violence: Naming and Identity in Postcolonial Bombay.* Princeton, NJ: Princeton University Press.

Herzfeld, Michael. 1985. *The Poetics of Manhood: Contest and Identity in a Cretan Mountain Village.* Princeton, NJ: Princeton University Press.

Jeffrey, Craig. 2010. *Timepass: Youth, Class, and the Politics of Waiting in India.* Stanford, CA: Stanford University Press.

Jeffrey, Craig, Patricia Jeffery, and Roger Jeffery. 2008. *Degrees without Freedom? Education, Masculinities, and Unemployment in North India.* Stanford, CA: Stanford University Press.

Kidambi, Prashant. 2007. *The Making of an Indian Metropolis: Colonial Governance and Public Culture in Bombay, 1890–1920.* Aldershot, England: Ashgate.

Kosambi, Meera. 1989. "Glory of Peshwa Pune." *Economic and Political Weekly* 24 (5): 247–250.

Lukose, Ritty. 2009. *Liberalization's Children: Gender, Youth, and Consumer Citizenship in Globalizing India.* Durham, NC: Duke University Press.

Mazumdar, Ranjani. 2001. "Figure of the 'Tapori': Language, Gesture and Cinematic City." *Economic and Political Weekly* 36 (52): 4872–4880.

McDuie-Ra, Duncan. 2014. "Being a Tribal Man from the North-East: Migration, Morality and Masculinity." In *Gender and Masculinities: Histories, Texts and Practices in India and Sri Lanka,* edited by A. Doron and A. Broom, pp. 126–148. Delhi: Routledge.

Osella, Caroline, and Filippo Osella. 2004. "Young Malayali Men and Their Movie Heroes." In *South Asian Masculinities: Context of Change, Sites of Continuity,* edited by Radhika Chopra, Caroline Osella, and Filippo Osella, pp. 224–261. New Delhi: Kali for Women and Women Unlimited.

———. 2006. *Men and Masculinities in South India.* London: Anthem Press.

Pune Municipal Corporation. 2014. "About Pune Municipal Corporation." August 26. http://www.punecorporation.org/about_us.aspx.

Ramaswami, Shankar. 2006. "Masculinity, Respect and the Tragic: Themes of Proletarian Humor in Contemporary Industrial Delhi." *International Review of Social History* 51 (S14): 203–227.

Ray, Raka. 2000. "Masculinity, Femininity, and Servitude: Domestic Workers in Calcutta in the Late Twentieth Century." *Feminist Studies* 26 (3): 691–718.

Rogers, Martyn. 2008. "Modernity, 'Authenticity', and Ambivalence: Subaltern Masculinities on a South Indian College Campus." *Journal of the Royal Anthropological Institute* 14: 79–95.

Roy, Ananya. 2008. *Calcutta Requiem: Gender and the Politics of Poverty.* New Delhi: Pearson Education.

Srivastava, Sanjay. 2004. "The Masculinity of Dis-location: Commodities, the Metropolis, and the Sex-Clinics of Delhi and Mumbai." In *South Asian Masculinities: Context of Change, Sites of Continuity,* edited by Radhika Chopra, Caroline Osella, and Filippo Osella, pp. 175–223. New Delhi: Kali for Women and Women Unlimited.

Waghorne, Joanne Punzo. 2004. *Diaspora of the Gods: Modern Hindu Temples in an Urban Middle-Class World.* Oxford, UK: Oxford University Press.

Watt, Carey Anthony. 2005. *Serving the Nation: Cultures of Service, Association, and Citizenship.* New Delhi: Oxford University Press.

CHAPTER NINE

Marriage and Reproduction in East Asian Cities

Views from Single Women in Shanghai, Hong Kong, and Tokyo

LYNNE NAKANO

Rapid economic growth in East Asian societies such as Japan, Hong Kong, China, Singapore, and South Korea has been accompanied by expectations of universal marriage, declining birthrates,[1] low extramarital birthrates,[2] and expectations that upon marriage women bear children and take primary responsibility for a family. This family pattern, however, appears to be challenged by the trend of rising ages at first marriage, resulting in large segments of the population of single women remaining single into their thirties, forties, and beyond. Women are marrying later across East Asia, and most noticeably in the region's largest cities. In 2012, the average age of first marriage for women was 29.0 in Hong Kong (Census and Statistics Department 2013), 29.3 in Japan (Statistics Bureau 2014), and 30.3 in Shanghai (Wang 2013). In the United States, in contrast, the average age of first marriage for women was just under 27 in 2014 (United States Bureau of the Census 2014). As a result, in these three societies, large percentages of women of childbearing age are single. Given their society's very low rates of extramarital births, it is highly likely that many of these women will not bear children. In Hong Kong in 2012, 38.6 percent of women aged thirty to thirty-four were single (Census and Statistics Department 2013, 62). In Japan, the figure for the same age group was 32 percent (National Institute of Population and Social Security Research 2011). In Shanghai in 2010, the numbers are lower, but rising.[3]

The parallel movement toward later marriage in these three cities raises questions about how women's views of gender and sexuality compare across societies, and why later marriage has occurred simultaneously in societies with different political and economic systems. A comparative study may shed light on these questions. This chapter explores single women's views of marriage and sexuality in Hong Kong, Tokyo, and Shanghai: three East Asian cities with relatively late ages of first marriage and large percentages of women who remain single beyond the age of thirty. These three cities have very different state systems and policies regarding women's role in reproducing the population. Shanghai, with the rest of China, adopted the one-child policy from 1979. The policy was relaxed in 2013 to allow couples to have two children if one parent was an only child. In fact, the restrictive policies turned out to be unnecessary in Shanghai as birthrates remained extremely low, at 0.8 per woman (Shan 2011), the lowest of any city in the world. Yet Shanghai's government does not worry about population depletion because its open borders allow massive flows of migrants into the city from other parts of China such that 38 percent or 8.89 million of the city's 23.02 million residents were migrants in 2010 (Jia 2011). The Shanghai government, as other urban areas in mainland China, controls city resources by strictly regulating the allocation of residence registration permits (*hukou*) that provide access to subsidized city services such as education and medical care (Jia 2011). Hong Kong, a Special Administrative Region (SAR) within China, does not follow China's one-child policy and does not attempt to control reproductive activities. The SAR government allows limited immigration from other parts of China, and attempts to attract elite immigration from China as a means to replenish the population and boost the economy. The Japanese government, meanwhile, does not directly control reproduction, but neither does it welcome permanent immigration, and thus in the government's view responsibility for social reproduction of the population falls upon married women, with expectations that single women should marry and contribute to reproducing the national culture, economy, and society. This chapter asks: Why do these societies with significantly different political systems share similar expectations of universal marriage, close associations between marriage and fertility, and delayed marriage?

This study views marriage as an integral part of state apparatus and a critical component of how a state regulates the reproduction of the society. States are actively involved in the intimate spheres of romance, love, and decisions to marry. Ryang (2006, 2) has argued that love in Japan may be viewed as a "political technology," and, drawing on Foucault, has approached love as a means to understand the effectiveness of the Japanese state as a "biopower, or a form of power that aggressively concerns itself with the life and death of a population." This approach helps to explain commonalities in the political technologies of rapidly developing East Asian economies and high rates of marriage seen in previous decades. To understand why single women's marriage strategies differ in the three societies, however, this chapter draws on Lee's (1998, 12) comparative study of factory workers in colonial Hong Kong and the clientalist state of Shenzhen. She argues that the two states play a minimal role in reproducing workers' labor power, and that we should consider the ways in which enterprises are organized to understand women's labor conditions (107). Similarly, this chapter argues that the governments of Tokyo, Hong Kong, and Shanghai, each with different policies for social reproduction, have relatively little effect on single women's decision making. To understand women's experiences, the chapter suggests that we need to consider the organization of marriage markets, employment, and families in each society.

Between 2000 and 2010, my research assistants and I interviewed one hundred never-married women between the ages of twenty-five and forty-five living in Shanghai, Hong Kong, and Tokyo. The women we interviewed worked in a range of occupations, but were primarily white-collar workers and slightly fewer than half had graduated from university. They were the elite of their societies in that they had significant opportunities to obtain an education and find interesting work. Their ability to work and earn enough to support themselves allowed them to choose to remain single. At the same time, these women's financial situation depended on their living arrangements; those who lived with their parents had a tremendous financial advantage given the high cost of housing in these cities, as they could pay much less to their parents than to a landlord (see Yamada 1999 regarding Japan). Those who lived alone because they had moved to the city from other regions had much higher expenses. In general, these women's experiences, while privileged, were nonetheless recognizable by other urban women in their societies as within the realm of familiar experience.

Commonalities in the capitalist developmental state may explain the similarities in marriage forms across the rapidly developing East Asian societies. These similarities include expectations of universal marriage and heterosexual orientation and few births outside of marriage. In the societies under study, women obtain high levels of education and are expected to work, yet their primary role is understood to be that of caring for family members within marriage. Marriage is critical because it is seen as the key to entering middle-class life and the beginning of women's primary role as a wife and mother. This is true even in Hong Kong and Shanghai where women are basically expected to continue working after childbirth.

In other words, in all three societies under study women are expected to marry. The women in Shanghai whom I interviewed were born after the start of the one-child policy, and most did not have siblings. They face tremendous pressure to do well in school, find good jobs, and to marry and produce a child; they are their parents' only hope of having a grandchild. Among women in Hong Kong and Japan, the pressure is less intense in large part because adult single women have siblings who may have already married and have children. Nonetheless, the vast majority of women I interviewed in all three cities said that they would like to marry or at least had not ruled out marriage. This finding reflects national surveys. In Japan, for example, a 2010 national survey found that 84 percent of single women aged thirty to thirty-four intended to marry within a year (National Institute of Population and Social Security Research 2011).

In the cities under study, women are expected to marry within a specific time period, generally extending from after their schooling is finished until they are twenty-nine. If a woman lets this time pass without getting married, she is considered to be unmarriageable, at least in the local marriage markets.[4] In Tokyo, it used to be said that women should marry by the age of twenty-five. Women were said to be like Christmas cakes that are sold on the 24th and 25th of December but lose their value on the 26th (see Brinton 1992; Creighton 1996). This term is no longer used, however, as women's average age of marriage has risen past twenty-five. Nonetheless, women in Tokyo and Shanghai said that they felt pressure to marry before the age of thirty. In Hong Kong, there are no set dates for marriage although women who hoped to marry wanted to do so before the age of thirty or thirty-five. The age limits for men are more relaxed because men basically need to have wealth to marry and a wealthy man may marry at almost any age.

In describing the matchmaking arena as a marriage market, I am not suggesting that love and romance are not important to these women (see Nakano 2014). On the contrary, women expected that their marriage would provide love, and they hoped that they would be romantically attracted to their spouses. I adopt Constable's (2003, 120) perspective that love and romance are intertwined with culture and politics. In other words, love and romance were inseparable from issues of family background, status, educational background, and financial resources.

In all three societies, a variety of negative terms are used by the media to describe women who have passed the expected age of marriage. In Japan, the media uses the term "parasite single" (*parasaito shinguru*) to describe single women who live with their parents. The term "loser dogs" (*makeinu*) has been used to describe single women since the 2006 publication of the book *The Distant Cry of Loser Dogs* by single woman Sakai Junko, who used the term to satirize the negative ways in which single women are viewed by society. In China, single women are described as "leftovers" (*shengnu*). Also in China, the phrase "third-type of human being" (*di san zhong*) refers to highly educated women such as PhD holders or medical doctors who are said to be unmarriageable and therefore no longer women due to their higher education; they therefore represent a new category of human being that is neither woman nor man. In Hong Kong, a woman over thirty is called a "Hong Kong woman" (*gong leui*) or "middle-aged woman" (*zhongleui*) and is stereotyped as being selfish, brand-obsessed, demanding, and critical of men. These terms do not reflect women's actual lives but should be understood as warnings by social conservatives that women should remain in service-oriented roles as wives and mothers.

In the three cities under study, methods for finding spouses differed significantly. In China, family members commonly help their single sons and daughters find partners by arranging "blind dates" (*xiangqin*). Internet dating sites are widely used in Shanghai and throughout China, especially among those who are not living in their city of origin and who thus lack hometown connections normally used to meet potential spouses. In Hong Kong, women rely less on family and commercial options, and prefer to meet partners through friends, hobby groups, or work. Tokyo has a large matchmaking industry that includes small dinner gatherings (*gōkon*), drinking parties, group activities, and online matching. Amateur or semiprofessional arranged matchmaking (*omiai*) is also available. Participation in such activities is so prevalent that it has been given a name in the Japanese media, *konkatsu,* a play on the word for the aggressive search for jobs (*shūshoku katsudō*) embarked upon by third- and fourth-year university students hoping to enter corporate life.

After speaking with dozens of women in each city, I found that women in all three societies generally accepted the institution of marriage as involving heterosexual romantic pairing, childbirth, and service to family members. Single women did not reject this idea of marriage, but described themselves as unsuitable for the institution or unable to find an appropriate partner. Even women who questioned their sexual orientation or described themselves as lesbians said that they had considered marriage as a life path. Many women I met thought that singlehood was a temporary stage that they could enjoy before they entered the restrictive institution of marriage. This chapter argues that differences in the ways in which women viewed gender and sexuality in the three cities emerged from state policies, family structures, and social and economic developments particular to that city. In introducing stories from women living in the different cities, the intention is not to imply that each woman represented her city; each woman only represented herself. Nonetheless, each woman's story provides insight into the experience of other single women living in the same city.

Shanghai

The women in Shanghai who had remained unmarried into their thirties were of the first generation to benefit from the increased availability of education following the end of the Cultural Revolution (1966–1976). Many had attended university and worked in white-collar jobs. In this sense, they were among China's elite. This group can be further divided into those who were native to Shanghai and thus possessed Shanghai residence registration, and those who were born outside of the city who did not possess such registration. As mentioned, in 2010, 8.98 million, or 38 percent of the city's 23.02 million residents, were migrants without Shanghai residence registration (Jia 2011). Shanghai natives had relatively secure futures. They usually lived with their parents, and thus could accumulate disposable income and feel secure that their medical costs and the costs of educating their children would be kept relatively low through the city's subsidized system. Those who did not possess Shanghai residency registration were in a more vulnerable position because they lacked local connections or access to local subsidized social services and needed to pay for housing and related living expenses.

Both natives and immigrants faced similar pressures to marry, usually most urgently from their parents. This pressure should be understood in the context of the marriage market in mainland China in which women and their families felt that women would be unmarriageable after the age of thirty. This pressure reflects the nature of the marriage market, but is also self-reproducing, as mass compliance with the expectation of marriage before thirty insures that the market retains a limited age range. A twenty-five-year-old Shanghai native explained the pressure to marry as follows:

> If our friends keep getting married, we keep getting [wedding] invitations, and we will feel pressure. Friends, family, colleagues from my company ask, "Where's your boyfriend?" It's better to marry by twenty-eight or thirty. Once you're over thirty, it becomes increasingly difficult. People start trying to set you up on blind dates. It starts at age twenty-three or twenty-four. There's pressure from family. At spring festival when all the relatives get together, the older people like to talk about our relationship and marital status.

Pressure is higher when women are the only child in the family as those women who had siblings reported that once a sibling married and had a child, their parents' attention focused on the grandchild and parental pressure eased. Women in Hong Kong and Tokyo were much more likely to have siblings, and these women also reported feeling less pressure after a sibling had married and had children. In spite of this pressure, the main reason why these women had not yet married was not because they resisted marriage itself but because they had not yet found a suitable mate. In Shanghai, the expectations for grooms are high. Men are expected to own a home or at least have enough funds to be able to buy one (usually with the help of their parents given the high prices of real estate in the city) before they may consider proposing. The popular phrase is that a man must have "a car, a house, and money" (*chezi, fangzi, piaozu*) if he wishes to marry. In addition, women expect to have feelings of attraction for the man. The main complaint among women I met was that there was no "feeling" or "spark" when meeting men. A woman who had participated in many blind dates arranged by friends, family, and commercial dating explained:

> In my blind dates, I found that the chemistry was just not right. I've also tried the group blind date where you have an eight-minute date. My friends and I wanted to try it because we watched *Sex in the City* and we thought it was interesting but it didn't work for any of us. One or two couples met from that but they didn't continue. The way it works is that men and women indicate their interest after meeting. If both are mutually interested, the company helps you to exchange phone numbers. In my case, none of the men in whom I expressed interest showed an interest in me.

The anxiety that Shanghai women felt about marrying on schedule was compounded by the expectation that they achieve success in the employment market in the same time frame. As mentioned, women in their twenties and thirties were the first generation of only children under China's one-child policy that began in 1979, and the first generation to receive education following the reopening of schools after the Cultural Revolution. While most young women complied with the enormous expectations that they marry on schedule, women who remained single were often waiting to find an appropriate person.

The marriage market requirements for women and expectations about women's sexual behavior were stricter in Shanghai than in Hong Kong and Tokyo. The Shanghai marriage market valued women for youth, beauty, and sexual inexperience. In China's cities, for example, hymen reconstruction surgery remains available (Wang 2008), but is relatively unknown in Hong Kong and Tokyo as virginity is not expected upon marriage. At the same time, women in Shanghai were the most expressive in relation to their sexual freedom as single women. A woman who had moved to Shanghai from Anhui province for university education explained:

> Because everything is so convenient, it makes it difficult for people to be devoted to love. The temptations are everywhere. Most of my friends have had one night stands. We feel that it is safe to have fun. It's like with sex toys. Before you use a sex toy, you would never think to use it. But after you use it, it becomes easy to use it. It is the same with one night stands. I've had one one-night stand, and I'm not afraid to do it again. The experience changed me. So it is harder for us to be truly devoted to love. I feel sorry about that.

In Shanghai, attitudes toward sexual behavior were the most extreme of the three cities, with some women entirely avoiding sexual activities before marriage while others openly discussed their experiences. This situation is not due to state policies, but to the recent openness of Chinese society to different lifestyles and ideas, and to the breakdown in family control over daughters' sexuality. Native Shanghai women who lived with their parents were under greater parental control and surveillance, and women who had come to Shanghai as immigrants without their families were more expressive about sexual freedoms.

Tokyo

The women I interviewed in Tokyo included both Tokyo natives and those who had come from outside of the city for education or work in their early twenties. As Yamada (1999) has noted, those who lived with their parents had financial advantages in that they did not pay rent, a great expense in the city. Those who had come from outside of the city had rented their own apartments and had considerably less disposable income. The women I interviewed were primarily in white-collar occupations and were from neither the richest nor the poorest backgrounds.

As the Japanese government does not welcome permanent immigration, conservative commentators view social reproduction as Japanese women's moral responsibility. This can be seen in comments by the former minister of health Yanagisawa Hakuo, who in 2007 described Japanese women as "birth-giving machines" (McCurry 2007). The women I interviewed dismissed such talk as ridiculous; they said that marriage was a choice, not a moral obligation. My research suggests that single women's views were not shaped by the state, but by the local employment and marriage markets. Because both employment and marriage in Japan required women's full commitment, single women felt that they could not continue to have a career if they married. A thirty-four-year-old Tokyo native who lived with her mother and worked for a national educational agency explained:

> Even though I've spent my life thinking about my career, I think in the future it would be good for me to marry and have children and a husband in the traditional sense. At this agency there are a lot of chances for people to be posted overseas. If it's a woman, she may take her children, but it's unheard of for her husband to go as well. When men go, their wives and families sometimes follow, although sometimes they go alone while their wife continues to work. I think I'd like to be the type that follows her husband overseas.

Despite her commitment to her education and career—she had graduated from a top university in Tokyo—she wanted to take on a traditional role of wife and mother. Due to the expectations placed upon workers at Japanese workplaces, she felt that marriage and career were incompatible, and she would have to choose one or the other. She recognized that marrying would result in the loss of freedoms such as eating out at restaurants and attending concerts, but the main reason she had not yet married was because she had not yet found an appropriate partner: "I wouldn't marry someone I didn't like just because I wanted to get married. Then I would consider that maybe this single life is not temporary and I'll settle down to a more permanent single life." Here she appears to assume that if she is unable to marry within the next few years, she will probably never marry. She accepts the narrow time frame of marriage based on the idea that the main purpose of marriage is procreation. Further, as in the case of women in Shanghai, women in Tokyo are not resisting the institution of marriage nor questioning the link between marriage and childbirth. Rather, they are refusing to marry until they find the right person. However, in Tokyo, women feel that marriage requires relinquishing their careers due to the rigidity of the employment market, lack of child care, and beliefs that mothers should care for their own young children.

In Tokyo, sexual experience is acceptable before marriage for women as well as men (Ueno 2003, 318). This delinking of sexual activity and marriage, however, did not result in a similar delinking of reproduction and marriage. The close link between marriage and reproduction can be clearly seen in cases of women who could not bear children. A woman who worked as a temporary dispatch worker for a financial institution was told by a doctor at the age of thirty that she would be unable to have children after having cysts removed from her uterus. Upon receiving the news, she decided that she should no longer participate in the Japanese marriage market because men would expect that marriage would bring children. "After the surgery, I lost confidence and didn't date anyone for three years," she said. In her early thirties, however, she decided to date foreign men who she thought would not care about her age or ability to bear children. She explained, "Japanese men immediately ask, 'How old are you?' but foreign men do not ask and do not seem to care." When I met her a few years later, however, she was married to a Japanese divorcee who had a child from his previous marriage. Her experience shows the strength of the expectation of fertility in first marriages, and also suggests the possibility of alternative marriage and romantic markets made available through rising divorce rates and the availability of non-Japanese partners.

Hong Kong

In Hong Kong, the women I met worked in white-collar occupations and had attended secondary school or university. The majority of women interviewed lived with their parents, a socially acceptable option that makes economic sense given the expensive housing market. Women I interviewed could be divided into two distinct categories. The older generation of women, over forty-five, had grown up at a time when many women quit school early to work in factories to support their siblings. The younger generation, under the age of forty-five, had more opportunities to study at university and embark on careers as they were able to take advantage of improvements and expansion in the secondary and tertiary institutions made by the British colonial government in the 1970s.

Public officials in Hong Kong occasionally encourage women to bear more children. In a 2005 radio address, the former chief executive of Hong Kong, Donald Tsang, urged couples to bear at least three children (Luk 2005). Yet later marriages and declining birthrates in Hong Kong are not viewed with the same degree of anxiety as in Japan because the Hong Kong government believes that the problem of depopulation can be solved by opening immigration to China's elite. The Hong Kong government regulates immigration from foreign states and controls immigration from China, its largest source of migrants. In 2010, for example, 43,000 mainlanders joined their families through the "One-Way Permit" scheme that imposes a daily entry quota of 150 persons (Information and Services Department 2010, 416). The government also launched programs such as the "Quality Migrant Admission Scheme" and the "Capital Migrant Admission Scheme" to admit mainlanders with special skills or substantial amounts of money to invest in Hong Kong. These schemes have not been very effective in attracting successful applicants, but they nonetheless reflect the Hong Kong government's perspective on reproducing the elite of the population.

Of the three cities, women in Hong Kong were under the least pressure to marry in part because their extended families provided them with social, financial, and emotional support. Single women in Hong Kong were involved in extended family affairs; they contributed money to parents or other siblings and their children, helped care for nieces and nephews, and benefitted from family financial support for their education and purchasing property. Hong Kong single women, unlike women in Shanghai, generally had several siblings, and reported feeling relatively free of pressure to marry and bear children if one of their siblings already had children. Family obligations sometimes even created unspoken pressure against marriage, as Hong Kong women who did not marry were able to continue to provide financial support to their families, support that would end if they married and needed to spend resources on their own children.

In spite of the reduced pressure to marry, as in the other cities Hong Kong women saw marriage as involving expectations of motherhood, and explained their eagerness to marry in terms of their desire to have children. Unlike Tokyo, however, where sexuality and marriage have become delinked, a significant number of informants in Hong Kong thought that sexual activity in principle should occur in marriage or in a committed relationship that leads to marriage. A thirty-two-year-old woman who worked as a secretary in an art academy said that she hoped to marry and have children. She explained her views on marriage as follows:

> I would like to be a mother. I would like at least two children. I really want to be a good mother. I really want a loving relationship [among family members] and a healthy family. I've read a lot of books on relationships such as *Boy Meets Girl* and *Kiss Dating Goodbye*. These are Christian books. They say that it is better not to date when you are immature; that you should get ready for marriage and that dating is not a game. You shouldn't have too much body contact when dating because that leads to sex. It's easy to have sex but that will ruin a relationship.

As a Christian, her views were more conservative than the average Hong Konger—Christians make up 11 percent of the population (Information Services Department 2014)—but her views would be recognized by other Hong Kong women as one kind of approach to marriage and sexuality. The tendency to restrict sexual activity to marriage among Hong Kong women may be a result of family structures in which the vast majority of adult single women continue to live with their parents and remain involved in extended family networks. Women in Tokyo and immigrant women in Shanghai were more likely to be living away from their parents and extended family networks, and were freer to experiment with sexual and romantic relationships outside of marriage.

Conversely, single women who did not want to have children or were beyond childbearing age in Hong Kong felt that they did not need to marry, and most of these older informants were not involved in romantic relationships. A forty-three-year-old civil servant explained that she did not need to have children or marry:

> Basically I like children but I don't feel that I need them. You have to spend a lot of time to raise children and education today is very important. There are many things that you need to teach them and it is a great responsibility. If you marry and have children you have to change your life. I've got-

ten accustomed to having my freedom. In the future I want to continue to
live the lifestyle that I'm living now.

She lived alone in an apartment she had purchased through a government home
ownership scheme, and although her parents had passed away, she was close to
her nieces and nephews, and felt supported by networks of friends and colleagues.
She felt that these sources of support were sufficient and she had consistently rejected offers of friendship from men, as she did not want to give them the "wrong
impression" that she was interested in marriage.

In Hong Kong, as in the other cities, the links between marriage and the physical body can be seen through the experiences of women who had encountered
health problems. The civil servant quoted above revealed that she had had a mastectomy as a result of breast cancer. She explained that although she received her
family's support in her decision to proceed with the mastectomy, not all women
were so fortunate. She had met a young woman whose family opposed mastectomy as they were concerned that it would affect her opportunities to marry. "This
made me angry," she said, "and I scolded her family." The woman's parents were
concerned that a mastectomy would challenge the completeness of the woman's
productive capacity and female form and thus threaten the woman's marriage-
ability. However, this conflict also reveals that the young, unmarried woman's
body is subject to family decision making as to how it may be passed on to a future husband.[5] The civil servant challenged the parents' strategy of placing marriage ahead of their daughter's health, but did not question their involvement in
managing their daughter's body.

Conclusions

This chapter has suggested that similarities in family forms—relatively late marriage, few children, low rates of childbirth outside of marriage, and association of
marriage with heterosexual pairing and childbirth—have emerged as part of the
political economy of East Asian societies experiencing rapid economic growth.
In all three societies, women felt pressured to marry within a particular time period and were expected to marry according to marriage markets that valued
youth, beauty, and fertility in women. The parallels between women's experiences
were indeed striking. However, this chapter has also argued that women's experiences of singlehood differed significantly in each society, and these differences
cannot be explained entirely by the state apparatus and policies. Rather, differences in women's experiences in the three societies were largely due to family

organization and expectations, local employment markets, patterns of migration, and housing arrangements.

In Shanghai, the pressure to marry is the most intense of the three cities in this study because of the expectations that women succeed in both marriage and employment markets in the same tight time frame, and the historical context in which single women in their thirties and forties are the first generation of educated women following the Cultural Revolution and the first generation of only children to reach marriageable age. In Tokyo, women felt that they would need to make a choice between career and family because of conflict between expectations of full-time maternal commitment to families and an employment market in a shrinking economy that privileged full-time, continuous employment. In Hong Kong, women were the least pressured to marry due to the protection of extended families, but their decisions regarding sexuality and marriage were framed in an ethical context in which a woman's sexuality was linked to marriage.

In discussing marriage, single women in all three societies looked inward and questioned their own appropriateness for the institution. They wondered whether they might not be lucky enough to find an appropriate person, whether they had become too accustomed to freedoms to endure restrictions, or whether they had personal or physical defects that made marriage impossible. They had internalized the requirements of the institution and questioned their ability to meet those requirements. Yet in this process, some also challenged fundamental assumptions in their societies. They found alternatives to reproductive marriage markets by finding partners through "secondary" marriage markets for foreign men and divorcees; they rejected marriage as the only path for women; and they questioned the relationship between sex and romantic love. These are significant developments in part because they occurred among women who basically wanted to marry and have families. In summary, the rise in singlehood in East Asia currently does not represent a radical rethinking of the triangular linkages of marriage, family, and reproduction. Rather, women are making a series of personal decisions and adjustments to remain single as they negotiate neoliberal capitalism's opportunities and limitations and the gendered expectations and values of their societies.

Notes and References

Substantial portions of the work described in this chapter were supported by a grant from the Research Grants Council of the Hong Kong Special Administrative Region, China (Project No. CUHK4018/02H). The research was also made possible by a 2001 Summer Grant for Research and a 2001–2002 Direct Grant awarded by the Chinese University of Hong Kong. I thank Moeko Wagatsuma, Chan Yim Ting, and Candy Lam for their assistance in conducting research.

1. The percentages of births outside of marriage stood at 2.1 percent in Japan in 2009 (Ministry of Health, Labor and Welfare 2012) and 8.3 percent in Hong Kong in 2009 (United Nations 2012). In the United States, in contrast, 40.6 percent of births occurred outside of marriage in 2008 (United Nations 2012).

2. Shanghai residents must comply with China's policy of one child per family, but the city's fertility rate of 0.8 per woman is much lower than the national average of 1.8 (Shan 2011) and significantly lower than the birthrate of 2.1 that is normally cited as the rate necessary to reproduce a population. Birthrates in Hong Kong are among the lowest in the world, falling to 0.9 in 2004 and then rising to 1.2 in 2011 (Census and Statistics Department 2014). The fertility rate in Japan has fallen steadily over several decades, from 3.65 in 1950 to 1.43 in 2013 (Statistics Bureau 2014).

3. In Shanghai in 2010, 20 percent of women aged fifteen and older were single, and women older than thirty accounted for 6.6 percent of all single women in 2010 compared to just 2.3 percent in 2000 (Yao 2011).

4. As I discuss later, some women turn to secondary markets of foreign or divorced men. By "secondary markets" I do not mean that divorced or foreign men are essentially less appealing or make poorer husbands. My meaning is that they are seen in these societies as secondary choices for a never-married woman.

5. In her discussion of commercialized sex (*enjo kōsai*) among teenaged girls in Japan, Ueno (2003, 319) argues that the reason teenaged prostitution causes so much embarrassment in Japan is because under patriarchy men cannot allow their women—that is, their daughters—to use their bodies at their own disposal. *Enjo kōsai* represents a challenge to this patriarchal view of women's sexuality because it reflects women's claiming of their bodies for themselves, yet it also represents women's continued oppression because these teenagers reinforce the structure of patriarchy that assigns value to their bodies (323).

Baidu Baike. 2014. "Shengnu." http://baike.baidu.com/link?url=TfntnBRcnWnRHUZjU R16yFM5lrkhmgbqM5yMZfXIBppaFVeBz5M4ULq0hQ56n99P.

Brinton, Mary. 1992. "Christmas Cakes and Wedding Cakes: The Social Organization of Japanese Women's Life Course." In *Japanese Social Organization,* edited by T. S. Lebra, pp. 74–107. Honolulu: University of Hawai'i Press.

Census and Statistics Department (Hong Kong). 2013. "Women and Men in Hong Kong: Key Statistics." http://www.statistics.gov.hk/pub/B11303032013AN13B0100.pdf.

———. 2014. "Population Estimates." http://www.censtatd.gov.hk/hkstat/sub/sp150.jsp ?tableID=004&ID=0&productType=8.

Constable, Nicole. 2003. *Romance on a Global Stage: Pen Pals, Virtual Ethnography and "Mail Order" Marriages.* Berkeley: University of California Press.

Creighton, Millie. 1996. "Marriage, Motherhood, and Career Management in a Japanese 'Counter Culture.'" In *Re-Imaging Japanese Women,* edited by A. Imamura, pp. 192–220. Berkeley: University of California Press.

Information Services Department (Hong Kong). 2010. *Hong Kong Year Book 2010.* http://www.yearbook.gov.hk/2011/en/pdf/E18.pdf.

———. 2014. *Hong Kong: The Facts.* www.gov.hk/en/about/abouthk/factsheets/docs /religion.pdf.

Jia, Feishang. 2011. "Policies Change as More Arrive." *Shanghai Daily,* May 4.

Lee, Ching Kwan. 1998. *Gender and the South China Miracle: Two Worlds of Factory Women.* Berkeley: University of California Press.

Luk, Eddie. 2005. "HK Administration Suggests 3 Children per Couple." *China Daily,* February 22.

McCurry, Justin. 2007. "Japanese Minister Wants Birth-Giving Machines, aka Women, to Have More Babies." *Guardian,* January 29.

Ministry of Health, Labor and Welfare (Japan). 2012. "International Comparisons." http://www.mhlw.go.jp/english/database/db-hw/FY2010/dl/live_births05.pdf.

Nakano, Lynne. 2014. "Single Women in Marriage and Employment Markets." In *Capturing Contemporary Japan: Differentiation and Uncertainty,* edited by S. Kawano, G. Roberts, and S. O. Long, pp. 163–182. Honolulu: University of Hawai'i Press.

National Institute of Population and Social Security Research (Japan). 2011. "Attitudes toward Marriage and Family among Japanese Singles." http://www.ipss.go.jp/site-ad/index_english/nfs14/Nfs14_Singles_Eng.pdf.

Ng, Teddy. 2005. "Call for Bigger Families." *Standard,* February 22.

Ryang, Sonia. 2006. *Love in Modern Japan: Its Estrangement from Self, Sex, and Society.* London: Routledge.

Sakai, Junko. 2003. *Makeinu no tōboe* (The distant cry of loser dogs). Tokyo: Kodansha.

Shan, Duan. 2011. "Census: China's Population Hits 1.37 Billion." *China Daily,* April 29.

Statistics Bureau, Ministry of Internal Affairs and Communications (Japan). 2014. "Statistical Handbook of Japan 2014." http://www.stat.go.jp/english/data/handbook/c0117.htm.

Ueno, Chizuko. 2003. "Self-Determination on Sexuality? Commercialization of Sex among Teenage Girls in Japan." *Inter-Asia Cultural Studies* 4 (2): 317–324.

United Nations. 2012. *World Fertility Report 2012.* http://www.un.org/en/development/desa/population/publications/dataset/fertility/wfr2012/MainFrame.html.

United States Bureau of the Census. 2014. https://www.census.gov/hhes/families/files/graphics/MS-2.pdf.

Wang, Yajun. 2008. "Love, Lies, and Loss: Young Women's Experiences of Abortion in China." MPhil diss., Chinese University of Hong Kong.

Wang, Zhenghua. 2013. "Average Marriage Age for Shanghai Women over 30." *China Daily,* February 28.

Yamada, Masahiro. 1999. *Parasaito shinguru no jidai* (The age of parasite singles). Tokyo: Chikuma Shobō.

Yao, M. 2011. "Choosing to Be Single (for Now)." *Shanghai Daily.com,* November 9.

CHAPTER TEN

Media, Sex, and the Self in Cambodia

HEIDI HOEFINGER

Introduction

As she cracked open a can of beer from her perch behind the bar, the diamond embedded in Leap's front tooth twinkled as she smiled and stated, "I want to be like you—a Western girl, a strong girl, a modern girl—like a movie star." Her resolve was palpable, yet discomforting. Leap owned her own Western-oriented hostess bar in Phnom Penh, Cambodia, where men from North America, Australia, and Europe came to drink and socialize with the array of Leap's female Khmer employees. A former "bar girl"[1] herself, she had married a Belgian customer she'd met while working, and was able to make socioeconomic advancements that enabled her to purchase her own bar.

Leap's comments reflect commonly shared views among many young women in Cambodia, which illustrate the uneasy collision between modernity, capitalism, feminism, global media, consumer culture, and their effect on identity construction. Global media foster desires to become "strong, modern, Western-like women" which drive many young women to migrate from the country to the city in search of independence, romance, and capital. Once there, many use sex and intimacy to cement materially fruitful relationships with Western men. Yet the women soon find that achieving a reconciliation between being "modern and individualized" and simultaneously "traditional and collectivist" can be very challenging.

Thus, my focus in this chapter is on the tensions and intersections between sex and intimacy, media and consumption, and the precarity of female "individualization" (Bauman 2001; Beck and Beck-Gernsheim 2002; Giddens 1991; Kim 2012a) in Cambodia. Through the lens of "professional girlfriends" and women employed in the Western-oriented hostess bar scene, I illustrate how sex and intimacy are used as a means to consume material goods, and how desires for consumption and individualization are heavily influenced by media and globalization (Kim 2012c; Thornham and Pengpeng 2012). Yet, due to the collective nature of Cambodian culture, combined with very strict gendered social codes, and contradictory messages from the state, this emphasis on individualization and "being modern" is a great site of anxiety for many women. The result is a constant shifting between multiple identities and subjectivities (Law 2000) and a constant (re)negotiation of the contradictions and ambivalences that surround not only this "precarious world of female individualization" (Kim 2012b; Nilan 2012) but also just daily life as female subjects in Cambodia, where women negotiate both the liberatory and constricting forces of globalization and neoliberal capitalism (Kim 2012a, 2012b).

However, despite experiencing constant contradictions around individualization, and relentless stigma for the decisions they make, I show how the women transgress the boundaries of respectability, challenge gendered double standards, and reconcile individualism and collectivity through subactivism (Bakardjieva 2009; Yue 2012), and by becoming proud patrons and providers for their families.

Although many scholars have written extensively about gendered expectations and double standards in Cambodia (e.g., Brickell 2011; Jacobsen 2008; Ledgerwood 1991; Tarr 1996), there is currently a dearth of literature that explores the ways in which gender and sexuality intersect with political economy, consumer culture, neoliberalism, feminism, and global media, and the resulting tensions these intersections create in relation to individualization and identity construction. And while female individualization in Asia was recently investigated in depth in an edited volume by Youna Kim (2012a) titled *Women and the Media in Asia: The Precarious Self,* research on Cambodia was noticeably absent. And finally, although sex and entertainment work in Cambodia (which includes hostess bar work) is often constructed in the literature and media as only ever exploitative and conflated with sex trafficking (e.g., E. Brown 2007; L. Brown 2000; Farley et al. 2012; Schwartz 2003), there is very little academic scholarship that presents women involved in sex and entertainment work with agency and self-determination (see Busza 2004; Derks 2008; Hoefinger 2013, 2011; Sandy 2014) and/or through the lens of resistance and activism (see Hoefinger 2014; Sandy 2013).

Therefore, in this chapter I address the many gaps in the literature by demonstrating the ways in which young Cambodian women involved in the sex and entertainment sectors actively negotiate the subsequent contradictions they face when not only their transnational relationships are impinged upon by both global and local social and economic factors (including gender, sexuality, political economy, media, and the state), but also their senses of self. This chapter is thus original and valuable for its nuanced exploration of media, sex, and precarious individualization in the Cambodian context, and for the ways in which these intersections are compared and contrasted with analogous phenomena in other countries.

Transactional Sex and Intimacy as Tools for Consumption

Hostess bars such as Leap's are Western-oriented bars located in urban areas of Cambodia where Khmer women act as hostesses to men from North America, Europe, Australasia, and increasing numbers of Malaysian, Japanese, and Singaporean men as well (Hoefinger 2013). The bars are highly sexualized environments where the woman dance and flirt with customers with the hope of getting drinks ordered for them. For every "ladies drink" purchased for them, they earn an extra $1 surcharge, which is added to their monthly salaries of approximately $60–$100.

The women may or may not have sex, but their goal is to form intimate, materially beneficial relationships with the men. Because of this, and strict gendered codes for women, they are often erroneously referred to as "broken women" (*srei kouc*) or "prostitutes," and their transnational relationships viewed as commercial. However, the commercial sex framework is not always an appropriate framework of analysis for these relationships, which are multilayered and complex, and often involve emotion and love. Nearly a decade of ethnographic research[2] has revealed that many women do not identify as sex workers, nor do they frame their quest for Western partners as "work." Inspired by the work of Viviana Zelizer (2005) and Mark Hunter (2002), I instead use a new vocabulary of "professional girlfriends,"[3] "transactional sex," and the "materiality of everyday relationships" to discuss the women and their relationships (Hoefinger 2013).

In his research on women in South African townships, Hunter (2002) uses transactional sex to outline gift-based sexual exchanges that exist outside of both local and Western definitions of prostitution. He points out that, although they are similar and sometimes overlap, transactional sex is different from prostitution in that "participants are constructed as girlfriends/boyfriends and not prostitutes/clients, and the exchange of gifts for sex is part of a broader set of obligations that might not involve a predetermined payment" (101). He goes on to compare sex linked to subsistence and sex linked to consumption and the intricate ways they coexist. "Subsistence sex" is sometimes referred to as "survival sex," which is used to secure the basic needs for daily living, such as food, shelter, and clothing. Certain scholars sometimes equate all forms of transactional sex with this—but Hunter makes it clear that in many cases it is more about a desire to consume material goods that are not necessary for survival, such as getting one's hair and makeup done at the salon every day, or getting new phones, designer bags, motorbikes, or even houses, school tuition, or visas. He refers to this as "sex linked to consumption," whereby sex is used as a tool in order to consume, but it is not considered "work" (101).

Although Leap was married and received the majority of her financial support from both her Belgian husband (who remained in Belgium for work), and the little income she earned from her bar, she actively sought out new foreign acquaintances while living on her own in Phnom Penh. She was highly skilled at employing certain tactics to capitalize most efficiently on her charm (Cressey 2005 [1932]) and bodily capital (Bernstein 2007; Hoang 2011) in order to attract potential partners. These strategies included appearing to be interested in banal conversation with the patrons of her bar, or communicating through flirtatious laughter when she didn't understand something; using eye contact, smiles, and suggestive gestures to flirt; making, or laughing at, sexual jokes or innuendos; physically touching or caressing patrons' shoulders, hands or thighs, or allowing herself to be touched, stroked, or hugged.

Leap relied on "deep acting," "emotion work" (Hochschild 2003 [1983]), and "performances of love" (Brennan 2004) in order to entice men into her intimate world. She was adept at making her clientele feel special, which caused many of them to become enamored and mark their relationship with her as different. Capitalizing on their racialized desires, she knew they would either be aroused by the "exoticized other" or express sympathy for the "impoverished other," depending on how she presented herself. Either way, she achieved her objective if she successfully secured relationships with them on some level. These relationships would range from platonic to sexual, but always involved the exchange of gifts for emotional and/or physical intimacy. Her efforts proved fruitful, as some of her more valuable rewards from her suitors included smartphones, gold jewelry, and a Range Rover. Leap and other bar workers and professional girlfriends like her utilized transactional sex and intimacy as tools to make socioeconomic advancements, and participate in global capitalist practices as modern, individualized consumers.

Media, Globalization, and Neoliberal Capitalism

Desires of young Cambodian women to "progress" and engage in neoliberal consumerism are heavily influenced by everyday media culture and globalization. Yet relatively recent political and economic changes in Cambodia make access to available employment opportunities for unskilled female workers difficult due to rigid gendered social codes and gendered inequities in the labor market (Kim 2012b).

In the 1970s Cambodia suffered a genocide under the Khmer Rouge communist regime during which an estimated 1–2 million people lost their lives (Chandler 1991, 2000; Kiernan 1996). That regime lost power in 1979, at which point there was a ten-year occupation by the Vietnamese, which was followed by the signing of the Paris Peace Accords of 1991. In a move toward reconciliation and liberalization—an estimated 20,000 United Nations international peacekeepers entered Cambodia, and many associate this period—known as the UNTAC[4] era (1991–1993)—with sexual permissiveness and depravity, corruption, inflation, increased rape and assault, increased prostitution, and the spread of HIV/AIDS—all apparently due the sudden appearance of wealth and foreign influence (Jacobsen 2008). In 1993 the first democratic elections were held, whereby the current prime minister, Hun Sen, and his Cambodian People's Party gained power, and have remained in power ever since—through a mix of patrimonialism and corruption (Jacobsen and Stuart-Fox 2013).

In the 1990s, there were sharp increases in industrialization and expansion, rural-to-urban migration, and changes in sexual culture. The Cambodian government opened up it markets and turned toward democracy and capitalism in order to pull itself out of the devastating black hole left behind after the Khmer Rouge and foreign occupation, but low-skilled and impoverished women, in particular, have not really benefited from this "progress." Instead, liberalization of the economy has left them with few options.

For the women in this study, many of whom were born in the rural countryside and have little education, opportunities to earn money are feminized and limited. These include staying in the country and farming or moving to the city to engage in factory work (textiles are the largest export in Cambodia, alongside tourism, and women make up 90 percent of the factory workforce; see International Labour Organization 2010), street trading (selling food or other goods on the street), domestic work (cleaning and child care), or sex/entertainment work. Often, female friends or relatives return to the countryside from the city with new phones and motorbikes, bedecked in jewelry and new clothes, and an "opportunity myth" (Brennan 2004) circulates. Girls hear of grandiose opportunities that are available in the big city, particularly when one forges relationships with foreigners. Curiosity mingles with global imagination (Appadurai 1991), and nascent desires for consumerism grow ever stronger.

Popular local and global media greatly contribute to this longing for Westernized consumption practices and individualization, as Leap explains: "I like everything Western. I wear bikini on beach, put on cream, and read magazine—just like on TV!" While commonplace in the urban areas, increasing numbers of households have televisions and Internet access via telephones in the countryside (due mostly to new wealth from feminized remittances). Karaoke videos, which appeared in Cambodia in the early 1990s, are filled with young women adorned with jewelry and "modern clothing" (e.g., that which exposes shoulders, legs above the knee, etc.).

Chinese, Thai, and South Korean "soap operas" are also influential, and tend to portray the dramatic love and romance between young urban couples from different social classes. Cambodian anthropologist Chou Meng Tarr (1996, 64) points out that while these soaps "offer a greater degree of autonomy for young people than the dominant discourses of Cambodian culture would sanction [they] are not completely at variance with what people expect in society. They are still very hierarchical in nature stressing the importance of both age and gender." And while popular media culture is influential in sparking aspirations for modernity, freedom, and independence, so too is corporate media.

Beer companies are a telling example of this influence. There is a glamorization of alcohol in Cambodia, whereby the ability to consume regular amounts, as well as the capacity to purchase it for others, signifies spending power, prestige, and status (Population Services International and Family Health International 2007; Tarr 1996). The branding and marketing of many of the local beers in particular are also closely linked to a sense of nationalism and pride. The slogan for the popular Angkor Beer, for example, is "My Country, My Beer," and images of modern, liberal young women are exploited in advertising campaigns.

In one popular Angkor Beer advertising poster found in drinking establishments throughout Phnom Penh, for example, a young Khmer female is centered at the front of the image, while her male counterpart is set slightly back. She is very light-skinned, which is generally considered aesthetically desirable in Cambodia and a form of higher social status (darker-skinned people are stereotyped as poor farmers, for example). She is wearing Westernized and revealing clothing, which is typically "nontraditional"—particularly because her shoulders are exposed. She looks directly into the camera and is smiling and happy as she holds her Angkor can in one hand, and a full pint of beer in the other. Beneath the image is the slogan "My Country, My Beer" in both English and Khmer. The messaging in this advertising is that it is fun, glamorous, and modern to drink, but most importantly that it is very Cambodian to drink—even for women. This messaging is confusing, and runs contrary to other messaging young women face about remaining respectable, moral, and "traditional"—the specifics of which are outlined below.

It was a heady mix of popular media, global imagination, opportunity myth, personal aspirations for economic power, independence, freedom, and self-fulfillment (Derks 2008) as well as a staunch sense of family obligation (which is embedded in Cambodian culture and related to Buddhist tenets of filial piety; see Jacobsen 2008; Ledgerwood 1990) that motivated the women in this study to leave their homes and migrate to urban areas for work. Arriving in the cities, they weighed their limited options within these very constrained environments, and after trying their hand at a few different things decided bar work was the most fruitful and lucrative—particularly because it enabled them to exploit relationships with Western men, from whom they benefited both materially and emotionally.

Leap and women like her tended to express a sense of freedom associated with their employment and relationships choices, and with modern consumer culture as depicted by the media. Women often stated that they liked their lifestyles in the bars because they could "be themselves"—whoever those selves were (Hoefinger 2013). Thus, they were actively working on projects of individualization. Informed by the work of Bauman (2001), Beck-Gernsheim (2002), and Giddens (1991) on identity and reflexivity in late modernity, I use the term "individualization" to refer to the "ongoing shift from a traditional gender role-oriented, collective, normal biography to a labour market-steered, elective, do-it-yourself biography" (Kim 2012b, 9). Yet, this quest for female individualism within the context of urban bar work is greatly at odds with the gendered regulatory practices of a society where "individualism is not placed at the heart of its culture" (Kim 2012b, 1) and where women are socially, culturally, and institutionally considered inferior to men.

Gendered Social Codes and Stereotypes

There is a very strong state-promoted sense of social morality in Cambodia, which is filled with gendered double standards. According to a popular Khmer proverb, "Men are like gold, women are like cloth." This reinforces the idea that men can be easily washed clean and have value; yet, women, once stained, can never be cleaned and lose value.

There are also very strict gendered rules in Cambodia that dictate proper behavior for women known as the *Cbpab Srei* (Women's Code) (Brickell 2011; Derks 2008; Jacobsen 2008; Tarr 1996). Written by elite men and monks from the fourteenth to the nineteenth centuries, they refer to the appropriate conduct, appearance, and comportment required of a woman:

> Walk softly, so not to sound like an animal
> Don't stray far from the family home
> Don't wear short skirts, low-cut blouses, or present yourself as alluring in any way
> Never act like a man or think yourself to be better than a man
> (adapted from Mai 2001)

If a woman accepts these rules, she will remain virtuous and ensure that the household is "peaceful, pleasant and enjoyable" (Ledgerwood 1990); this is her "duty" as a Khmer woman.

While the Woman's Code is no longer taught in school and memorized, its message is still strong and reproduced in daily life. Women are seen to be the natural bearers of Cambodian tradition and morality (Brickell 2011; Derks 2008; Ledgerwood 1990). This has been made explicit in a formalized state-sponsored "morality projects." On International Women's Day in Phnom Penh in 2010, for example, Prime Minister Hun Sen announced that the Ministry of Women's Affairs and the National Committee for Promoting Social Morality, Women's Value, and Khmer Families were introducing a new initiative titled "Jointly Improving Women's and Youth Potential for Social Development," in which youth (as well as women) were now "officially" responsible for (the burden of) improving "economic and socio-cultural conditions, tradition, and customs of Cambodia" (Hun 2010).[5]

For the women in my study, this, in addition to backlashes related to the 2008 antitrafficking law[6] resulted in increased and arbitrary policing of clothing in bars, where some women were randomly charged fines of up to $200 for wearing short skirts. Hostess bars with dancing poles or platforms were given fines between $10,000 and $20,000, despite the fact that these fines are completely discriminatory and based on "moral codes" rather than any formalized Cambodian laws that criminalize clothing, poles, stages or dancing (Hoefinger 2013). On Valentine's Day—which is an increasingly popular Western holiday taking hold in Cambodia—there are often state-sponsored campaigns on TV and radio and actual physical policing of guesthouses aimed at keeping young people from having sex together on that day. On Valentine's Day in 2012, the Phnom Penh municipal police chief went so far as comparing youth sex to "anarchy" (see Titthara and Worrell 2012). These measures are punitive and extreme, yet the messages women receive in media are contradictory, as highlighted above.

Audrey Yue (2012) really captures the messiness of these various contradictions, particularly in relation to state governance, with her concept of "illiberal pragmatism," which refers to the "ambivalence between rationality and irrationality, liberalism and non-liberalism that regulates the pragmatic interventions of government" (237). Through an examination of female blogging in Singapore, she concludes that nations construct themselves as modern by providing the necessary material conditions for women to progress socioeconomically, but at the same time these gendered nation-building strategies ensure that women structure their life decisions around family, which ultimately works to reinforce patriarchal state power. A similar phenomenon is at work in Cambodia.

Negotiating Contradictions and the Illusion of Choice

While it is critical for Cambodian women to maintain their dignity and virtue by adhering to social codes—one being not to stray far from home—they are also responsible for improving economic and sociocultural conditions, which *requires* them to leave home and work. Thus, they face a contradiction between economic liberalism and entrepreneurialism on the one hand and authoritarian modes of governance and strict social codes dictating women's lives on the other, which unsurprisingly leaves them feeling very confused and ambivalent (Kim 2012b; Nilan 2012; Yue 2012).

Though the women achieve a sense of freedom and choice from their migration to the city and employment in bars, Martin and Lewis (2012) and Thornham and Pengpeng (2012) point out that within the hegemonic system of neoliberalization, the language of "choice" and "empowerment" is often an illusion. Freedom and individuality are promoted in the image of the "new woman" who engages with consumer culture but this "new woman" is not really free and mobile but instead always constrained by the fashion and beauty complex (Dewey 2012; McRobbie 2009; Shaw and Lin 2012), which is a form of gender regulation that requires them to remain within the strict confines of a stereotypical yet unattainable femininity that is based on relentless self-monitoring, self-improvement, self-branding and self-promotion (Hambelton 2012, 2013; Wu 2012). Yet it is also a femininity that requires that life decisions are structured around the family—despite all the emphasis on individualization. All of this ultimately works to re-traditionalize women and reinforce patriarchal state power (Martin and Lewis 2012).

Kim explains (2012b, 8), "Nation-building strategies of gendered state policies encourage women to identify as members of families and to structure life decisions around the family, rather than gender-based individualized identity, which ultimately works to reinforce state/male power as the only agent able to deal with difficult modernizing conditions not of its own making." Thus, for Khmer women, the process of individualization, and the associated discourses of "choice-based selfhood" that are promoted by the media may actually involve reinscriptions of older forms of ascribed gendered identity, and essentialist understandings of women's roles and femininity because the media is ultimately engineered, manufactured, and controlled by the state (Martin and Lewis 2012).

However, Yue (2012, 251) points out that although compliant female subjects are produced whose practices resonate with gendered state policies, it is through subactivism that these female subjects demonstrate resistance through everyday small-scale political and ethical decisions. According to Maria Bakardjieva (2009,

92), subactivism is "a kind of politics that unfolds at the level of subjective experience and is submerged in the flow of everyday life. It is constituted by small-scale, often individual, decisions and actions that have either a political or ethical frame of reference (or both) and are difficult to capture using the traditional tools with which political participation is measured." I argue it is through such subactivism that Cambodian professional girlfriends and bar workers grapple with contradictions around individualization, gender roles, and social expectations.

Subactivism

A key goal of this chapter is to illustrate the ways women are negotiating all these contradictions and ambivalences that exist at the uneasy intersection of what Pam Nilan (2012) describes in her study of young Muslim woman in Indonesia and Malaysia as individualized modernity and institutionalized morality. These specific binaries include freedom/constriction, submission/emancipation, Westernized sexual culture/Buddhist asceticism, and moral virtue/having fun (Nilan 2012). By acting as taboo-breaking "phallic girls" (McRobbie 2009), which involves working at night in bars, wearing provocative clothes, "sexy" dancing, drinking alcohol, doing drugs, flirting with foreigners, and having premarital sex, bar girls are directly challenging and defying "traditionally" constructed meanings of Khmer womanhood, respectability, and family honor in their pursuit of becoming modern, individualized, "strong" girls. They are seen to have disregarded the gendered social roles 100 percent and are thus stigmatized as the epitome of "bad women," "broken women" and even subhuman in some cases (Lind van Wijngaarden 2003).

Paradoxically, however, by financially and materially fulfilling their financial obligations to their families through using sex and intimacy as a tool to materially benefit from foreign men, they can sometimes salvage their tarnished reputations. Leap paid for her siblings' school tuition, and bought her family a car and big house with Western amenities (such as a new fridge that sat empty because her family were not accustomed to using one). Because of her spending power, English skills, and her exposure to the global community, Leap was even sometimes accorded an almost celebrity-like status—the "movie star" she always longed to be. By conspicuously displaying their wealth and generosity to their families and friends, women gain prestige, which is then further bestowed on their family members through the system of patronage.[7] Through this mechanism, some women ultimately become proud patrons in their own families, and thus experience simultaneous stigma and praise as they are embroiled in a type of "double value system" (Hoefinger 2013).

Therefore, in these women's projects of "becoming modern," there is not a complete repudiation of tradition, religious beliefs, morals, or institutions of marriage and extended family support. As noted above, there is a strong degree of collectivism in Cambodian culture, and there is a need to move away from homogenizing assumptions about detraditionalization as always being linked to highly individualized freedom of choice (Nilan 2012). Many bar workers do still desire to remain closely tied to tradition, their homes, and to local ways of life. And as Edward and Roces (2000, 10–11) note, the contemporary woman in Asia simultaneously "straddles between tradition and modernity, victimization and agency, between being a subject and an object." As I have argued elsewhere, "Women are, at once, 'symbols of progress and modernity' (Derks 2008: 13), yet traditional 'culture bearers par excellence' (Ledgerwood 1990: 2); they '(de)stabilize putatively traditional ideals of Cambodian womanhood' while 'resituat[ing] them in the contemporary period' at the same time (Brickell 2011: 437). Gilroy (1993) identifies this as the active adoption of a 'double consciousness', which not only connotes a bridged way of thinking, but also a bridged appearance, behaviour, and way of speech" (Hoefinger 2013, 127).

The women's lives and identities are becoming "hybridized" as they embrace "glamorous modernity," which, James Farrer (2005 [1999], 481), in his study of transnational sexual encounters in Chinese discos, defines as "a global culture celebrating consumption, fashion and sexuality in which youth on every continent participate, reinforcing an emergent global hegemony of consumer values." Here, consumption should not be seen as erosion of culture (as it often is), but rather as part of the creation of "social and cultural identities" (Miller 1995, 156). For the bar workers and professional girlfriends in this study, the act of utilizing sex and intimacy as tools to buy new clothes or pay for their siblings' tuition can be seen as a space not only for identity construction, but also sharing, bonding, altruism, personal exchange and pleasure (McRobbie 2009), and could also be viewed as a form of subactivism.

Thus, despite the women possibly being complicit feminine subjects, they actually make use of make use of style, information technology, intimacy, and the global fashion and beauty complex in order to create hybridized identities that incorporate elements of both Khmerness and Westernness. Participation in the bar girl subculture allows them to also create their own families and subcultural alternative kinship networks for support and survival that in many ways are similar to Judith Butler's (1993) queer kinship. Thus, while the women might represent a paradox in terms of their behaviors and the expected social ideals, they also represent a bridge between them, and, as such, are agents of change (Hoefinger 2013).

Conclusion

To conclude, while the state's growing emphasis on autonomy is at times at odds with more collectivist modes of living and being that are traditionally practiced within Cambodian culture and while this creates a new arena of anxiety for the women, who are left negotiating both the liberatory and constricting forces of globalization; and while the concept of "free choice" within neoliberal capitalism doesn't really exist, women use subactivism within the bar girl subculture to actually resist and subvert patriarchy while often remaining within the context of the existing sexual and gendered status quo. By migrating from their homes to work in cities, and following in the footsteps of their sisters before them, many young Khmer women are unapologetically resisting the constricting demands of the contemporary social codes that require them to remain compliant and submissive. And while women's experiences are heterogeneous and vary greatly across the sex and entertainment sectors, it could be argued that by utilizing men for their own material benefits, some women are undermining the unidirectional exploitation discourse by blatantly "exploiting back" (Hoefinger 2013, 2014). Despite experiencing constant contradictions around individualization, and unremitting stigma for the decisions they make, they transgress the boundaries of respectability, challenge gendered double standards, and reconcile individualism and collectivity by becoming proud patrons and providers for their families.

As Yue (2012) concludes, the illiberal pragmatism that governs identities and new subjectivities can also facilitate new practices that are both complicit with and resistant to it at the same time. In other words, compliant female subjects are produced whose practices resonate with gendered state policies, yet through subactivism these female subjects demonstrate resistance through everyday political and ethical decisions that "traverse the private/public and self/collective" (251). Thus, these new female subjectivities—who take the shape of professional girlfriends and bar girls in Cambodia—are at once "hegemonic, complicit *and* transgressive" (252, italics added).

Notes and References

1. "Bar girl" is a term the women self-reference with.
2. The data presented in this chapter was collected during intensive immersion-based ethnography in the hostess bar scene in Phnom Penh between 2003 and 2012, and from interviews and conversations with over one hundred cis-gendered female workers.
3. I define "professional girlfriends" as women who engage in multiple overlapping transactional gift-based relationships via a performance of intimacy in order to gain material benefits and support their livelihoods. For more, see Hoefinger (2011, 2013).

4. UNTAC stands for the United Nations Transitional Authority in Cambodia.

5. See Hun Sen (2010) for a copy of this speech.

6. Under pressure from (and with the help of) the U.S. Department of State, new antitrafficking legislation was implemented by the Cambodian government in order to meet the standards imposed by the U.S. government's annual Trafficking in Persons (TIP) report. The Law on Suppression of Human Trafficking and Sexual Exploitation was enacted in February 2008 and has since caused a negative backlash for people working in the sex and entertainment sectors. For more on the backlash, see Human Rights Watch (2010).

7. All of Cambodian society is organized through a system of patronage whereby "followers [attach] themselves to a person of higher status. . . . Patrons and clients are locked in a system of unequal exchange. . . . Patrons have power and influence, and can distribute resources to and provide protection for their clients. Clients in turn provide loyalty and personal assistance which contributes to the patron's power" (Ledgerwood 1990, 16).

Appadurai, Arjun. 1991. "Global Ethnoscapes: Notes and Queries for a Transnational Anthropology." In *Recapturing Anthropology: Working in the Present,* edited by R. G. Fox, pp. 191–210. Santa Fe, NM: School of American Research Press.

Bakardjievaa, Maria. 2009. "Subactivism: Lifeworld and Politics in the Age of the Internet." *Information Society: An International Journal* 25 (2): 91–104.

Bauman, Zygmunt. 2001. *The Individualized Society.* Cambridge, UK: Polity.

Beck, Ulrich, and Beck-Gernsheim, Elisabeth. 2002. *Individualization.* London: Sage.

Bernstein, Elizabeth. 2007. *Temporarily Yours: Intimacy, Authenticity and the Commerce of Sex.* Chicago: University of Chicago Press.

Brennan, Denise. 2004. *What's Love Got to Do With It? Transnational Desires and Sex Tourism in the Dominican Republic.* Durham, NC: Duke University Press.

Brickell, Katherine. 2011. " 'We Don't Forget the Old Rice Pot When We Get the New One': Gendered Discourses on Ideals and Practices of Women in Contemporary Cambodia." *Signs: Journal of Women in Culture and Society* 36 (2): 437–462.

Brown, Eleanor. 2007. *The Ties That Bind: Migration and Trafficking of Women and Girls for Sexual Exploitation in Cambodia.* Phnom Penh: International Organization for Migration.

Brown, Louise. 2000. *Sex Slaves: The Trafficking of Women in Asia.* London: Virago Press.

Busza, Joanna. 2004. "Sex Work and Migration: The Dangers of Oversimplification: A Case Study of Vietnamese Women in Cambodia." *Health and Human Rights* 7 (1): 3–21.

Butler, Judith. 1993. *Bodies That Matter: On the Discursive Limits of "Sex."* New York: Routledge.

Chandler, David. 1991. *The Tragedy of Cambodian History: Politics, War and Revolution since 1945.* New Haven, CT: Yale University Press.

———. 2000. *A History of Cambodia.* 3rd ed. Boulder, CO: Westview Press.

Cressey, Paul. 2005 [1932]. "The Life-Cycle of the Taxi-Dancer." In *The Subcultures Reader, Second Edition,* edited by K. Gelder, pp. 35–35. New York: Routledge.

Derks, Annuska. 2008. *Khmer Women on the Move: Exploring Work and Life in Urban Cambodia.* Honolulu: University of Hawai'i Press.

Dewey, Susan. 2012. "'To Do Whatever She Wants': Miss India, Bollywood and the Gendered Self." In *Women and the Media in Asia: The Precarious Self*, edited by Y. Kim, pp. 204–219. London: Palgrave Macmillan.

Edwards, Penny, and Mina Roces, eds. 2000. *Women in Asia: Tradition, Modernity and Globalization*. St Leonards, Australia: Allen and Unwin.

Farley, Melissa, Wendy Freed, Kien Srey Phal, and Jaqueline Golding. 2012. "A Thorn in the Heart: Cambodian Men Who Buy Sex." Paper presented at "Focus on Men Who Buy Sex: Discourage Men's Demand for Prostitution, Stop Sex Trafficking." Phnom Penh: Cambodian Women's Crisis Center and Prostitution Research and Education.

Farrer, James. 2005 [1999]. "Disco 'Super-Culture': Consuming Foreign Sex in the Chinese Disco." In *The Subcultures Reader*. 2nd ed., edited by K. Gelder, pp. 479–490. New York: Routledge.

Giddens, Anthony. 1991. *Modernity and Self-Identity: Self and Society in the Late Modern Age*. Stanford, CA: Stanford University Press.

Gilroy, Paul. 1993. *The Black Atlantic: Modernity and Double Consciousness*. London: Verso.

Hambleton, Alexandra. 2012. "Women and Sexual Desire in the Japanese Popular Media." In *Women and the Media in Asia: The Precarious Self*, edited by Y. Kim, pp. 115–129. London: Palgrave Macmillan.

Hoang, Kimberly Kay. 2011. "'She's Not a Low-Class Dirty Girl!': Sex Work in Ho Chi Minh City, Vietnam." *Journal of Contemporary Ethnography* 40 (4): 367–396.

Hochschild, Arlie Russell. 2003 [1983]. *The Managed Heart: Commercialization of Human Feeling, 20th Anniversary Edition*. Berkeley: University of California Press.

Hoefinger, Heidi. 2011. "Professional Girlfriends: An Ethnography of Sexuality, Solidarity and Subculture in Cambodia." *Cultural Studies* 25 (2): 244–266.

———. 2013. *Sex, Love and Money in Cambodia: Professional Girlfriends and Transactional Relationships*. London: Routledge.

———. 2014. "Re-Evaluating Anti-Trafficking—Cambodian Feminisms and Sex Work Realities." *Hysteria: A Collection of Feminisms* 3: "Abjection."

Human Rights Watch (HRW). 2010. *Off the Streets: Arbitrary Detention and Other Abuses against Sex Workers in Cambodia*. Phnom Penh: HRW.

Hun, Sen. 2010. "Keynote Address at the 99th Anniversary of International Women's Day," Phnom Penh. http://www.cnv.org.kh/.

Hunter, Mark. 2002. "The Materiality of Everyday Sex: Thinking beyond 'Prostitution.'" *African Studies* 61 (1): 99–120.

International Labour Organization (ILO). 2010. *Research Snapshot: Garment Workers Tracking Survey*. Phnom Penh: ILO.

Jacobsen, Trude. 2008. *Lost Goddesses: The Denial of Female Power in Cambodian History*. Vol. 4. Copenhagen: NIAS Press.

Jacobsen, Trude, and Martin Stuart-Fox. 2013. "Power and Political Culture in Cambodia." Asia Research Institute Working Paper Series, no. 200. Singapore: Asia Research Institute of the National University of Singapore.

Kiernan, Ben. 1996. *The Pol Pot Regime: Race, Power and Genocide in Cambodia under the Khmer Rouge, 1975–79*. New Haven, CT: Yale University Press.

Kim, Youna, ed. 2012a. *Women and the Media in Asia: The Precarious Self*. London: Palgrave Macmillan.

———. 2012b. "Introduction: Female Individualization and Popular Media Culture in Asia." In *Women and the Media in Asia: The Precarious Self*, edited by Y. Kim, pp. 1–27. London: Palgrave Macmillan.

———. 2012c. "Female Individualization? Transnational Mobility and Media Consumption of Asian Women." In *Women and the Media in Asia: The Precarious Self*, edited by Y. Kim, pp. 31–52. London: Palgrave Macmillan.

Ledgerwood, Judy. 1990. "Changing Khmer Conceptions of Womanhood: Women, Stories and the Social Order." PhD diss., Cornell University.

Lind van Wijngaarden, J. W. 2003. *Broken Women, Virgins and Housewives: Reviewing the Socio-cultural Contexts of Sex Work and Gender in Cambodia*. Bangkok: UNESCO.

Mai, Minh. 2001. *Cbpab Srei-proh*. Translated by S. Pou. Phnom Penh: Phsep pseay juon koan khmei.

Martin, Fran, and Tania Lewis. 2012. "Lifestyling Women: Emergent Femininities on Singapore and Taiwan TV." In *Women and the Media in Asia: The Precarious Self*, edited by Y. Kim, pp. 53–76. London: Palgrave Macmillan.

McRobbie, Angela. 2009. *The Aftermath of Feminism: Gender, Culture and Social Change*. London: Sage.

Miller, Daniel. 1995. "Consumption and Commodities." *Annual Review of Anthropology* 24: 141–161.

Nilan, Pam. 2012. "Young Women and Everyday Media Engagement in Muslim Southeast Asia." In *Women and the Media in Asia: The Precarious Self*, edited by Y. Kim, pp. 77–95. London: Palgrave Macmillan.

Population Services International and Family Health International (PSI/FHI). 2007. *Let's Go for a Walk: Sexual Decision-Making among Clients of Female Entertainment Service Workers in Phnom Penh, Cambodia*. Phnom Penh: PSI/FHI.

Sandy, Larissa. 2013. "International Agendas and Sex Worker Rights in Cambodia." In *Social Activism in Southeast Asia*, edited by Michele Ford, 154–169. London: Routledge.

———. 2014. *Women and Sex Work in Cambodia: Blood, Sweat and Tears*. London: Routledge.

Schwartz, Abigail. 2003. "Sex Trafficking in Cambodia." *Columbia Journal of Asian Law* 17: 371–422.

Shaw, Ping, and Chin-yi Lin. 2012. "Move Freely: Single Women and Mobility in Taiwanese TV Advertising." In *Women and the Media in Asia: The Precarious Self*, edited by Y. Kim, pp. 130–142. London: Palgrave Macmillan.

Tarr, Chou Meng. 1996. *People in Cambodia Don't Talk about Sex, They Simply Do It! A Study of the Social and Contextual Factors Affecting Risk-Related Sexual Behaviour among Young Cambodians*. Phnom Penh: Prepared for UNAIDS by the Cambodian AIDS Social Research Project.

Thornham, Sue, and Feng Pengpeng. 2012. "'Just a Slogan': Individualism, Post-Feminism and Female Subjectivity in Consumerist China." In *Women and the Media in Asia: The Precarious Self*, edited by Y. Kim, pp. 96–114. London: Palgrave Macmillan.

Titthara, May, and Shane Worrell. 2012. "A Vigilant Valentine's." *Phnom Penh Post,* February 14.

Wu, Jing. 2012. "Post-Socialist Articulation of Gender Positions: Contested Public Sphere of Reality Dating Shows." In *Women and the Media in Asia: The Precarious Self,* edited by Y. Kim, pp. 220–236. London: Palgrave Macmillan.

Yue, Audrey. 2012. "Female Individualization and Illiberal Pragmatism: Blogging and New Life Politics in Singapore." In *Women and the Media in Asia: The Precarious Self,* edited by Y. Kim, pp. 237–254. New York: Palgrave Macmillan.

Zelizer, Viviana A. 2005. *The Purchase of Intimacy.* Princeton, NJ: Princeton University Press.

CHAPTER ELEVEN

Islam, Marriage, and Yaari

Making Meaning of Male Same-Sex Sexual Relationships in Pakistan

AHMED AFZAL

In this chapter I employ a cultural analysis to explore cultural constructions of male same-sex sexual relationships in Pakistan. My ethnographic research focused on Pakistani Sunni Muslim men from the Punjabi ethnolinguistic community and tracks several of these men over the course of almost two decades (from 1994 to 2013). These men resided in extended family households in high-density, lower-middle-income localities in the metropolis of Rawalpindi in Pakistan. They were employed in a variety of professional settings. Aamir worked as a clerk at a governmental agency.[1] Aamir's partner, Sohail, owned his own grocery store. Javed worked as an assistant manager at a large department store. Faisal was a full-time cab driver. The youngest of my interlocutors, Reza, had just recently completed high school and was working as a receptionist at a four-star hotel.

The commonality between these men extended beyond shared ethnolinguistic and classed identities to the realm of sexuality: all of these men were involved in sexual relationships with other men. Significantly, none self-identified as "homosexual" or "bisexual." As I learned, such categorizations of a fixed sexual identity had very little meaning in their lives and did not encapsulate their construction of a fluid, culturally informed male sexuality that permitted sexual relationships with both women *and* men. Critical components of such a culturally constructed male sexuality include the absence of gender anxiety regarding engaging in sex with other men, the desire for heterosexual marriage and family, and adherence to Islam.

Drawing on the life experiences and narratives of my interlocutors, I explore cultural constructions of a nonheteronormative male sexuality and everyday negotiations of religion, gender, and sexuality through the following set of interrelated questions. How do these men craft gendered identities and selfhoods that disavow labels such as "homosexual," "bisexual," and even "heterosexual" and are premised on a fluid sexuality? How is religion intertwined with such presentations of self? How are these relationships structured? How are notions of marriage and sexual intimacy reconfigured in these same-sex sexual relationships? And finally, what are the cultural scripts that explain this fluidity? I focus on three intersecting registers in making meaning of these male same-sex sexual relationships: a) assertions of religious belonging; b) conceptions of marriage and familial obligations; and c) cultural scripts of homosociality, notably the concept of *yaari* (friendship).

This chapter contributes to recent studies of nonheteronormative sexualities in contemporary Muslim communities (e.g., Gaudio 2009; Hendricks 2009; Jama 2008; Kugle 2003, 2014; Massad 2007; Merabet 2014; Roscoe and Murray 1997; Whitaker 2006). Following such scholarship, the research presented here also belies common misunderstandings of contemporary Muslim cultures and societies as inherently intolerant of same-sex sexual desire, intimacy, and relationships and instead illuminates spaces for accommodation of same-sex sexual relationships and intimacies. Covering Muslim communities in Africa, the Middle East and the Arab world, South Asia, Europe, and the United States, the above scholarship documents the experiences of gay communities cross-culturally and globally, and their modes of activism to claim rights, visibility, and space as nonheteronormative subjects.

In *Living Out Islam: Voices of Gay, Lesbian, and Transgender Muslims*, an exemplary study that characterizes the recent scholarship, religious studies scholar Scott Siraj al-Haqq Kugle (2014) draws on the narratives and biographies of queer Muslim activists in Canada, Europe, South Africa, and the United States to illuminate the varied appropriations of Islam as a source of capital in fashioning nonheteronormative selfhoods and activism. As the biographies included in Kugle's important and necessary work demonstrate, lesbian, gay, and transgender Muslims who reside in modern secular democratic nation-states do not reject Islam and instead actively engage with religious tradition by reinterpreting the Qur'an. Several of Kugle's interlocutors participate in lesbian and gay Muslim groups and seek out coreligionists in an effort to reconcile their nonheteronormative sexuality with a professed belonging to Islam. As these biographies reveal, the lesbian, gay, and transgender experience is deeply varied as it is continuously shaped and reshaped by specificities of individual life experiences and the broader sociocultural, historical, and political contexts.

Other studies in the canon elaborate practices of place-making and everyday negotiations of sexuality, citizenship, and belonging. For example, in *Queer Beirut*, anthropologist Sofian Merabet (2014) draws on the narratives of gay men to illuminate the appropriations and contestations of urban space in the production of queer cultures in post–civil war Lebanon. Merabet deftly employs ethnography to explore the spatial, the temporal, and the embodied in the formation of queer spaces and socialities. The notion of "zones of encounter," that is, "particular urban locations that foster attempts, with various levels of success, to transcend spatio-temporal fixities" (5) in the production of queer spaces and socialities, foreground the analysis in the volume. *Queer Beirut* offers valuable insights about the complexities of queer lives in contemporary Beirut and is a significant experimental ethnography about sexuality, citizenship, and belonging in the Middle East.

In spite of the importance of this scholarship, most of these studies employ Western epistemologies of sexuality and focus on queer cultures and on men who self-identify as gay, bisexual, or transgender. Unlike the subjects in these studies, my interlocutors disavowed such self-labeling in fashioning nonheteronormative subjectivities and selfhoods. Their life experiences and narratives demonstrate how a range of sexualities are produced and enacted in the non-West and compel a rethinking of the pervasive reliance on Western epistemologies in making meaning of nonheteronormative subjectivities in contemporary Muslim communities and societies. I argue that these sexual cultures do not reflect a premodern sexuality, unfettered by what Middle East scholar Joseph Massad (2007) has termed the "Gay International"; that is, the globalization of Western categories of sexual identification and the production of modernity among nonheteronormative communities in the non-West. Rather, these sexual cultures are complexly intertwined with transnational religious revivalist movements, globalization, and engagements in the neoliberal economy.

To be clear, in contemporary Pakistan the global flows of people, media, technologies, ideologies, and finances have in fact contributed to the emergence of Western gay communities and lifestyles. It is beyond the scope of this chapter to elaborate on these emergent gay communities. It must be noted, however, that recent interdisciplinary scholarship on contemporary South Asia has begun the important task of documenting gay lives at the intersection of globalization, the transnational flow of ideologies around sexuality, and traditional forms of authority and knowledge (e.g., Bhattacharyya and Bose 2007; Dave 2012; Narrain and Bhan 2006; Shahani 2008).

Two caveats are in order before continuing further. One, the data presented in this chapter reflects a culturally constructed male sexuality through the lens of a very specific group of men; that is, Punjabi Muslim men who reside in the city of Rawalpindi and with whom I interacted during the period of my ethnographic research. My intention in this chapter is to ground the analysis within the specificities of the individual experiences and narratives of my interlocutors. I follow anthropologist Richard Parker's (1999) analysis of emerging gay communities in Brazil and similarly approach the narratives in this chapter as "a collection of fragments, slices of life, bits and pieces" (23) rather than a totalizing or definitive account of nonheteronormative male sexualities in contemporary

Pakistan. Relatedly, the omission of lesbian and bisexual Pakistani women in this chapter is primarily due to my lack of exposure to female interlocutors. Research on nonheteronormative Muslim women is an important and essential project. Recent scholarship on same-sex sexual relationships among women in South Asia serves to fill such gaps in knowledge and provides important directions for future research (e.g., Gopinath 2005; Thadani 1998; Vanita 2001).

Two, in several places in this chapter, I draw on analyses of male sexuality in Bangladesh and India in the discussion of the broader contexts that shape male same-sex relationships and intimacies in Pakistan. The slippage between Bangladesh, India, and Pakistan is intentional. The inclusion of Bangladesh- and India-centered research highlights the similarities in cultural constructions of nonheteronormative sexualities across South Asia. Significantly, studies of male same-sex sexual relationships and intimacies in Bangladesh and India demonstrate the regional circulation of shared cultural idioms around sexuality that transcend the geographical borders of the postcolonial South Asian nation-states.

Religion and Nonheteronormative Selfhoods

In this section, I explore the negotiations of sexuality with religious self-identification as Muslim and assertions of belonging to the Muslim *ummah*, "a transnational supra-geographical community of fellow Muslims that transcends nationality and other bases of community" (Kibria 2011, 4). My interlocutors for this research belong to the dominant Sunni sect of Islam and are practicing Muslims. For these men, religion is a central facet of their identity and community life. For example, most of my interlocutors observed the alcohol prohibition, prayed regularly, and participated in the activities of their congregations at their local mosques. Most had also received religious education, notably reading the Qur'an as adolescents and during their teenage years.

The salience of religion extended beyond ritual and education, and was also apparent in their presentations of public self. For example, Faisal, a cab driver, had placed stickers with Qur'anic verses on the back windshield of his taxicab. Islamic prayer beads adorned the car's rearview mirror. On one occasion, when I asked Faisal about these adornments, he had replied: "My cab is my place of work, you know. By doing this, I feel that Allah blesses my business." Faisal's comment here invokes similar sentiments regarding the increasing salience of religion in shaping the work environments that were made by my interlocutors during the course of my research on Pakistani ethnic businesses in the United States (Afzal 2010, 2014b). Significantly, these similarities in worldviews demonstrate how transnational religious ideologies intersect with individual lived experiences and practices of subjectification in multiple sites, and link homeland and diaspora.

For my interlocutors, religion also shaped sexual intimacy. Faisal refrained from engaging in oral sex, perceiving it to be polluting and un-Islamic, and also abstained from sexual intercourse during the month of Ramadan, when Muslims fast from sunrise to sunset. Faisal, as well as several of my other interlocutors, also refrained from sexual relations during the call to prayers five times a day.

The centrality of Islam in fashioning selfhood among my interlocutors intersects with ongoing revivalism in Islam globally (Afzal 2010, 2014a, 2014b; Asad 2003; D'Alisera 2004; Kibria 2011). Revivalist movements in Islam, such as those associated with Wahabi Islam emanating from Saudi Arabia, sustain literalist interpretations of homosexuality in Islam. These literalist interpretations characterize Islam as a religious tradition and as a faith that "explicitly condemns homosexuality, which is addressed through the parable of Prophet Lut in the Qur'an" (Jaspal and Siraj 2011, 183). These literalist interpretations positively affirm and reward heterosexuality and denounce, criminalize, and punish any public expressions of homosexuality, foreclosing the possibility of accommodation of same-sex eroticism, love and relationships in Islam. These readings of the Qur'an also represent homosexuality as a Western import (Rahman 2010) in spite of the rich and varied repertoire of same-sex eroticism and relationships in South Asia and Muslim societies historically. For example, Roscoe and Murray (1997), in one of the few cross-cultural analysis of mostly Orientalist historical, anthropological, and literary texts produced in the Muslim world, make visible the many occurrences of same-sex sexual eroticism, love, and relationships and belie literalist interpretations of Islam.

Most scholarship on homosexuality and Islam takes as its starting point the literalist interpretations as the irrevocable and absolute truth without due consideration of the geopolitical, economic, and social contexts that shaped religious forms of knowledge (see, e.g., Doi 1984; Duran 1993; Jamal 2001; Yahya 2000; Yip 2004). Moreover, this scholarship scarcely, if at all, examines the historical contingency of scriptural knowledge, such as the rise of revivalist movements in Islam in the late twentieth century and the early twenty-first century. Equally, this scholarship only cursorily relates the production of scriptural knowledge to its interaction with lived experience, or the "variance in how homosexual conduct existed or exists and was or is understood in Islamic societies" (Rahman 2010, 950). Providing insights into hegemonic understandings in the West regarding the impossibility of accommodation of same-sex desire in Islam and in Muslim countries, and its intersection with production of the Muslim-as-terrorist following 9/11, Jasbir Puar (2007, 13–14) states, "Queer secularity most virulently surfaces in relation to Islam because Islam, the whole monolith of it, is often described as unyielding and less amenable to homosexuality than Christianity and Judaism, despite exhortations by some queer Muslims asserting sameness with Christian and Jewish counterparts."

Indeed, research by Muslim scholars such as Kugle (2003) provides compelling insights into accommodations of same-sex sexual eroticism and relationships in Islam historically. Going against the grain of dominant interpretive understandings of nonheteronormative sexualities and Islam, Kugle instead argues:

> In comparison with many other religious traditions . . . Islam is a religion that has evaluated sexual life positively. Articulating the integral relationship between spirituality and sexuality is one way that the Prophet Mohammad challenged his society. It remains for us, today, to continually struggle with that challenge. The system of norms, rules, and laws created by Muslims in the past does not absolve us of this challenge. . . . Muslims in pre-modern times certainly were not shy about discussing matters of sex. (190–191)

Writing about the experience of being Muslim and gay, Shahid Dossani (1997, 236) states, "I find it hard to imagine being able to live a mentally peaceful life, content with one's gay nature, in a Muslim country." Significantly however, in Dossani's assessment, "Overall there does not seem to be as much fear and hatred of homosexuality in the Qur'an as gay Muslims and others generally tend to think there is" (236).

In spite of the denigration of homosexuality in literalist interpretations of Islam, this had not led to a rejection of religion or even a distancing from religious life and sources of authority for my interlocutors. Rather, Islam is central to their lives, which ruptures scholarly interpretations of Islam and Muslim communities as a monolith incapable of nonheteronormative accommodation. Although literalist interpretations dominate the scholarship, critiques of this view show how literalist interpretations of homosexuality in the Qur'an and the *hadith* (sayings attributed to the Prophet Mohammad and perceived as a definitive source of Islamic knowledge) have increasingly co-opted alternative representations and understandings of homosexuality in Islam.

Structuring Male Same-Sex Sexual Relationships

Among my interlocutors, the salience of Islam in fashioning selfhoods intersected with an individually negotiated and highly variable repertoire of same-sex sex-

ual intimacies that disavow homosexual self-labeling. For example, Javed, an assistant manager at a departmental store, said to me: "I would never even think
about being with any other man except my childhood friend. We had been friends
for so long that it seemed only natural that we would eventually 'be together [sex-
ually].' But, I would never cross the line with someone else." Javed's sentiments
demonstrate the possibility of reinscribing close friendships as sites for a *natural*
sexual intimacy. Similarly configured friendships also appear in the literature on
nonheteronormative sexualities in contemporary South Asia (e.g., S. Khan 1997;
Merchant 2000; Ratti 1992; Vanita and Kidwai 2001). For example, a study of men
who have sex with men in Bangladesh includes the following narrative:

> We were friends for a long time and then started flirting and making jokes
> about how attractive we found each other. . . . One evening we were at his
> house and were lying on his bed and talking. The next thing I knew we
> were hugging each other madly. We took off each other's clothes and made
> out for hours. Our affair continued for a year. . . . Emotionally and physi-
> cally we were close as any lovers. (S. Khan 1997, 12)

Studies of male sexualities cross-culturally have illuminated the enactment
of a range of culturally constructed nonheteronormative sexual identities and behaviors. For example, anthropological studies of male sexuality in South American cultures (e.g., Carrier 1976; La Fountain-Stokes 2009; Lancaster 1988; Parker
1986, 1999; Taylor 1986) provide rich theoretical and ethnographic insights into
constructions of sexuality premised on sexual roles; that is, active or passive, rather
than sexual identity; that is, homosexual, bisexual, or heterosexual. Studies of men
who have sex with men in the West similarly show the limitations of using Western epistemologies of sexuality to describe sexual behaviors that preclude homosexual self-labeling (e.g., Blumstein and Schwartz 1990; Byne 1997; De Cecco and
Elia 1991; Hencken 1984; Humphreys 1970; Stein 1997; Weinberg 1978). The culture of "down-low" among African-American men in the United States is an important example of a culturally conceived nonheteronormative male sexuality
(King 2004). The term refers to heterosexual, married African-American men who
engage discreetly in sexual activities with other men but do not self-identify as
homosexual or bisexual.

My ethnographic research with Punjabi men like Faisal, Sohail, Aamir, Javed,
and Reza revealed similar configurations of male sexual desire and relationships
(Afzal 2005). For my interlocutors, sexual relationships with other men were exemplified by clearly articulated active and passive sexual roles for both partners.
The active sexual role is defined by the sexual act of penetration, and the passive

role is assumed by the partner who is penetrated. The active partner's engagement in the sexual act posed no threat to his masculinity or manhood, nor to his social identity as an implicitly heterosexual male. In fact, his ability to penetrate *both* women *and* men sexually contributed to an elevated status within the close circle of friends who were privy to these sexual relationships. The passive partner, on the other hand, remains vulnerable to being undermined as not a "real man," his masculinity and manhood sometimes in question. The act of being penetrated sexually—culturally conceived as feminine—contributes to a feminization of the passive male partner, at least in the realm of sexual intimacy. Not surprisingly, within such a cultural configuration of same-sex male desire, sexual relations between men become loosely modeled on established local patterns of gendered male-female marital relationships in patriarchal societies like Pakistan.

Although most of my interlocutors appropriated established local patterns of heterosexual, male-female marital relationships in organizing same-sex sexual relationships, the repertoire of acceptable sexual activities was individually negotiated and varied from couple to couple. The men mutually established and negotiated the boundaries of sexual play including kissing, oral sex, and penetration with their partners. Javed, for example, shared that his boyfriend was uncomfortable with kissing on the lips. Reza's repertoire of sexual activities was limited to caressing, kissing, and oral sex. "I cannot bare the idea of being penetrated. I think I am more passive because I wouldn't want to penetrate my [male] partner either," he told me during one of our more candid conversations at his home.

Despite such assertions of the naturalness of same-sex sexual intimacy and individually negotiated sexual roles within such relationships, all of these men planned to eventually marry a woman and raise a family. The desire for marriage and children may well be characterized as a familial and societal expectation and as conformity to dominant societal gender roles. Complicating this characterization, most Punjabi men I met *wanted* to marry and raise a family. Over the course of my research, I came to appreciate that for these men, marriage and children were integral to their sense of a masculine self and adulthood, and social status within their communities. Sexual relationships between men appeared to have their own valued place; however, these relationships did not replace the desire for heterosexual matrimony, a subject that I discuss more fully below.

Marriage and Same-Sex Sexual Intimacies

I had first met Aamir in 1994 through an acquaintance and we quickly became friends. Aamir became a valuable interlocutor in my research on same-sex sexual relationships between men in Pakistan (Afzal 1995, 2005). As I learned over the course of the several months after meeting Aamir, he had been involved in a monogamous sexual relationship with Sohail, a friend since they were teenagers. Aamir and I were sitting outside of Sohail's grocery store when I asked Aamir whether he intended to get married. He seemed perplexed by my question. "What do you mean, if I'll get married? Of course, I'll get married! I want to get married. . . . Don't I want to have children?"

"What about Sohail?" I asked.

"Sohail will get married also," Aamir replied.

"Will you still be with Sohail after you get married?" I asked wanting to press the issue of how same-sex sexual relations could coexist with a desire for a marital life with a woman.

"Sohail is my *jaan* (life/beloved). . . . I could never be without him. . . . You know, I once went to see Sufi sahib, a saint, whom my family visits for counsel. I did not even mention Sohail by name to Sufi sahib but just told him that that I was in love with someone. Sufi sahib already knew. It was almost as if he could see inside my heart. He told me, 'I know you are in love with a man.' If I could, I would marry Sohail."

During a visit to Pakistan in the summer of 2012, I met Aamir for the first time after almost ten years. Much had changed in Aamir's life since we had last met. He had settled into a comfortable life and started his own business—a DVD rental store. He had married and was the proud father of two young girls and a boy. The passage of time showed in his appearance—his hairline had thinned considerably and the previously taut and muscled physique had given way to a portly stomach that he still carried well on his five feet eleven frame. In spite of these changes, his long sexual relationship with Sohail of over fifteen years had continued through both their marriages.

Faisal was also among the several men with whom I became close friends during the course of my research. He had completed high school in Rawalpindi and after several months looking for a job in the private and public sectors, took out a loan to purchase a taxicab. When I met Faisal in 1994, he had been driving his taxicab for over two years and often worried about his financial situation. Faisal had been romantically involved with a young woman with whom he had attended high school. However, his love affair came to an abrupt end when his girlfriend's working-class parents discovered their relationship and decided that Faisal could not provide the upward economic mobility they wanted for their daughter. The relationship could not withstand the pressure from her parents and ended soon afterward.

It was almost a year after the relationship ended that Faisal met Salim, a junior-level executive at a local hotel in Rawalpindi. Faisal's taxicab route brought him regularly to the hotel. Over a period of several months, Faisal and Salim became friends, often spending the evenings together going for long drives in Faisal's cab. However, their relationship changed on a weekend trip to a hill resort. They shared a hotel room on the trip and according to Faisal, one thing led to another and they ended up having sex. Faisal had never had a sexual relationship with a man before Salim. When I asked Faisal about his relationship with Salim, he did not express any gender anxiety about being involved with another man.

"No, never. . . . Never been with a man, and neither had Salim," Faisal told me as we sat in his cab one late evening. "I am being completely honest with you. I had never thought about having sex with another man. My girlfriend was my first love. I thought I would marry her, but her parents opposed our marriage. After my relationship ended, I just did not think I would ever be able to love someone as passionately again. . . . I have only loved two people like this—my girlfriend and now Salim."

"Do you think you'll get married?" I asked him.

"I know that in America, men live together as couples but we can't do that here. Can you imagine if I was living together with Salim? If I weren't living in Pakistan, I would marry Salim. I would perform all duties of a husband, and Salim my wife."

"Would you continue your relationship with Salim after you marry?" I asked.

"Of course, my love and feelings for Salim don't have anything to do with marriage."

My interlocutors perceived marriage as a sacred duty and believed that social stigma would become attached to those who remained single beyond a certain age. Given such understandings of marriage, even men who might eroticize a person of their own gender and *prefer* a same-sex sexual relationship feel the pressure to marry (Agha 1999; B. Khan 1992; S. Khan 1997). However, it would appear that marriage provides these men with the freedom to establish and maintain same-sex sexual relationships. Discussing bisexuality in India, Ramakrishnan (1996, 4) argues that "it doesn't matter, once these [familial] duties are fulfilled, who . . . you [have sex with]. So long as it is done discreetly and you don't talk about it." Indeed, by 2012, all of my interlocutors—Aamir, Sohail, Faisal, Reza, and Javed—had married and were raising young families, assuming the role of husband and father. Yet, for all of the desire for marriage and heterosexual procreation, such societal and familial expectations had not precluded same-sex relationships for them. As noted above, Aamir and Sohail were still involved in a sexual relationship in 2012, and told me that their wives knew of their "friendship." "We don't really talk about it. Where's the need?" Sohail said to me when I asked if his wife was privy to his relationship with Aamir. This arrangement could be said to subordinate women, demonstrate male privilege in patriarchal societies, and rupture conceptions of marriage as the sole site for the production of sexual intimacy, pleasure, and desire.

It would be erroneous, however, to construe such same-sex sexual relationships between men as male privilege or as a compromised expression of homosexual desire that cannot be expressed publicly and mobilized into a public identity. For men like Aamir, Sohail, Faisal, Reza and Javed, having a wife and children formed the basis of their social status within their family, kin, and community. It was not their sexual relationships and intimate friendships with men, no matter how much pleasure they may have derived from them, that gave meaning and validation to their *public* social life. Writing on Pakistani male sexuality, Badruddin Khan (1992, 94) states, "the meaning and purpose of life has its root in loyalty to family, in protecting its honor and stature, in procreation, and in caring for children." Indian gay rights and HIV/AIDS activist and writer, Shivananda Khan (1997) similarly notes:

> Whether husband and wife get along with each other is strictly secondary to whether they breed well. If a husband takes care of his family's security needs and bears many children, what he does for personal sexual satisfaction is uninteresting to everyone involved, so long as he is discreet. It is certainly not discussed. It simply does not matter. It is quite irrelevant and—so long as it is kept a private matter—tolerated. (95)

Given this configuration of filial and community obligations, and societal expectations, Shivananda Khan (1997) argues that homosexual behavior is almost uninteresting:

> It does not create children, nor does it add to the potential of children in the family's resource base. . . . Sex in general is interesting primarily because of its impact on family, rather than its potential for individual pleasure or carnal fulfillment. (95)

As evidenced from the discussion in this section, marriage confers social status and illustrates the assumption of traditional gender roles expected of adult men in mainstream Pakistani society. However, doing so had not displaced the desire for same-sex sexual intimacies in my interlocutors. Given this configuration of gender and sexuality, what does one make of the salience of these friendships that sometimes extend to the realm of sexual intimacy and endure in spite of marriage? As I discuss below, cultural scripts such as the term *yaar* (friend) provide an important register in understanding the potential of same-sex friendships to become transformed into sites for the production of intimacy.

Yaari (Friendship): Cultural Scripts and the Eroticizing of Male Friendships

There are several interchangeably used words for "friend" in Urdu, among them *dost, humsafar, saathi,* and *yaar.* For example, in an autobiographical chapter in one of the first anthologies of the gay and lesbian experience in South Asia (Ratti 1993), one contributor, a gay Indian male using the pseudonym Ayyar, describes his quest for the ideal relationship in the following manner. Ayyar's (1993) description underscores the subversive potential of the term *yaar* to encapsulate sexually intimate friendships:

> Over the past few years I have come to realize that my meandering path through romance, sexual liaisons, and friendship has been, and still is, but a search for a singular relationship that can encompass all three of these elements. Such a bond is embodied in the concept of *yaari.* A *yaar* is an individual with whom one feels a deep, almost intangible connection. . . . For me a *yaar* embodies elements of both a friend and a lover, and I yearn for just such a connection with a man in my life. . . . There is really no English equivalent for this concept, no word that approaches its breadth and depth. *Friend* is not enough. *Buddy* is superficial, reeks of Budweiser beers and backslapping in bars. . . . A world of romantic images revolves around *yaari.* There are tales of *yaars* dying for one another. Even a wife must many a time take a backseat to a man's *yaar.* (167)

The subversive potential of the term *yaar* to encapsulate same-sex sexual relationships underscores the permissibility of such relationships in South Asia, and also speaks to conceptions of homosexual behaviors that preclude homosexual labeling. According to psychologist Joel Hencken (1984, 56), "For more involved relationships, 'special friendships' and love may be emphasized so that the relationship is seen as an expression of unique feelings for the partner that have no implications for sexual identity." Writing about the exchange of Holi (the Indian festival of color) greeting cards among Hindu men in the city of Banaras in India, anthropologist Lawrence Cohen (1995, 418) states that the men he interviewed spoke "not only of play . . . but of *pyar mohabbat,* of love and of the passions of the heart." Cohen notes that drawings of erect phallus did not refer to the world of the "the doer and the done to." Instead, "he [the sender] had drawn it from life and was offering it, as Penis, to another. *Holi* was here the possibility of penetration being a gift" (418). Badruddin Khan (1992) expresses a similar romanticized account of relationships between men in South Asia when he states:

> Love between men is, in fact, exalted, and tenderness, affection, and deep friendships are not uncommon. Unlike the macho backslap that passes for camaraderie in the West, men frequently hold hands while walking, and it is not uncommon to see men embracing. (99)

Close male friendships carry erotic potential in part because of the cultural permissibility of intense male bonding that is expressed in single-sex institutions such as schools or through socialization that brings together young men and creates gendered public cultures of leisure activities, entertainment, sociality, and living, for example eating, working, and sleeping together. The permissibility of same-sex sexual desire in intimate friendships may also be due to "the close emotional bonding and physical affection between male friends while discouraging premarital heterosexual social life" (Dynes and Donaldson 1992, xii).

Homosociality is also culturally reinforced, exalted, and glorified in South Asian popular culture, notably in mainstream Indian films, one of the primary sources of mass entertainment in India and elsewhere in South Asia, including Pakistan (Gopinath 1997, 2005). The themes of several popular films center on the almost sacredness of male friendships for which men willingly sacrifice the love of their beloved (a woman) for the love of their friend (a man). An anthropologist who lived with a Tamil family in southern India during the 1980s suggests that such themes in mainstream Indian feature films were continually reproduced in social relations and vice versa (Trawick 1992). Homosociality also extends to poetry and popular songs that "talk of undying friendship between men [and] are part of the repertoire of popular verse" (B. Khan 1992, 99). According to the eighteenth-century Urdu poet Abru, for example, "He who avoids the boy and desires the woman is not in love but a man of lust" (Naim 1979, 130).

The cultural acceptance and the social reinforcement of homosociality and male bonding contribute to the lack of gender anxiety regarding sex relationships and intimacy between close male friends. Cohen (1995, 417) states that the intense homosociality is defined not through "homosexual panic but through mutuality and *dosti* (friendship)." Cohen argues that homosociality holds the potential to collapse playfulness and penetration into a single desire. As such, sexual activity is transformed into a *khel* or *masti* (play) allowing sex to be conceptualized as an appropriate and acceptable facet of male friendships. As Cohen suggests:

> Different men may articulate the boundaries of friendship and play differently. . . . The boys and men who play around with friends their own age and of similar backgrounds must negotiate this mutual terrain of play. (417)

Gendered spaces of male sociality and the production of intimate and close male friendships in popular culture contribute to friendships with flexible boundaries. Yet, the sexual intimacies that are forged between men do not fit categorizations and self-labeling such as homosexual, bisexual, or heterosexual. Moreover, these relationships do not replace the desire for a heterosexual marital relationship and the performance of traditional gender roles as married men. Instead, sexually intimate male friendships coexist with the ideals of marriage, family, and children.

Conclusion

The cultural constructions of male sexuality and same-sex sexual relationships and eroticism in Pakistan discussed in this chapter do not reflect a premodern, "prior condition before assimilating into a [modern] gay identity" (Manalansan 2003, 186). Indeed, my interlocutors demonstrated considerable knowledge of gay rights in the West. For example, in the fall of 2012, when I met Aamir upon returning from the United States after almost a decade, he remarked to me: "I hear that there is a lot of momentum for gay marriage in the United States." He paused before adding, "It's different here." Aamir's remark was significant for two reasons. One, his knowledge of the political and public support around gay marriage in the United States indicated an awareness of same-sex sexual relationships globally, something which is often elided in analyses of "traditional" systems of culturally constructed sexualities in the non-West. Second, Aamir's reflection that "it's different here" indicates an understanding of how patterns of homosocialities vary cross-culturally and of how they are circumscribed by cultural context.

In this chapter, I have explored cultural constructions of male same-sex sexual relationships and eroticism in contemporary Pakistan. I examined three intersecting registers for making meaning of male same-sex sexual relationships: a) assertions of religious self-identification and belonging; b) conceptions of marriage and familial obligations; and c) cultural scripts of homosociality and sexually intimate friendships. The analysis shows how a range of sexualities are produced and enacted in the non-West, belying common misunderstandings of Muslim cultures and societies as inherently intolerant of nonheteronormative subjectivities and selfhoods. Rather, drawing on the life experiences of Pakistani men, the research presented in this chapter illuminates spaces for accommodation of same-sex sexual relationships and intimacies in contemporary Muslim cultures and societies at the intersection of everyday negotiations of religion, gender, and sexuality.

Notes and References

1. In keeping with established protocol for confidentiality in social science research, I have changed the names and certain identifying details for all interlocutors referenced in the essay.

Afzal, Ahmed. 1995. "Public Policy Limitations: The Individual, the Family and AIDS in Pakistan." *Development* 2: 61–63.

———. 2005. "Family Planning and Male Friendships: Saathi Condom and Male Same Sex-Sexual Desire in Pakistan." In *Culture and the Condom,* edited by Karen Anijar and Thuy DaoJensen, pp. 177–205. New York: Peter Lang.

———. 2010. "From an Informal to a Transnational Muslim Heritage Economy: Transformations in the Pakistani Ethnic Economy in Houston, Texas." *Urban Anthropology* 39 (4): 397–424.

———. 2014a. "Being Gay Has Been a Curse for Me": Gay Muslim Americans, Narrative and Negotiations of Belonging in the Muslim *Ummah.*" *Journal of Language and Sexuality* 3 (1): 60–86.

———. 2014b. *Lone Star Muslims: Transnational Lives and the South Asian Experience in Texas.* New York: New York University Press.

Agha, Sohail. 1999. "Sexual Behavior of Truck Drivers in Pakistan: Implications for AIDS Prevention Programs." Working Paper No. 24. PSI Research Division: Washington, DC.

Asad, Talal. 2003. *Formations of the Secular: Christianity, Islam, Modernity.* Stanford, CA: Stanford University Press.

Ayyar, Raj. 1993. "Yaari." In *A Lotus of Another Color: An Unfolding of the South Asian Gay and Lesbian Experience,* edited by Rakesh Ratti, pp. 167–174. Boston: Alyson.

Bhattacharyya, Subhabrata, and Brinda Bose. 2007. *Phobic and the Erotic: The Politics of Sexualities in Contemporary India.* New Delhi: Seagull Press.

Blumstein, Philip, and Pepper Schwartz. 1990. "Intimate Relationships and the Creation of Sexuality." In *Homosexuality/Heterosexuality: Concepts of Sexual Orientation,* edited by David P. McWhirter, Stephanie Ann Sanders, and June M. Reinisch, pp. 307–320. New York: Oxford University Press.

Byne, William. 1997. "Why We Cannot Conclude That Sexual Orientation Is Primarily a Biological Phenomenon." *Journal of Homosexuality* 34 (1): 73–80.

Carrier, Joseph M. 1976. "Cultural Factors Affecting Urban Mexican Male Homosexual Behavior." *Archives of Sexual Behavior* 5 (2): 103–124.

Cohen, Lawrence. 1991. "*Holi* in Banaras and the *Mahaland* of Modernity." *Gay and Lesbian Quarterly (GLQ)* 2: 399–424.

D'Alisera, JoAnn. 2004. *An Imagined Geography: Sierra Leonean Muslims in America.* Philadelphia: University of Pennsylvania Press.

Dave, Naisargi. 2012. *Queer Activism in India: A Story in the Anthropology of Ethics.* Durham, NC: Duke University Press.

De Cecco, John P., and John P. Elia. 1991. "A Critique and Synthesis of Biological Essentialism and Social Constructionist Views of Sexuality and Gender." *Journal of Homosexuality* 24 (3–4): 1–26.

Doi, A. R. I. 1984. *Shari'ah: The Islamic Law.* London: Ta-Ha.

Dossani, Shahid. 1997. "Being Muslim and Gay." In *Que(e)rying Religion: A Critical Anthology,* edited by Gary David Comstock and Susan E. Henking, pp. 236–237. New York: Continuum.

Duran, K. 1993. "Homosexuality and Islam." In *Homosexuality and World Religions,* edited by A. Swidler, pp. 181–197. Philadelphia: Trinity Press International.

Gaudio, Rudolf. 2009. *Allah Made Us: Sexual Outlaws in an Islamic African City.* New York: Wiley-Blackwell.

Gopinath, Gayatri. 1997. "Nostalgia, Desire, Diaspora: South Asian Sexualities in Motion." *Positions* 5 (2): 467–489.

———. 2005. *Impossible Desires: Queer Diasporas and South Asian Public Cultures.* Durham, NC: Duke University Press.

Hencken, Joel D. 1984. "Conceptualizations of Homosexual Behavior Which Preclude Homosexual Self-Labeling." *Journal of Homosexuality* 9 (4): 53–63.

Hendricks, Pepe, ed. 2009. *Hijab: Unveiling Queer Muslim Lives.* Cape Town: African Minds.

Humphreys, L. 1970. *Tearoom Trade: Impersonal Sex in Public Places.* Chicago: Aldine Press.

Jama, Afdhere. 2008. *Illegal Citizens: Queer Lives in the Muslim World.* Bloomington, IN: Salaam Press.

Jamal, Amreen. 2001. "The Story of Lot and the Qur'an's Perception of the Morality of Same-Sex Sexuality." *Journal of Homosexuality* 41 (1): 1–88.

Jaspal, Rusi, and Asifa Siraj. 2011. "Perceptions of Coming Out among British Muslim Gay Men." *Psychology and Sexuality* 2 (3): 183–197.

Khan, Badruddin. 1992. "Not-So-Gay Life in Karachi: A View of a Pakistani Living in Toronto." In *Sexuality and Eroticism among Males in Moslem Societies,* edited by Arno Schmitt and Jehoeda Sofer, pp. 93–104. New York: Haworth Press.

Khan, Shivananda. 1997. *Perspectives on Males Who Have Sex with Males in India and Bangladesh.* London: Naz Foundation.

Kibria, Nazli. 2011. *Muslims in Motion: Islam and National Identity in the Bangladeshi Diaspora.* New Brunswick, NJ: Rutgers University Press.

King, J. L. 2004. *On the Down Low: A Journey into the Lives of "Straight" Black Men Who Sleep with Men.* New York: Broadway Books.

Kugle, Scott Siraj al-Haqq. 2003. "Sexuality, Diversity, and Ethics in the Agenda of Progressive Muslims." In *Progressive Muslims: On Justice, Gender and Pluralism,* edited by Omid Safi, pp. 190–234. Oxford, UK: One World.

———. 2014. *Living Out Islam: Voices of Gay, Lesbian, and Transgender Muslims.* New York: New York University Press.

La Fountain-Stokes, Lawrence. 2009. *Queer Ricans: Cultures and Sexualities in the Diaspora.* Minneapolis: University of Minnesota Press.

Lancaster, Roger N. 1988. "Subject Honor and Object Shame: The Construction of Male Homosexuality and Stigma in Nicaragua." *Ethnology* 27 (2): 111–125.

Manalansan, Martin. 2003. *Global Divas: Filipino Gay Men in the Diaspora.* Durham, NC: Duke University Press.

Massad, Joseph. 2007. *Desiring Arabs.* Chicago: University of Chicago Press.

Merabet, Sofian. 2014. *Queer Beirut.* Austin: University of Texas Press.

Naim, C. M. 1979. "The Theme of Homosexual Love in Pre-Modern Urdu Poetry." In *Studies in the Urdu Ghazal and Prose Fiction,* edited by Mohammad Umar Memon. Madison: South Asian Studies, University of Wisconsin.

Narrain, Arvind, and Gautam Bhan. 2006. *Because I Have a Voice: Queer Politics in India.* New Delhi: Yoda Press.

Parker, Richard. 1986. "Masculinity, Femininity, and Homosexuality: On the Anthropological Interpretation of Sexual Meanings in Brazil." In *The Many Faces of Homosexuality: Anthropological Approaches to Homosexual Behavior,* edited by Evelyn Blackwood, pp. 155–163. New York: Harrington Park Press.

———. 1999. *Beneath the Equator: Cultures of Desire, Male Homosexuality, and Emerging Gay Communities in Brazil.* New York: Routledge.

Puar, Jasbir. 2007. *Terrorist Assemblages: Homonationalism in Queer Times.* Durham, NC: Duke University Press.

Rahman, M. 2010. "Queer as Intersectionality: Theorizing Gay Muslim Identities." *Sociology* 44 (5): 1–18.

Ramakrishnan. 1996. "Bisexuality: Identities, Behaviors and Politics." *Trikone,* April.

Ratti, Rakesh, ed. 1993. *A Lotus of Another Color: An Unfolding of the South Asian Gay and Lesbian Experience.* Boston: Alyson Publications.

Roscoe, Will, and Stephen O. Murray, eds. 1997. *Islamic Homosexualities: Culture, History, and Literature.* New York: New York University Press.

Shahani, Parmesh. 2008. *Gay Bombay: Globalization, Love and (Be)longing in Contemporary India.* New Delhi: Sage.

Srivastava, Sanjay. 2004. *Sexual Sites, Seminal Attitudes: Sexualities, Masculinities and Culture in South Asia.* New Delhi: Sage.

Stein, Terry S. 1997. "Deconstructing Sexual Orientation: Understanding the Phenomena of Sexual Orientation." *Journal of Homosexuality* 34 (1): 81–86.

Taylor, Clark L. 1986. "Mexican Male Homosexual Interaction in Public Contexts." In *The Many Faces of Homosexuality: Anthropological Approaches to Homosexual Behavior,* edited by Evelyn Blackwood, pp. 117–136. New York: Harrington Park Press.

Thadani, Giti. 1998. *Sakhiyani: Lesbian Desire in Ancient and Modern India.* London: Cassell Press.

Trawick, Margaret. 1992. *Notes on Love in a Tamil Family.* Berkeley: University of California Press.

Vanita, Ruth. 2001. *Queering India: Same-Sex Love and Eroticism in Indian Culture and Society.* New York: Routledge.

Vanita, Ruth, and Saleem Kidwai, eds. 2001. *Same-Sex Love in India: Readings from Literature and History.* London: Palgrave Macmillan.

Weinberg, T. S. 1978. "On 'Doing' and 'Being' Gay: Sexual Behavior and Homosexual Male Identity." *Journal of Homosexuality* 4 (9): 143–156.

Whitaker, Brian. 2006. *Unspeakable Love: Gay and Lesbian Life in the Middle East.* Berkeley: University of California Press.

Yahya, H. 2000. *Perished Nations.* London: Ta-Ha.

Yip, A. K.-T. 2004. "Embracing Allah and Sexuality? South Asian Non-Heterosexual Muslims in Britain." In *South Asians in the Diaspora,* edited by K. A. Jacobsen and P. Pratap Kumar, pp. 294–310. Leiden, the Netherlands: Brill.

CHAPTER TWELVE

Racialization of Foreign Women in the Transnational Marriage Market of Taiwan

HSUNHUI TSENG

Introduction

Taiwan's close economic ties with mainland China and Vietnam in the 1990s gave rise to the trend of transnational marriages. The trend extended from specific groups of people, such as veterans and businessmen, to ordinary people in the late 1990s and grew rapidly in the early 2000s. According to one survey, the rate of transnational marriages peaked at 31.86 percent in 2003.[1] To restrain the trend, the government adopted a stricter visa interview policy from 2005 and banned profit-oriented brokerage in 2008, which, along with the economy turning sluggish, led to the decline of transnational brokered marriage in Taiwan.

Why did Taiwanese men begin to marry foreign women in such large numbers? The imbalance between the sexes of the marriageable population, the discordance between the raising of women's feminist consciousness and the expected gender relations in mainstream society, as well as industrialization and urbanization that damaged the economies of rural areas and traditional industries are commonly recognized factors that triggered large numbers of men of rural origin and lower social status to look for foreign brides from developing countries (Hsia 2002; Tian and Wang 2006; Tsay 2004). At the peak of the economic boom in the early 2000s, several brokering companies started businesses introducing Ukrainian women to Taiwanese men as an alternative to brides from China and Vietnam. These new businesses challenged the assumption that only marginalized, lower-class men looked for foreign brides since marrying a Ukrainian woman was hardly affordable for ordinary white-collar workers, let alone the blue-collar working class.[2]

It would seem that the abovementioned macro factors cannot account for the trend alone. If we calculate the costs of marrying foreign brides from different regions, we find large discrepancies. I argue that it is the cultural logic of racial hierarchies behind matchmaking pricing; that is, white women are considered more valuable than Asian women. It is important to look at the political economy of the imaginary of racial hierarchies in Taiwan to see how they are embodied in the individual's decision making and further legitimated by the market mechanism.

Although the market for Ukrainian brides in Taiwan soon declined, the phenomenon allows us to look into the cultural and political economic factors that heavily influenced the dramatic changes in the market. In the past decade there have been many studies on transnational marriage in Asia (Constable 2003, 2005; M. Lu 2008; Thai 2005; Wang and Chang 2002), yet very few deal with gender politics through the workings of market mechanisms and brokerage. Looking at the operation of the brokerage gives us insight into how the influx of marriage migrants was facilitated by the perceived cultural and political economic affiliations between Taiwan and the bride-sending countries. It also helps us create a clear picture of how the practices of gender inequality and sexualization of foreign women conform to the existing imaginary of racial order in the global hierarchy.

In this chapter, I pay particular attention to how marriage brokering companies, based on their perception of the public imaginary of what desirable wives ought to be, constructed images of foreign women differently according to their countries of origin, especially during times of intense market competition. I examine the racialization and stratification of foreign women in the matchmaking process and argue that this social imaginary of the racial order has to be understood through both a political economic and a historical lens.

Matchmaking Trips: Vietnam and Ukraine

Having waited for a long time, I finally gained agreement from both the marriage broker, Huigo,[3] and his two clients, Guoching and Yanpo, to join their matchmaking trip (*xiangqintuan*) from Taiwan to a remote village in Quảng Ninhin province in northeast Vietnam[4] in 2005. Guoching was thirty-eight years old and worked as an administrator of the warehouse of a publishing house. Yanpo was twenty-nine years old. He had graduated from a national university and was an engineer working for a computer company.

We arrived at the village around ten in the morning the next day. As our car slowly approached the destination, numerous villagers were standing by the sides of the muddy and bumpy road watching us. Children were running around the car and caused obstruction from time to time. It seemed that the entire village was rather busy and excited on that day due to our visit. When we got to the house where the matchmaking meeting was going to be held, there were more than fifty young women waiting outside. The oldest were twenty-three years old.

We sat in the living room of the small house. Dung, a local matchmaker who served as Huigo's business partner, Guoching, and Yanpo sat together on one side of the table, and left the other side for "interviewees." Two women were arranged to come in at a time. Dung served as an interpreter and also raised questions for both sides. Questions revolved mainly around three points: personal information, family background, and housework capability. The male clients asked questions throughout the meeting, although the women could raise questions as well. The meeting ended after three hours, and both Guoching and Yanpo got their brides. After having lunch, Dung drove us to visit the brides' parents to ask for agreement to their daughters' marriage. After meeting all of the family members, simple engagement ceremonies were held on the spot. Then the couple went out of the house to meet people, take pictures, and receive congratulations.

Guoching and Yanpo returned for the visa interview in Hanoi a couple of weeks later. Their interviews were coincidently arranged on the same day that I was allowed to observe the process. Owing to Yanpo's educational background, the consular officer ceaselessly asked him with misgiving why he wanted to marry a foreign wife. "You should be able to find a wife of good quality in Taiwan with your good conditions!" he said. After Yanpo and his wife left, the official expressed to me his deep concern about the increasing rate of transnational marriages in Taiwan:

> "Why are there so many Taiwanese men coming to Vietnam to look for wives? We have so many good women in Taiwan. Do Taiwanese people not understand the meaning of the old Chinese saying, *feishui buluo wairentian* (one should prevent nourishing water in his farmland from flowing into others')? You know, I'm surprised by the increasing number of cases in which the Taiwanese husband has a good educational background and good job, like the guy you just saw, in recent years!"

Indeed, during my fieldwork from 2005 to 2007, I encountered quite a few other men like Yanpo, university graduates with a good salary, also interested in having a foreign wife. These cases seem to suggest that, despite the fact that lower-class men constitute the majority of consumers in the commodified transnational marriage market, the numbers of men with more economic and social capital participating in the market have increased.

A Flash in the Pan: The Emergence of Ukrainian Brides

When the market was most active in the early 2000s, some marriage brokering companies began introducing women from Eastern Europe, mainly Ukraine, to Taiwanese men. This was seen as a golden business opportunity as the brokers believed white women would be targeted by middle- to upper-class men who had no time for courtship, such as engineers working in industrial parks. After the news of the brokering business in Eastern European brides hit the mass media, it attracted tremendous attention from the public.

The phenomenon challenged the stereotypical images of transnational brokered marriages in three ways. First of all, these white women, unlike brides from China or Southeast Asia, were never depicted as poor opportunists who use marriage as a strategy for a better life. Instead, they were often promoted for their sexy appearance, high educational level, and language skills, characteristics thought to be helpful in improving the population quality of the next generation in Taiwan. Second, they were intended for upper-middle-class men and therefore had a much higher market price than brides from other Asian countries. The cost of marrying a Ukrainian woman was about three to four times the cost of marrying a Vietnamese or Chinese woman. Besides, it was widely believed that marital life with a Ukrainian would involve far greater expenses. In other words, men without considerable economic means or inheritable property would not be regarded as eligible candidates for marrying Eastern European women. Last, these white women were not expected to play the traditional role of housewife as most Asian wives are when marketed to Taiwanese men. This discrepancy implies that men's expectation of women's role in the household and gender relations in the marriage varies with race and/or nationality.

In contrast to the way in which matchmaking is practiced in Vietnam, the procedure of introducing a Ukrainian woman to a Taiwanese man is much more complex and costly. To get a sense of how the business operated, I went on another matchmaking trip organized by a brokering company to Kiev, Ukraine, in 2005. The group I joined consisted of only three members: the broker, the client, and me. The client, Yangze, was a son of a landowner family. He was forty-two and worked as a foreman at a construction company. He had been impressed by a TV interview featuring the broker, Mr. Chu. After registering with Mr. Chu, he had been put in touch with several women, and had finally decided to meet Natasha after corresponding with her for several months. Yangze was told that if he was not satisfied with Natasha after meeting her in person, he could meet other potential brides. Contrary to my expectation, Yangze refused Natasha after they had spent a night together. Yangze gave me a simple reason that shocked me a lot. He said that Natasha did not meet his expectations of *jinsimao* (blonde hair cats),[5] as she was neither blonde nor as sexy as her picture in the catalog. As a result, he asked Mr. Chu to arrange other women for him to meet after Natasha left the next day.

I was very surprised by the way Mr. Chu positioned his client in relation to the Ukrainian bride candidates in the matchmaking process. The expected gender relation was the complete opposite of that between Taiwanese clients and Asian bride candidates. For example, all of Yangze's meetings were dinners at luxurious restaurants with only one candidate at a time. We were given instructions regarding how to behave in a proper manner at the dining table, how to eat and drink, what to say and not to say, and other Western etiquette that Mr. Chu thought we should follow. We were both asked to behave and speak with caution so as not to lose face in front of the candidates, whom Mr. Chu thought to be "Western" and more "civilized" than Taiwanese.

As noted above, the Eastern European bride fever did not last long, and successful cases were very few.[6] Despite its transience, however, it did cause a sensation. For instance, to attract the public's attention, one proprietor held a public dating event close to an industrial park for interested men to meet several Ukrainian women who had been invited to Taiwan. These women were arranged to stand on stage and play interactive games with a crowd of men standing in front of the stage. One newspaper used half a page to report this event and the new foreign bride trend with the compelling title "Wukelan jiaren, Taiwanlang xiang qianshou! (Taiwanese Men Want to Hold the Hands of Ukrainian Beauties!)" (Pan 2003). This scenario is reminiscent of another piece of sensational news about Vietnamese women being displayed in front of a Mazu temple as being "for sale" by a marriage broker in 2004. The marriage broker arranged for several Vietnamese women who were interested in marrying Taiwanese men to come to Taiwan. In contrast to the treatment the other broker offered to his Ukrainian women, unfortunately, these Vietnamese women ended up being peddled in the streets and displayed in public with a price of NT$320,000 (about $10,000) for on-site transactions. According to a news report, interested men could just pay and take a woman away with them (Apple Daily 2004). This incident resulted in the opposition of women's rights advocates deploring the overt practice of "selling women."

The differences in the ways marriage brokers operated according to the origin of their brides encouraged me to explore further the racial hierarchy among these foreign women: Why were Eastern European women represented as "modern" subjects in relation to Asian women as "backward" ones? How does racial ideology interact with class distinctions to differentiate the value of foreign brides in the marriage market?

Racialized Bodies: How Are Foreign Women Advertised?

A piece of doggerel that has circulated widely on the Internet since 2004 jokes about the reason why many Taiwanese men turn their back on local women and seek foreign women, especially from China and Southeast Asia. It crudely differentiates Taiwanese brides from foreign brides by delineating the former as arrogant and avaricious, in opposition to the latter who are docile and easily satisfied, with little consumption desire. Here are some excerpts:

> *When looking for foreign brides:* Women line up for men to choose!
> *When looking for Taiwanese brides:* Men have no choice but to be chosen!
> *Foreign brides:* Honey, please take me to supermarkets and night markets!
> *Taiwanese brides:* Honey, please take me to Japan and USA!
> *Foreign brides:* Honey, I want a cake on my birthday!
> *Taiwanese brides:* Honey, I want a diamond on my birthday!
> *Foreign brides:* Cleaning the house whenever they have time.
> *Taiwanese brides:* Doing nothing!
> ("Why are there so many Taiwanese men looking for foreign brides?")[7]

By using contrasts such as wanting to go to supermarkets/night markets vs. Japan and the United States, and diligence vs. laziness in doing housework to represent the different perceptions of foreign and local brides, this text has provoked much discussion on blogs and brokers' websites. Many men expressed their approval of the content by sharing the same feeling of being tramped (*cai*) by Taiwanese women. For many of them, it is their sense of male dignity and masculinity that primarily triggers them to consider marrying foreign women from developing countries (Tian and Wang 2006). Portrayed as men's essential characteristic, this sense of male dignity is manipulated by brokers. Many men looking for Vietnamese brides shared similar concerns for their marriage. Despite being economically powerful they were often culturally weak due to a lack of socially recognized masculinity. Besides masculinity, the need for free labor is also an important factor triggering men to look for foreign brides, a demand that crosses class distinctions. For example, for men who own a small factory or farm, money is not an issue when getting married. What is important, rather, especially for those who have parents or children to be cared for at home, is finding a wife who is willing to support them by contributing both free productive labor and reproductive labor at work and home.

Before profit-oriented matchmaking was completely banned in 2008, it was easy to find advertisements online or to see them in the streets. Many brokering companies knew well how to manipulate the cultural logic of love in packaging their bride candidates. They assumed and homogenized all foreign women from developing countries as docile and domestic so as to make them ideal wives in the traditional sense. One brokering company promoted their bride candidates by calculating for men the benefit of getting married to a woman from China or Vietnam:

> First, she can work and earn NT$20,000 [about $625] a month. The total income of the household increases NT$240,000 [about $7,500] per year. Second, she will sleep with you. You do not need to find women outside. It saves you NT$80,000 [about $2,500] per year. Third, she can do housework, cooking and doing laundry for free. It saves you NT$10,000 per month and NT$120,000 [about US$3,750] per year. Fourth, she can give birth to a child. Producing a male heir to continue the family line is invaluable. In total, you can get a benefit of NT$300,000–400,000 [about $9,375–$12,500] per year. Why don't you get married?

Although using this kind of degrading language to promote foreign brides drew reproach in society, it did reflect the ideal marriage that many Taiwanese men dream of; that is, "buy one (wife) get one free (labor)." More interestingly, these two groups of women could further be differentiated from each other according to their "racial traits." For example, Huigo maintained that Chinese brides are cleverer than Vietnamese brides, while Vietnamese brides are more obedient and trustful. Mr. Lin, a manager of a brokering company that also did business in both Chinese and Vietnamese brides, expressed the same opinion:

> "If the client is more introverted and his personality is less masculine, we will probably suggest him considering Vietnamese rather than Chinese brides. Here is our reason. For example, Chinese brides more likely request more than Vietnamese brides do. It is because their economic condition is better than Vietnamese on the average. Plus, they speak Chinese so they can argue with you. You will find sharing the same language would be good for some people yet bad for others."

Indeed, in my observations of matchmaking meetings, in Vietnam most bride candidates agreed to do housework and domestic tasks without negotiation and considered them the wife's obligation; whereas in China, more women reached agreement through negotiation. While it is true that sharing the same language makes it easier for Chinese women to bargain with Taiwanese men, the impact of a nation's economic capability also influences women's accumulation of social capital. After China's economy became prosperous and attractive to foreign capital, Chinese women started to enjoy better living conditions than before. A flood of Taiwanese enterprises entering China gave these women more opportunities to meet and compare Taiwanese men of different backgrounds. Therefore, Chinese bride candidates hold relatively more bargaining power and are more "difficult" than their counterparts from Southeast Asia in the eyes of the brokers.

The Power of Image

Yet these kinds of culturally twisted narratives for emphasizing foreign brides' domestic capability were never utilized by advertisements for Eastern European brides. Comparing web pages from two brokering companies' websites reveals how the reproductive labor of women from different regions is considered.

In the catalogs, Vietnamese women are presented through snapshots taken on the spot one after another. They have no makeup and their hair is not styled. They wear plain dresses and shy smiles and there is no attempt to make them look sexually attractive. By stark contrast, Ukrainian women are presented in glamour shots with full makeup, styled hair, and fine clothes. Enchanting poses and facial expressions make them look more like celebrities than housekeepers. Romantic attraction thus appears as a reference to distinguish Eastern European brides from Vietnamese brides, and a cue for male clients to consider what type of wife they want and what they can afford.

Left: A screenshot of a Taiwanese marriage brokerage website (www.vnn.com.tw) showing Vietnamese bride candidates taken June 15, 2006. *Right:* A screenshot of a Taiwanese marriage brokerage website (www.crosinternational.com.tw) showing Ukrainian bride candidates taken June 15, 2006.

Interestingly, photographic portraits of bride candidates in the catalog mean different things to consumers/suitors according to the cultural framework in which the portraits are positioned and through which the consumers view them. In the "mail-order bride" market of the United States, glamour shots of Russian brides never threaten American men's confidence in Russian women's traditional values but enhance their belief that Russian women possess the virtues of domesticity, passivity, and patience while still being sexy and hyperfeminine (Patico 2010). In the context of Chinese society, women gesturing in an alluring way or showing certain body parts in a photograph would seldom be associated with the image of an ideal wife but more with that of licentious woman. The Ukrainian women gazing at the lens/men with sexy and confident poses therefore means they are far from being the model of "traditional" and "passive" women in the Chinese context. By contrast, Vietnamese women's plain dress, stiff, standing posture, and shy smile makes them desirable as traditional housewives who lack modern subjectivity and consumer desire and whose self can only be realized through helping her husband and teaching her children (*xiangfujiaozi*). This lack is constructed, discursively and visually, as if it can only be fulfilled through a love connection with a man who can rescue her from the catalog world and bring her into the real world.

Many studies have mentioned how nostalgia for "tradition" is at work in creating men's desire for foreign brides (Halualani 1995; Robinson 1996; Simons 2001; Tolentino 1999; Wilson 1988), and how brokering companies manipulate nostalgic discourses and fit foreign women's bodies into the discursive framework (Patico 2010; Tolentino 1999). As Rolando Tolentino (1999, 59) observes, to maintain the U.S. nuclear family fantasy, "the functional third-world woman's body is made symptomatic of the ideal first-world male nuclear family narrative." In the same vein, Jennifer Patico (2010, 33) criticizes brokering companies for their reductive and objectifying rhetoric that homogenously positions all American male clients as consumers of Asian or East European "tradition," docility, or desperation and that ignores other dimensions of the gender crisis that also account for men's desire of foreign brides, such as excessive individualism and materialism, and the American culture of divorce. Similarly, most Asian bride brokering companies I encountered knew well how to manipulate men's nostalgia for the traditional gender relations in preindustrial Taiwan, and link the realization of "bringing nostalgia back to reality" to men's vision of romantic love.

The strategies that appeal to men's masculinity through the idea of "rescuing/ conquering" women and nostalgia, however, were never seen in Ukrainian bride advertising. As mentioned above, Ukrainian brides are promoted in Taiwan not in terms of tradition but, on the contrary, in terms of modernity and cosmopolitanism, which is embodied in their higher educational background and their stereo-typical appearance: blonde and tall. The contradictory perceptions of Eastern European women in the United States and Taiwan shows us how the cultural logic of value and desire varies from one society to another and how this has led to different sentiments toward foreign women as ideal wives in different social contexts.

Stratification of Foreign Brides: Quality?

In contrast to the guaranteed happy ending when Taiwanese men travel to select a Vietnamese bride, not every man interested in marrying an Eastern European woman realized his dream. According to Mr. Chu, men who wanted to become his clients had to go through the following process: online registration, a tele-phone interview, and then a face-to-face interview. They had to be single with a stable job and high income, and own real estate. The client was granted access to the entire online bride catalog only when he passed the examination and paid the membership fee.

However, this kind of filtering mechanism was never adopted by Asian bride brokering companies. Asian bride brokers usually recruited as many clients as pos-sible without stipulating any requirements for their backgrounds. Unlike choos-ing a Ukrainian bride, which required correspondence between both sides for a period of time before meeting in person, choosing a Vietnamese or Chinese bride was far more straightforward. The client did not even need to know who he was going to meet prior to his departure on the matchmaking trip. In most cases, the bride catalog existed only for the client's reference and as proof that the broker had the "ability" to provide that number of bride candidates.

For Mr. Chu, Asian brides, especially those from Southeast Asia, were not comparable with Eastern European brides due to their huge difference in "qual-ity." How Ukrainian brides were promoted is illustrated by a newspaper interview he gave (Hsiu 2003). In that interview, Mr. Chu claims that all of the women listed in the catalog held at least college degrees.[8] By comparison, the educational back-ground of Asian brides was never recognized as important human capital, even though some do receive higher education, especially Filipina brides.

Eastern European brides' language ability was also highlighted as a selling point. In the same interview, Mr. Chu stated that "marrying Eastern European women allows our next generation to grow up in a bilingual environment, which is important for Taiwan's internationalization." He misled readers here by imply-ing English and Chinese bilingualism rather than Ukrainian (or Russian) and Chinese bilingualism. Mr. Chu claimed most Ukrainian women could speak

English well, but in fact, Filipina brides generally speak English more fluently—a skill that is never promoted by brokers in relation to their advantages. The differing treatment of foreign brides reflects male clients' different expectations of the role of their future mates and conforms to the social imagination of racial/ethnic division of labor in Taiwan. For example, Filipina women are associated with domestic workers while Ukrainian women are associated with models. The gendered racialization and stratification of others has been observed both in the labor market (Anthias and Yuval-Davis 1983; Lan 2006; Palmer 1989; Parreñas 2001) and in the marriage market (M. Lu 2008, 99–100). The racialized representation of foreign Asian brides as less cultivated and romantic than white Eastern European brides conforms to the Western-centric logic of a global racial hierarchy in Asian people's minds.

The incompatibility between Taiwan native-born brides and those from Vietnam and China is very often ascribed to the latter's low quality of cultural cultivation, in spite of the common belief that they share a lot of cultural similarities with Taiwanese. To improve their quality, Asian brides are asked to learn and internalize the host culture and lifestyle. Contrary to this "cultural racism" (Balibar and Wallerstein 1991), Ukrainian brides are treated as coming to "rescue" Taiwan with their sought-after genes.

If cultural similarity and the political economic relationships between Taiwan and the bride-sending countries in Asia were the background for the booming transnational marriage brokerage, what could be the background for the transient yet sensational Ukrainian bride craze, considering that neither cultural affiliation nor close political economic cooperation exists between the two countries? What so intrigued Taiwanese men about the possibility of having a Ukrainian bride? What kind of desire was it?

The Myth of Whiteness: A Historical Lens

"Wow, it is too romantic to be true!" When I chatted with young men about Ukrainian bride brokerage, I often saw a strange smile appear on their faces. Because there was no guarantee of marriage, clients had to pay for one trip after another until they find a suitable bride. Plus, during the period of correspondence, they also needed to spend money on gifts and flowers and translation if both sides could not use English. So it was not affordable for ordinary white-collar men. Yangze, in order to make the trip to Kiev, had spent almost NT$1,000,000 (about $31,000) on relevant expenses before I met him.

In spite of this great expense, Yangze still wanted to give it a try. He told me that he was originally going to find a Vietnamese wife to take care of his old mother, but after watching Mr. Chu's interview on TV, he changed his mind. "How come you changed your mind so dramatically? How about your mother? Do you expect your Ukrainian wife to take care of your mom?" I asked, and his answer surprised me: "But I think it is also good to have someone practice English with me and lead me to the Western world. . . . In the past I could only imagine white women's bodies through reading novels, watching TV and movies, but now I can touch them physically. Even if I cannot find one eventually, it will still be an un-forgettable memory in my life. It is thus worthy."

It is clear how the differentiation of body values between Eastern European brides and Asian brides is made along the class and race/ethnicity lines. The huge difference in their market prices cannot be accounted for only by the visible costs such as paperwork, travel expenses, and service quality; there is also, I argue, the exchange value of women's bodies created by "white fetishism" that frequently lurks in Taiwanese men's thoughts. Generally speaking, one of the major reasons for Taiwanese men to find a foreign wife from developing Asian countries through brokers is to maintain the mechanism of labor reproduction in the family, while the selling point of a Ukrainian bride is their sexiness and cultural capital, the value of "modernity." This disparity suggests that Taiwanese men who dream of marrying Eastern European women are not concerned about their future wife's domestic capability but their sexuality and whiteness, the homogeneously imag-ined high cultural taste that can bring glory to the match.

During the short-lived craze, Eastern European women became more and more visible to the public thanks to the mass media, and their sexy appearance drew the public's attention. In the past decade, increasing numbers of women from Ukraine and Russia have found work as dancers and models in the Taiwan enter-tainment industry. A few have even become well-known TV stars. Some are in-volved in the sex industry, which has been reported by the mass media. These at-tractive women help the stereotypical construction of *jinsimao*, the exotic women who used to only appear in movies and novels but are now available in the real world.[9]

For Yangze, marrying an Eastern European woman signified appropriating her whiteness, the magic power that can boost men's cultural capital and sym-bolic power. The psychosexual dynamics in transnational gender politics may be understood in the light of Frantz Fanon's famous analysis of black men's white complex in the postcolonial context:

I wish to be acknowledged not as Black but as white . . . who but a white woman could do this for me? By loving me she proves that I am worthy of white love. I am loved like a white man. I am a white man. Her noble love takes me onto the road of self realization—I marry white culture, white beauty, white whiteness. When my restless hands grasp those white breasts, they grasp white civilization and dignity and make them mine. (Fanon 1967 [1952], 63)

Yet how could Fanon's analysis of this inferiority complex make sense in our case when there was no such historical contact between Taiwan and Eastern European countries? Where do the desire and complex come from and what does whiteness mean to Taiwanese? I suggest that the desire for Eastern European women should be analyzed in the context of the formation of American and Eurocentric discourses in the contemporary history of Taiwan, the history of how white culture—mainly American culture—was introduced to Taiwan and became a symbol of modernity for people to pursue. I argue that the desire is created based on the chain of misrecognition, a simplified logic of the myth that all Ukrainians are blonde/white; all whites are from the United States; the United States is a perfect example of modernity; modernity is desirable; and therefore Ukrainian women are desirable.[10]

As Chen Kuan-Hsing (2001) has shown, in Taiwan and East Asia in general modernization is very often interpreted as "Westernization" and has been used interchangeably with "Americanization" ever since the United States gained its power and influence on the region in the postwar era. The long-term relationship based on America's military and economic assistance to Taiwan after World War II paved the way for the latter to follow the steps of the former toward modernization. Taiwanese imaginings of American society and American lifestyle thereby triggered many people's "American dream," a dream that does not fade away even though Taiwan has successfully developed into one of the newly industrialized countries in Asia. The collective imagination of modernization appearing in daily life becomes the individual's desire to be Westernized and participate in global capitalist consumption through consuming goods from the West, such as European luxury brands and American pop culture, the practice of "imagined cosmopolitanism" (Schein 1994, 149).[11] In this formula, English proficiency was perceived as an index of an individual's degree of modernization and internationalization. One can say that the Taiwanese imaginary of the West is by and large formed through knowledge of the United States. People imagine Westerners through the stereotype of Americans—Caucasian Americans—obtained from the mass media and then extend the stereotype to all others who look "American." The conflation of Eastern European women and Caucasian American women into the same category of "white" women is actually the practice of Occidentalism, the cultural practice through which the West is homogeneously and exotically represented with the same logic of what Edward Said (1978) criticizes as Orientalism.

While Occidentalism is common practice in Asian societies, its expressions vary from country to country as a result of different historical and geopolitical influences. In his research on Chinese identity, Sheldon Lu looks into what Fredric Jameson called the "geopolitical unconscious"; that is, the vision of the social, the public, and the national-within-the global, through the tales and images in media representations (S. Lu 2000, 29). Lu analyzed Chinese masculinity in Chinese soap operas and found Chinese men are always positioned as the owners of power and capital, and white women are the "subalterns" subject to the men's gaze and desire (Barmé 1999; S. Lu 2000, 34). For example, Russian women who migrate to China for jobs and wealth are depicted as romantic, innocent, and fragile subjects who heavily rely on Chinese men.[12] This image is very different from its counterpart in Taiwan, which sheds light on how white women are consumed by the national imagination in different geopolitical contexts. The comparison with representational politics across the strait shows the importance of taking into account the history of imagination when exploring the embedding of imaginaries in geopolitical and economic structures. From this cross-strait example we can see how the political and cultural logic of the Cold War has shaped and dominated people's imaginaries and sentiments differently in the postwar era, even up to today.

Conclusion

Due to the decline of Taiwan's economy in recent years and a stricter immigration policy, the demand for foreign brides in Taiwan has cooled. The high-profile brokering companies discussed in this chapter did not exist at the time of writing. In addition to these political economic factors, other social forces have caused the demand to fall and therefore we cannot simply assume that Taiwanese men no longer desire foreign brides as ideal wives. I am not trying to say that all Taiwanese men are "foreign bride dreamers." Yet it cannot be denied that an imaginary of a racial hierarchy among foreign women is pervasive in society, and the transnational marriage market is the venue where cultural racism can most easily be perceived.

I have shown how a racial hierarchy is in consonance with class distinctions in the marriage market through the representation of foreign women in Taiwan. Resonating with what Tiantian Zheng has emphasized in the introduction to this book, this study also suggests that gender and sexuality in a society have to be understood within its own cultural context, which is very often influenced by its political economic relationship with others. In the same manner, I have unraveled the cultural logic of the racialization and stratification of foreign women in the transnational marriage market of Taiwan through analyzing Taiwan's direct and indirect political economic relationships and cultural contacts with the bride-sending countries. Only through revealing these dimensions, I argue, can we trace the causes of social mentalities and seek to deconstruct the gender inequality in the marriage market and in society.

Notes and References

1. Survey by the Department of Statistics, Ministry of the Interior, Taipei, Taiwan.

2. Marrying a Ukrainian woman would cost approximately $25,000 to $30,000 or even more, while marrying a Vietnamese woman would cost only $7,000 to $8,000. The cost of marrying a Ukrainian woman in Taiwan is about 1.6 times that in the United States (Peterson 2003, 109).

3. To protect the privacy of research subjects, all names in this chapter are pseudonyms.

4. Although marriage brokerage is more popular in the south, Huigo still made trips to the north and claimed that it was a "new virgin land" for bride hunting.

5. Taiwanese people liken Eastern European women to golden-haired cats, implying that they are as tempting as cats.

6. Since the brokers I contacted always refused to reveal the number of their successful cases to me, my conjecture is that the numbers were low.

7. Article from the Bunny Forum website. For the full version, please see http://bonny .com.tw/bbs/viewthread.php?tid=12241.

8. In fact, the education system of Ukraine is different from that of Taiwan and it is problematic to conflate the degrees of one system with those of the other.

9. For more discussion on how Western women and Asian women are represented in the East and West, respectively, see Ling (2002).

10. I would like to thank my friend Tzu-I Chung for helping to clarify my thinking here.

11. I do not deny Japanese colonial influence on today's Taiwan. However, when speaking of "connecting to the world" and "being cosmopolitan," American culture and English are more valued.

12. These scenarios sharply contrast to the Soviets' brutal treatment of China. Soviet demands that China pay back its debts caused widespread hardship and hunger in the late 1950s and early 1960s. China's generosity is emphasized through Chinese men's heroic behavior toward Russian women in the soaps (S. Lu 2000, 35).

Anthias, Floya, and Nira Yuval-Davis. 1983. "Contextualizing Feminism: Gender, Ethnic and Class Divisions." *Feminist Review* 15: 62–75.

Apple Daily. 2004. "當街叫賣越女「保固一年」 [Peddling Vietnamese brides with a one-year warranty in the streets]." *Apple Daily,* November 6.

Balibar, Etienne, and Immanuel Maurice Wallerstein. 1991. *Race, Nation, Class: Ambiguous Identities.* London: Verso.

Barmé, Geremie R. 1999. *In the Red: On Contemporary Chinese Culture.* New York: Columbia University Press.

Chen, Kuan-Hsing. 2001. "America in East Asia: The Club 51 Syndrome." *New Left Review* 12: 73–87.

Constable, Nicole. 2003. *Romance on a Global Stage: Pen Pals, Virtual Ethnography, and Mail-Order Marriages.* Berkeley: University of California Press.

———. 2005. *Cross-Border Marriages: Gender and Mobility in Transnational Asia.* Philadelphia: University of Pennsylvania Press.

Department of Statistics, Ministry of the Interior, Taiwan. 2003. "04. The Number of Marriage by Nationality, Age, and Education 結婚按國籍年齡教育程度." http://www.moi .gov.tw/stat/gender.aspx.

Fanon, Frantz. 1967 [1952]. *Black Skin, White Masks.* New York: Grove.

Halualani, Rona Tamiko. 1995. "The Interesting Hegemonic Discourses of an Asian Mail-Order Bride Catalog: Philipina 'Oriental Butterfly' Dolls for Sale." *Women's Studies in Communication* 118 (1): 45–64.

Hsia, Hsiao Chuan. 2002. 流離尋岸: 資本國際化下的「外籍新娘」現象 [Looking for the shore: The "foreign bride" phenomenon in the capital internalization]. Taipei, Taiwan: A Radical Quarterly in Social Studies Journal Press.

Hsiu, Shu-Fen. 2003. 仲介烏克蘭新娘，台灣郎婚啦 [Ukrainian bride brokerage dazes Taiwanese men to get married]. *Chinatimes Express,* September 11.

Lan, Pei-Chia. 2006. *Global Cinderellas: Migrant Domestics and Newly Rich Employers in Taiwan.* Durham, NC: Duke University Press.

Ling, Lily H. M. 2002. *Postcolonial International Relations: Conquest and Desire between Asia and the West.* Basingstoke, England: Palgrave.

Lu, Melody Chia-wen. 2008. "Gender, Marriage and Migration: Contemporary Marriages between Mainland China and Taiwan." PhD thesis, University of Leiden.

Lu, Sheldon H. 2000. "Soap Opera in China: The Transnational Politics of Visuality, Sexuality, and Masculinity." *Cinema Journal* 40 (1): 25–47.

Palmer, Phyllis M. 1989. *Domesticity and Dirt : Housewives and Domestic Servants in the United States, 1920–1945.* Philadelphia: Temple University Press.

Pan, Shuting. 2003. "烏克蘭佳人, 台灣郎想牽手 [Taiwanese men want to hold the hands of Ukrainian beauties]." *United Daily News,* May 28.

Parreñas, Rhacel Salazar. 2001. *Servants of Globalization: Women, Migration, and Domestic Work.* Stanford, CA: Stanford University Press.

Patico, Jennifer. 2010. "Kinship and Crisis: The Embedding of Economic Pressures and Gender Ideals in Postsocialist International Matchmaking." *Slavic Review* 69 (1): 16–40.

Peterson, V. Spike. 2003. *A Critical Rewriting of Global Political Economy: Integrating Reproductive, Productive, and Virtual Economies.* London: Routledge.

Robinson, Kathryn. 1996. "Of Mail-Order Brides and 'Boys' Own' Tales: Representations of Asian-Australian Marriages." *Feminist Review* 52: 53–68.

Said, Edward W. 1978. *Orientalism.* New York: Pantheon Books.

Schein, Louisa. 1994. "The Consumption of Color and the Politics of White Skin in Post-Mao China." *Social Text* 41: 141–164.

Simons, Lisa Anne. 2001. "Marriage, Migration, and Markets: International Matchmaking and International Feminism." PhD diss., University of Denver.

Thai, Hung Cam. 2005. "Clashing Dreams in the Vietnamese Diaspora: Highly Educated Overseas Brides and Low-Wage U.S. Husbands." In *Cross-Border Marriages: Gender and Mobility in Transnational Asia*, edited by Nicole Constable, pp. 145–165. Philadelphia: University of Pennsylvania Press.

Tian, Jingying, and Hongzen Wang. 2006. "男性氣魄與可「娶」的跨國婚姻: 為何台灣男子要與越南女子結婚? [Masculinity and "marriageable" women in the transnational marriage: Why Taiwanese men want to marry Vietnamese women]." 台灣東南亞學刊 [*Taiwan Journal of Southeast Asian Studies*] 3 (1): 3–36.

Tolentino, Rolando B. 1999. "Bodies, Letters, Catalogs: Filipinas in Transnational Space." In *Transnational Asia Pacific: Gender, Culture, and the Public Sphere*, edited by Shirley Lim, Larry E. Smith, and Wimal Dissanayake, pp. 43–68. Urbana: University of Illinois Press.

Tsay, Chinglung. 2004. "Marriage Migration of Women from China and Southeast Asia to Taiwan." In *(Un)tying the Knot: Ideal and Reality in Asian Marriage,* edited by Gavin W. Jones and Kamalini Ramdas, pp. 173–191. Singapore: National University of Singapore.

Wang, Hong-zen, and Shu-ming Chang. 2002. "The Commodification of International Marriages: Cross-Border Marriage Business in Taiwan and Vietnam." *International Migration* 40 (6): 93–116.

"為何很多男生都喜歡外籍新娘呢? 外籍新娘有哪些優點呀? [Why are there so many Taiwanese men looking for foreign brides? What advantages do they have?]" 兔兔電腦論壇 [Bunny Computer Forum]. Accessed June 4, 2007. http://bonny.com.tw/bbs/view thread.php?tid=12241.

Wilson, Ara. 1988. "American Catalogues of Asian Brides." In *Anthropology for the Nineties: Introductory Readings,* edited by Johnnetta B. Cole, pp. 114–124. New York: Free Press.

Contributors

Ahmed Afzal is a lecturer in the Department of Anthropology, Geography, and Ethnic Studies at California State University, Stanislaus. His research interests include globalization and transnationalism, South Asian and Muslim immigrants in the United States, the anthropology of mass media, cross-cultural gender and sexuality, urban life, and the anthropology of Pakistan. He is the author of *Lone Star Muslims: Transnational Lives and the South Asian Experience in Texas* (New York University Press, 2014).

Kevin Carrico is a postdoctoral fellow at Stanford University's Center for East Asian Studies. He is currently completing an ethnography of the construction and reconstruction of Han identity and tradition in contemporary urban China.

Nana Okura Gagné is an assistant professor in the Department of Japanese Studies at the Chinese University of Hong Kong. Her research interests include gender and sexuality, exchange and consumption, and globalization and neoliberalism in Japan and the United States. Her work has been published in *Asian Anthropology, American Ethnologist, Ethnography,* and the *Journal of Language and Communication.*

Danielle Antoinette Hidalgo is an assistant professor of sociology at California State University, Chico. Her areas of interest include gender and sexuality, sociology of the body, globalization, and disaster studies. She coedited *Narrating the Storm: Sociological Stories of Hurricane Katrina* (Cambridge Scholars Publishing, 2007) and her work has appeared in the *Journal of Bisexuality, Sociological Spectrum,* and the *Journal of Family Issues.*

Heidi Hoefinger is an adjunct lecturer in the Institute of South East Asian Affairs' South East Asian Comparative Semester program based in Phnom Penh, Cambodia. Her areas of expertise include gender and sexuality, sexual subcultures, transnational relationships, sex work, drug use, migration, deportation and "intimate" ethnography, with a focus on Cambodia and Southeast Asia.

Madhura Lohokare is a doctoral candidate in cultural anthropology at Syracuse University. Her areas of interest cover the anthropology of space, masculinity, urban informality, and the politics of knowledge. Her doctoral research investigates the processes through which the social and physical spaces of neighborhoods in urban India produce their young male inhabitants as gendered subjects.

Lynne Nakano is a professor in the Department of Japanese Studies at the Chinese University of Hong Kong. She is the author of *Community Volunteers in Japan: Everyday Stories of Social Change* (Routledge, 2004) and is currently working on a book manuscript about the life strategies of single women living in Tokyo, Shanghai, and Hong Kong.

John Osburg is an assistant professor of anthropology at the University of Rochester and is the author of *Anxious Wealth: Money and Morality among China's New Rich* (Stanford University Press, 2013). His research interests include capitalist and consumer culture, morality, political corruption, gender and sexuality, and Han Chinese patronage of Tibetan Buddhism.

Tracy Royce is a graduate student in the Sociology Department at the University of California, Santa Barbara. Her research interests include gender, sexualities, conversation analysis, violence against women, and weight bias and discrimination. Her work has been published in *Archives of Sexual Behavior, International Journal of Sexual Health,* and *The Fat Studies Reader* (NYU Press, 2009).

Hsunhui Tseng is an assistant professor in the Gender Studies Program at the Chinese University of Hong Kong. Her research interests include transnational marriage, migration and modernity, human trafficking, and the politics of representation and identity. Her work has appeared in the *Hong Kong Journal of Social Science, Human Trafficking in Asia: Forcing Issues* (Routledge, 2013), and *Cross-Currents: East Asian History and Culture Review.*

Danning Wang is adjunct assistant professor in the Anthropology Department at the Chinese University of Hong Kong. Her research interests include family and gender studies in China and East Asia. She coedited *Gender and Family in East Asia* (Routledge, 2013).

Xia Zhang is an assistant professor in the Department of Sociology and Anthropology at Manhattanville College. Her research interests include Chinese masculinities, labor, migration, youth culture, new media, globalization, and modernity in contemporary China. Her work has appeared in *International Labor and Working-Class History* and she is currently working on a book manuscript titled *Carrying Out Modernity: Migration, Work, and Masculinity in China* based on her dissertation research.

Tiantian Zheng is a professor of anthropology at the State University of New York, Cortland. She is the author or coauthor of eight books, including *Red Lights: The Lives of Sex Workers in Postsocialist China* (University of Minnesota Press, 2009; winner of the 2010 Sara A. Whaley Book Prize from the National Women's Studies Association), *Ethnographies of Prostitution in Contemporary China: Gender Relations, HIV/AIDS, and Nationalism* (Palgrave Macmillan, 2009; winner of the 2011 Research Publication Book Award from the Association of Chinese Professors of Social Sciences in the United States), and *Tongzhi Living: Men Attracted to Men in Postsocialist China* (University of Minnesota Press, 2015).

Index